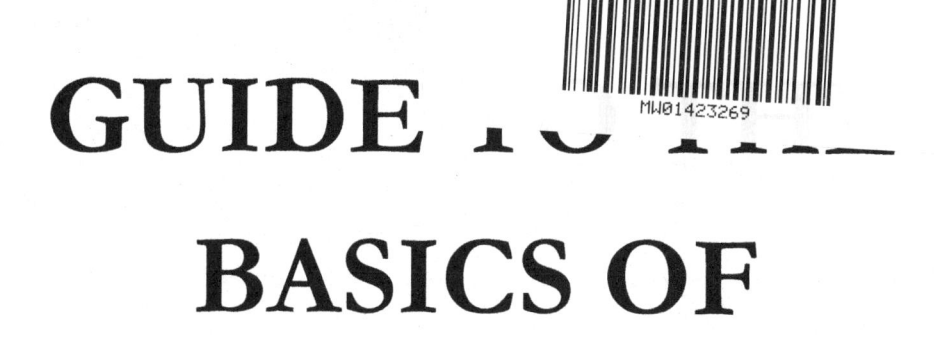

GUIDE TO THE BASICS OF ONTARIO FAMILY LAW

A Short and Easy-To-Understand Guide to Separation, Divorce, Child and Family Law Issues, the Family Court Process and the Alternatives to Court

JOHN P. SCHUMAN, C.S.

LL.M., LL.B., B.A.H., AEMCA

Certified Specialist in Family Law, Family Lawyer and Mediator

4th Edition

Copyright © 2018 John P. Schuman

All rights reserved. No part of this publication may be reproduced or transmitted in any form or by any means, electronic or mechanical, including photocopy, recording or any information storage and retrieval system without permission in writing from the publisher.

Requests for permission to make copies of any part of the work should be directed to the publisher or, in the case of material reproduced here from elsewhere, to the original copyright holder.

Library and Archives Canada Cataloguing in Publication

Schuman, John, 1971-
The Guide to the Basics of Ontario Family Law, 4th Edition / by John. P. Schuman
Includes bibliography references

ISBN 978-0-9867993-8-9

1. Attorney and client.   2. Domestic Relations – Ontario   3. Law – Family Law - General

4th Edition

Printed in Canada

Every reasonable effort has been made to acquire permission for copyrighted materials used in this book and to acknowledge such permissions accurately. Any errors or omissions brought to the publisher's attention will be corrected in future printings.

This book does not constitute legal advice. If you need legal assistance, please see a lawyer. Each case in unique and a lawyer with good training and sound judgment can provide you with advice tailored to suit your specific situation and need

Contents

Introduction	3
How to Use This Book	4
Part 1: Road Map Through the Various Paths in Separation and Divorce: Court, Negotiation, Mediation, Arbitration, Collaborative Practice and Others Options	9
Does Ontario Family Law Even Matter to You?	9
Are You Married?	10
Are You Common Law?	11
How Do You Know If You Have Children Together?	12
How Do You Know if You are Separated?	13
What Happens After Separation? Is it Always Nasty?	14
Keeping it Simple: Negotiations and Separation Agreements	15
What is a Divorce? How Do I Get One? What Does It Mean?	17
Do I Need a Divorce if I Am Not Legally Married?	20
Can I Get Divorced in Ontario?	21
The Usual Steps in Ontario Family Court Proceedings	21
How to Start a Court Proceeding	24

Applying for a Divorce (Pleadings)	24
Parenting Affidavits Show that the Children Will Be Safe	25
Financial Statements – The Most Basic Way to Show What You Have	26
Financial Disclosure – The Foundation for Court Cases Involving Money	27
Practical Tip: Disclosure	30
What If I Ignore a Family Court Application Against Me?	31
Your First Time in the Court House: The Mandatory Information Program	32
First Meeting with a Judge: The Case Conference	33
Having a Judge Decide Matters Temporarily: Motions	34
Finding Out Your Spouse's Position: Disclosure and Questioning	36
Stuck in an Impasse: Settlement Conferences and Moving to Trial	39
Planning an Orderly Trial at Trial Management Conferences	40
Preparing for Trial is a Big, Difficult Job	40
One Last Attempt to Avoid the Big Battle: the Pre-Trial	41
Being Reasonable Helps: The Advantage of Offers to Settle	42
Trial: The Big Show Down	44
How to Get a Formal Court Order	47

John P. Schuman, C.S., Family Lawyer, Mediator and Arbitrator

What Do You Do If You Did Not Like The Decision? Appeal	47
People Are Often Unhappy in Court – The Reasons to Consider Alternatives	49
Court Takes the Decision Making Away from the Separated Spouses or Parents	49
Court Resources Are Limited and Limit the Judge's Knowledge of the Family	50
Courts Can Only Deal With Legal Issues – Not Emotions or Feelings	50
Court Will Make Disagreements Worse Before Anything Is Resolved	50
Court is Expensive and Time Consuming	51
Court is Public: Everyone Can See Your Dirty Laundry	51
But Sometimes You Have to Go to Court…	52
Ways to Avoid Big Nasty Fights: Alternative Dispute Resolution (Mediation and Arbitration) and the Online Child Support Calculation Service	52
Choosing ADR and Screening the Parties Before the Process	52
Mediation	53
When Going to Mediation, You Need to Speak to a Lawyer First	54
Family Arbitration	57
Mediation/Arbitration	59
Parenting Coordination is ADR for Difficult Situations	60
Family Arbitration Awards Are Binding on the Parties	60
What to do if the Arbitrator "Got it Wrong"	61
Collaborative Practice – "Divorcing Without Wrecking the Kids"	63

John P. Schuman, C.S., Family Lawyer, Mediator and Arbitrator

When It's "Just Math" – Resolving Child Support Through the Online Service	66
Should the Children be Involved in the Process?	68
Practical Tip: Getting Your Child's Voice Before the Court	70
After a Court Hears a Child, the Child Must Do What the Court Orders	71
There are Always Exceptions to Rules and Different Paths to Take	71
Part 2: What You Really Need to Know Before Making Any Decisions after Separation: The Basic Family Law Issues	**73**
Who Gets the Kids? Parenting (Custody/Access) Issues	75
Who Makes the Decisions? – The Legal Definition of Custody	76
Access Parents Still Have a Right to Information	78
Giving up Your Rights – the Concept of De Facto Custody	79
Joint Custody and When It Can Be Ordered	80
Moving With the Kids	81
What To Do If A Parent Disappears With the Kids	82
Getting Professional Help Making Parenting Decisions	83
Child Support- Who Pays and How Much?	86
"It's Not My Kid" – Child Support and Non-Biological Children	86
Extraordinary Expenses Are Not Included in Base Child Support	88
Back to (paying for) school: child support and post-secondary education	90

John P. Schuman, C.S., Family Lawyer, Mediator and Arbitrator

Child Support When There Are Children Living with Both Parents	92
Child Support in Various Parenting Situations	93
Important Tax Considerations for Child Support: Yes - Child Support Impacts Tax	94
Self-Employed? Your Income For Child Support May Be Greater Than Your Income On Your Tax Return	95
Quitting Your Job To Avoid Support Does Not Work	97
The Thorny, and Often Misunderstood, Issues Around Spousal Support (Alimony)	97
Spousal Support Is Not Child Support - It Does Not Change with the Payer's Income	101
Trying to be Predictable: the Spousal Support Advisory Guidelines	102
Ignoring Support Orders Can Really Hurt: Support Enforcement	104
Property Matters (How the Family's Assets and Debts Are Divided)	107
Common Law Couples Do Not Share in Each Other's Property under the Family Law Act.	107
Married Couples Share Some of the Value of Some Property	108
Can I Be Liable for My Spouse's Debts?	111
The Problems Surrounding Pensions in Divorces	112
Canada Pension Plan	112
Defined Contribution Pensions	113
Defined Benefit Pensions	114
Pensions and Spousal Support	116
Stock Options Are Great –Except in Divorce Proceedings	117

John P. Schuman, C.S., Family Lawyer, Mediator and Arbitrator

There's No Place Like a Matrimonial Home (or Homes)   118

Forcing Your Ex-Partner Out: Partition and Sale of Property   121

What to Do If Everything So Far Does Not Help: Other Remedies   122

Stopping Your Spouse From Giving Everything to Someone Else: Preservation Orders   126

How to Get Paid Pursuant to a Non-Support Order   126

Bankruptcy Can Change Everything or Nothing   127

Protecting the Safety of You and the Kids: Restraining Orders 131

You Can't Put it Off Forever – There are Limits on How Long You Can Ask For Things   133

Death May Not Change Anything in Family Law   136

A Special Note about Last Wills and Testaments – Why Everyone Needs One   138

Sometimes Family Law Is Not About Family Law   139

Part 3: Going Back.... Changing an Order or Agreement   141

What Can Be Changed and What Cannot   143

Changing Child Support Is Expected and Often Easy   143

Annual Changes to Child Support for Self-Employed People Can Be Difficult and Expensive if the Parties Do Not Cooperate   147

Child Support Can Change for Reasons Other than Income 148

John P. Schuman, C.S., Family Lawyer, Mediator and Arbitrator

When Parenting Plans Break Down: Changing Custody and Access	149
"I Need More" or "I'm Out of Money": Changing Spousal Support	150
Changing Dismissals of Spousal Support and Lump Sum Spousal Support Orders	152
Obtaining Support Contrary to the Terms of an Agreement	152
Agreeing to Review Spousal Support	155
Changing On-Going Support Where There is No Set Review Date	156
The Uphill Battle: Changing Property and Lump Sum Damages Payments	158
Ensuring Continued Safety: Changing and Continuing Restraining/Non-Harassment Orders	159
The Risk of Asking for a Change to an Order or Agreement	160
I Need a Change! What Do I Do? How to Change a Final Court Order	160
Making a Change That Is Complex or Based on Contested Facts	162
How Do I Change Our Agreement?	163
Going Back Again and Again (and Again…. And Again…)	166
"My Ex Won't Follow the Rules!" - Going Back Because the Other Party Is Not Following the Order, Arbitration Award or Agreement	167
Judges Do Not Like Changing Temporary Orders Before Trial	169

John P. Schuman, C.S., Family Lawyer, Mediator and Arbitrator

Part 4: Last Things First: Planning Your New Life Together With Cohabitation Agreements & Marriage Contracts ("Pre-nups")   171

    What a Marriage Contract or Cohabitation Agreement Can Do   172

    What a Marriage Contract or Cohabitation Agreement Cannot Do   174

    Avoiding Making A Bad Deal That Will Not Hold Up   176

    Imposing Punishment for Cheating and Other Lifestyle Clauses   179

    Why You Should Never Negotiate A Marriage Contract Right Before the Wedding   179

    Be Fair, and Careful, About Support Terms   180

    An Ontario Marriage Contract or Cohabitation Agreement May Not Work Some Place Else   182

    "We Didn't Mean It": Abandoning the Contract   182

    A Deal is Still A Deal   183

Part 5: Accusations of Child Abuse or Neglect – What to Do, What Not to Do and When: A Brief Discussion of Child Protection (Cases Brought by Children's Aid Societies)   185

    You Need Help To Avoid Serious Trouble   186

    What To Do When A Children's Aid Society Calls To Investigate   188

    The Basis for the CAS Going to Court: A Child Being In Need Of Protection   192

    Children Can Be Taken From Their Parents Very Quickly   194

John P. Schuman, C.S., Family Lawyer, Mediator and Arbitrator

Who Can Ask to Care for Kids: People Entitled to Participate at Child Protection Court	195
Allowing Children to Have a Voice in Their Future in Child Protection Proceedings	196
Meeting With a Judge Right After the Kids Are Taken Away	197
It is Nobody Else's Business: Child Protection Matters Are Private	198
You Are Entitled to Know: Important Rules for Disclosure	198
What the Judge Can See and When: The Rules of Evidence are Different in Child Protection Proceedings	200
Deciding the Child's Future at Trial	201
There Are Only a Few Orders a Court Can Make When a Child is in Need of Protection	202
How the Judge Decides What Final Order is Right to Protect a Child	204
Checking if the Child is Okay: Reviewing the Child's Status	205
The Last Chance: Appeals	205
Avoiding Court: Alternative Dispute Resolution in Child Protection	206
Sharing the Love and Growing a Family: Adoption	209
Stranger Adoptions	209
Relative Adoptions	211
Conclusion: Avoid Saying "I Should Have Done That" – Know Your Options from the Beginning	213
Separation Does Not Necessarily Mean War	213

John P. Schuman, C.S., Family Lawyer, Mediator and Arbitrator

Separation Does Not Have to Hurt the Kids	214
Knowing the Law Helps a Lot	214
Marriage Contracts Say Good Things about a Marriage	215
Parents With a Little Bit of Knowledge Keep Their Kid in Child Protection Cases	215
Last Thoughts	216
Appendix A: 10 Guaranteed, Sure-Fire Ways to Anger a Judge or Otherwise Blow Your Case in Family Court	217
Appendix B: Top 10 Reasons to Get a Family Law Lawyer	221
Appendix C: Why Lawyers Charge by the Hour (and Why Cost is Often Impossible to Predict)	225
Appendix D: Questions and Answers about Alternative Dispute Resolution (Mediation, Arbitration and Collaborative Law/Practice)	229
Where to Find Out More: References and Bibliography	233
Statutes (Family Law Legislation)	233
Court Decisions	234
Other Useful Reference Available On the Internet:	235
Helpful Books about Separation, Divorce, Children and Family Court	236
Parenting Resources	236
Index	237
About the Author	249

John P. Schuman, C.S., Family Lawyer, Mediator and Arbitrator

Preface

Your deeds are your monuments.

-R J Palacio, Wonder, 2012
spoken by the character, Mr. Browne
referencing an Egyptian Tomb Inscription

How a person makes difficult decisions can make a lasting impact on everyone around. That is especially true when the decisions relate to some aspect of family law, and the people around are children who are observing the example and modelling themselves after how the adults around them make decision. Not only can those decisions directly affect the children, but they also can teach children how to make similar decisions in their lives. In that way, the "deeds become monuments." And for this reason employing the "precepts" that are popular among the younger generation can be doubling meaningful.

It is our choices that show what we truly are, far more than our abilities.

~J.K. Rowling, Harry Potter and the Chamber of Secrets, 1999,
spoken by the character Albus Dumbledore

The choices that adults make when in family changes or crisis can create or minimize conflict, and inflict or avoid harm to the spouses, parents, children and extended families. What path a person chooses in these difficult circumstances can make all the difference both in that person's life and the life of all the people around him or her. Often the choice is between protecting those people, including children, or standing up for principles. While it is

John P. Schuman, C.S., Family Lawyer, Mediator and Arbitrator

important to stay true to his or her beliefs and set an example in protecting those beliefs, protecting other people, especially children is also important. We know that conflict can hurt everyone around. So, an important lesson for children to learn is to "pick your battles" and principles are really only important when they protect others from harm. In life, the impact we make those around us is not by being correct in our beliefs, but in making life better for others.

So, in considering action in any difficult situation, consider one of the "precepts" being shared through all forms of media by children, as they are sharing it:

> *If given the choice between being right and being kind...*
> *#ChooseKind*

~Dr. Wayne Dyer

John P. Schuman
Toronto, Ontario
January 2018

John P. Schuman, C.S., Family Lawyer, Mediator and Arbitrator

Introduction

Take a deep breath. If you are reading this book, you are probably someone who is either going through a major change in your family life, or you know someone who is. A separation, a divorce, or a child abuse investigation is a stressful major life event. The fact that you probably don't know what is going to happen next or have a good grasp of Family Law only adds to that stress. Both at initial meetings, and over the course of representing Family Law clients, our clients ask us many of the same questions. This guide will answer the basic questions most people have in these difficult situations and provide a general and simple guide to non-Family Law lawyers about what to expect, from a legal standpoint, when preparing a marriage contract or cohabitation agreement, after a couple separates, or when a children's aid society starts child protection proceedings in court.

    This book is the product of helping, and answering the questions of thousands of clients with their family law situation. Those clients are going through a difficult time due to their separation, need for a marriage contract, or involvement with a children's aid society investigation. Almost none of those clients had any significant understanding of Family Law or the steps that they had to take. Those clients come to the author, John Schuman, as an Ontario Family Lawyer/mediator who has advocated before every level of court in Ontario and the Supreme Court of Canada. They have heard that he has more than ten years of experience dealing with complex financial matters in divorce and has a reputation for concern and advocacy for children. They come looking for a greater depth of knowledge of Family Law and how to get the best results in their situation.

John P. Schuman, C.S., Family Lawyer, Mediator and Arbitrator

Family law is special in that almost every case presents unique people and circumstances. The law applies differently to different people in different situations. This guide cannot say how the law will apply in any particular case. It also does not cover how Family Law works outside of Ontario. There can be significant differences in Family Law in other jurisdictions. This guide will give a brief explanation of the most important issues in Ontario Family Law and answer the most common questions that Family Law clients ask.

Although this guide covers all the basics of Ontario Family Law, it is important to remember "there is an exception to every rule". This guide does not address the exceptions. Sometimes judges in Family Law matters prefer a common sense approach over a strict application of the law, so it can be difficult to predict what decision a judge will make in any particular case. It is only possible to say what will usually happen if a judge is asked to make a particular type of decision. To understand how the law could apply to your specific situation, and what your best options are for resolving your Family Law matter, you must discuss that position with a lawyer. Contact information for the Family Law department at Devry Smith Frank LLP is on the back cover of this guide.

How to Use This Book

This guide consists of five main parts and several appendices. Part 1 describes the process that couples have to follow after they separate. It explains when a couple is legally separated, and what steps separated partners should take to move forward. It discusses the negotiation of a separation agreement, the use of mediators to assist in resolving issues, and when it is necessary to go to court. The guide then outlines the steps involved in a Family Law proceeding, from the first filing of documents, to trial, and then the hearing of appeals. Most couples will never go through all of the steps; they settle along the way. The first part of this guide will help separated couples decide whether to settle, because it will let them know what they are in for before they move to the next step. There is also a discussion of the alternatives to going to court: alternative dispute resolution (mediation and arbitration) and Collaborative Family Law. This first part of this guide also includes a description of how the voices of children might be heard in a Family Law case.

Part 2 of this guide discusses the main issues in Family Law. It outlines issues related to the custody and parenting of children, child support, spousal support, and property issues, from the equalization of net family property for married spouses, to more complicated property issues that can arise. The second part also discusses the significance of matrimonial homes

---

John P. Schuman, C.S., Family Lawyer, Mediator and Arbitrator

and what spouses can and cannot do with them after they separate. Finally, this part explains why it is important for separated couples to create new wills.

Part 3 of this guide is about going back to court (or negotiations, mediation or arbitration) because the original resolution must be changed. It is not possible to change every final resolution of a Family Law matter. A court will only change a final resolution if certain circumstances exist. Part 3 explains what can be changed and when. It also addresses going back to court because one party is not following an order, arbitration award, or agreement.

Marriage contracts and cohabitation agreements are the subject matter of Part 4. Ontario allows parties to have marriage contracts (which are also known as "pre-nups") and cohabitation agreements. However, the parties must follow several strict rules for a court to enforce those agreements when the parties separate. This chapter explains what marriage contracts and cohabitation agreements are, what they can do, and the rules that parties must follow to ensure they are enforceable. This section comes after Part 2 because for parties to properly understand their marriage contract or cohabitation agreement, they must understand the laws to which they are opting out.

Part 5 of this guide gives a very brief introduction to child protection cases. Child protection cases, which are the cases in which a children's aid society intervenes in a family's life, are also considered a branch of Family Law. However, child protection cases are quite different from cases between spouses or other family members. This section briefly explains what happens when a children's aid society starts a court proceeding to intervene in a family and what steps everyone involved should be taking.

> *Throughout this guide, the fictitious characters, Desmond and Molly, help explain how the ideas in the text work in real life. Desmond owns a store. Molly is in a band. They have two children. Desmond and Molly are going through a separation and divorce.*
>
> *These examples show how the law affects Desmond and Molly's situation. Since even small details can affect the outcome, you should not assume that your case would be the same as theirs. It is still important to talk to a lawyer for guidance, even if your case looks a lot like Desmond and Molly's situation.*

John P. Schuman, C.S., Family Lawyer, Mediator and Arbitrator

The conclusion of this book sums up the most important points to remember from each chapter. Those points are not specifics about law or court procedure. The most important things to remember are the best ways to think about the situation that you (or your friend) find yourself in when you need Family Law advice. Thinking about your situation the right way is the first step to making everything easier.

This guide also has appendices focused on practical advice. Appendix A explains under what circumstances a person in the middle of a Family Court proceeding is sure to lose her case. It explains what not to do in Family Court. Of course, by doing the opposite, it is possible to do well in Family Court.

Appendix B explains why it is important to retain a Family Lawyer after separating. After reading this guide, the reader should have a better understanding of how complex Family Law is and just how essential it is to have a legal expert when working through Family Law issues. This Appendix also explains the many additional reasons for having a Family Law lawyer.

Appendix C explains how Family Lawyers bill, and what separated couples can do to avoid paying lots of money to their lawyers.

Appendix D answers some common question about alternative dispute resolution (ADR) processes such as mediation, arbitration and collaborative law/practice. Since ADR is often quicker, less expensive and less emotionally damaging than court, many separating couples are choosing these processes instead. Although the ADR processes are addressed throughout this guide, this Appendix provides a quick reference guide.

Appendix E contains a list of references. It is not a formal bibliography, because there are pinpoint citations through the text to allow readers to link exact references to the concepts in the text. Appendix E gives the reader a starting point to find out more information about Family Law matters. It includes Internet addresses Ontario's Family Law legislation, a few of the most important court decisions that apply in Ontario, and some good reference texts for non-lawyers.

This guide contains footnotes throughout. These footnotes provide citations for the legal authorities for the comments in this guide. They reference both the statutory laws and court decisions. The purpose of these footnotes is to help the reader ask follow-up questions about the content of this guide. It is easier for the reader to ask questions about how a particular law

John P. Schuman, C.S., Family Lawyer, Mediator and Arbitrator

or court decision affects his or her situation if the reader knows which law or court decision he or she is asking about.

The readers of this guide should find it useful and informative. It is designed to be a reference that people can use throughout their Family Law matters, and perhaps even pass on to their friends and colleagues later. Until those friends and colleagues read this guide, or speak at length to a Family Lawyer, they probably do not know enough about Family Law, nor the options that are available to them.

John P. Schuman, C.S., Family Lawyer, Mediator and Arbitrator

John P. Schuman, C.S., Family Lawyer, Mediator and Arbitrator

Part 1: Road Map Through the Various Paths in Separation and Divorce: Court, Negotiation, Mediation, Arbitration, Collaborative Practice and Others Options

Does Ontario Family Law Even Matter to You?

Ontario Family Law and the mechanisms it provides to resolve conflict do not apply to everyone. Family Law legislation in Ontario applies to three types of people when they are living separate and apart: The three types of people – who are called either "spouses" or "parents" under the law are:

1. People who are married;

2. People who are living common law;

3. People who have a child together.

The legal implications and procedures for when a Children's Aid Society becomes involved due to child abuse or child neglect is also considered to be Family Law in Ontario. However, that is covered in Part 5 of this book. The Court process in those cases is similar to the description below in this Part.

This Part of the book will go over the procedures for separated spouses and parents. How Family Law applies to married couples through marriage contracts is the subject of Part 4.

People who think they are separated must first determine whether they were "spouses" because they were they married, living common law or are "parents" because they have children together? If they do not fall into one of those categories, then Ontario Family Law may not apply to them.

Are You Married?

People usually know if they are married because there was some form of wedding. But to be legally married in Ontario, there are certain rules. They are:

1. The spouses must have a marriage licence or their church-published banns.[1]
2. The spouses must be over the age of 18, or over the age of 16 and have parental consent[2] or have a judge dispense with the need for parental consent.[3]
3. Both spouses must have the mental capacity to marry and must not be intoxicated by liquor, drugs or something else.[4]
4. The spouses must not be siblings, or half-siblings, or parent and child, grandparent and grandchild, or great-grandparent and great-grandchild.[5]
5. The officiant who solemnizes the marriage must be authorized to solemnize marriages.[6]
6. The marriage must only involve two people, unless it was solemnized in another jurisdiction that recognizes polygamous marriages as valid.[7]

If a couple does not follow all the above rules when they are married in Ontario, they may not be legally married. However if the spouses believed, in good faith, that they had met all the requirements to be married, Ontario Family Law treats them as married even if their marriage may be void.[8] But if two people have a wedding and deliberately do not follow the above rules because they intended to *not* be legally married, they are not married under Ontario Law.

---

[1] *Marriage Act,* R.S.O, 1990, c. M.3, s. 4.
[2] *Marriage Act,* R.S.O, 1990, c. M.3, s. 5(1), 5(2), as amended.
[3] *Marriage Act,* R.S.O, 1990, c. M.3, s. 6.
[4] *Marriage Act,* R.S.O, 1990, c. M.3, s. 7.
[5] *Marriage (Prohibited Degrees) Act,* S.C. 1990, c. 46, s. 2(2) as amended.
[6] *Marriage Act,* R.S.O, 1990, c. M.3, s. 20(1), as amended.
[7] *Family Law Act,* R.S.O. 1990, c. F-3, s 1(2).
[8] *Family Law Act,* R.S.O. 1990, c. F-3, s 1(1), as amended.

John P. Schuman, C.S., Family Lawyer, Mediator and Arbitrator

Are You Common Law?

In Ontario (the law is different in other jurisdictions), two people are living common law for Family Law purposes if:

1. they have lived together continuously for a period of three years or more; or
2. they are the natural or adoptive parents of a child and they have "cohabitated" for any period of time.[9]

All being "common law" means under Ontario Family Law is that the partners can claim spousal support from each other. It does not give them any rights to each other's property.[10] The definition of "common law" is different for other areas of law (such as for income tax purposes or employment benefits).

"Living together continuously" or "cohabitating" does not necessarily mean moving in together and sleeping in the same bedroom every night. Two people can be "cohabitating" while living in separate places, if they intend to be in a common law relationship, but it is circumstances alone that keep them apart. Many married couples spend lots of time apart, but they still intend to be "together" and the same principle applies to common law couples. In the case of military personnel, spouses can be apart for months or years, but they are not separated because they intend to remain common law. Similar circumstances exist where a spouse lives in a nursing home to receive care but the other spouse either chooses or cannot afford to live in the nursing home. What matters are the parties' intentions with regard to the relationship. Similarly, a "one night stand" does not count as cohabitation (except for the purposes of restraining orders[11]). A series of "one night stands" would similarly not count, unless the parties intended to be in a common law relationship.

---

[9] *Family Law Act*, R.S.O. 1990, c. F-3, s 29, as amended.
[10] The definition of spouse for property division only includes married couples: *Family Law Act*, R.S.O. 1990, c. F-3, s 1(1), as amended.
[11] *Family Law Act*, R.S.O. 1990, c. F-3, s 46(2)(b), as amended.

John P. Schuman, C.S., Family Lawyer, Mediator and Arbitrator

How Do You Know If You Have Children Together?

People who are the natural or adoptive parents of a child, or who have demonstrated a settled intention to treat a child as his or her own are subject to the child support[12] and custody/access provisions of Ontario Law even if they have never lived together.

If you are not certain whether you are the parent of a child, or you are not certain whether another person is the other parent of your child, you can get an order requiring DNA testing. A person can refuse to participate in DNA testing. However if a person refuses, the court can simply assume that person is, or is not, the parent based on that refusal, depending in part on the apparent reasons for refusing.[13]

It is possible for someone who is not biologically related to a child, or has not adopted the child, to be considered a parent of that child if that person treats that child as his or her own. This means more than treating the child with "common courtesy" or acting as a babysitter. To be considered a 'parent; of a non-biological or adopted child, a person must have consciously and firmly decided to treat the child as his or her own and that intention must have been demonstrated by the person's actions. Some actions that a person can take to demonstrate that he or she intends to be a parent to a child include, but are not limited to: having the child participate in the parent's extended family in the same manner they would a biological child; providing financially for the child; disciplining the child as a parent; telling the child, the family, the world, either explicitly or implicitly, that he or she is responsible as a parent to the child; and the existence and nature of the child's relationship with their biological parents.[14]

When people are "together" as a couple, they do not need to turn to Family Law, or the courts, to decide issues between them. They work things out "together." It is only when people separate that Family Law, Family Courts and the alternatives to court come into play.

---

[12] *Family Law Act,* R.S.O. 1990, c. F-3, s 1(1), as amended.
[13] *Children's Law Reform Act,* R.S.O. 1990, c. C-12, s. 10 as amended.
[14] *Chartier v. Chartier,* [1999] 1 S.C.R. 242 at paras 38-42. (S.C.C.)

John P. Schuman, C.S., Family Lawyer, Mediator and Arbitrator

How Do You Know if You are Separated?

At the end of a relationship, people often want to know whether they are legally separated and whether there is anything that they need to do to be legally separated. The date on which a couple separates is an important one in Ontario Family Law. The date of separation is the date on which support obligations usually commence. It is also commonly used as the 'valuation date' - the date as of which the parties' Net Family Property is determined, which governs how the value of their assets will be divided.

There is no formal process in Ontario to recognize spouses as being separated. Ontario Law says that cohabiting spouses are separated when a reasonable observer[15] would conclude that they are no longer living together as spouses and "there is no reasonable prospect that they will resume cohabitation." (For non-cohabiting couples, the date is the day when a reasonable observer would believe that the relationship was over). The date of separation is not necessarily the date when the parties start living in separate residences, although that is a very strong indication that the couple is separated. Couples can be living "separate and apart under the same roof". Many couples continue to live in the same residence after their relationship is over either for economic reasons or "for the sake of their children". By the same token, some couples remain married even though they have to live in separate residences much of the time because of their jobs or for other reasons. If a court has to determine whether these couples are married or separated, the judge has to ask whether an objective observer, who knows what is going on in the parties' lives, would believe that they were still living as a couple or the relationship was over. Some factors that the court considers include:

- if they are living under the same roof, whether they share the same room,
- whether the parties go out together as a family,
- whether they eat meals together,
- whether they vacation together,
- whether the parties have separated their finances,
- whether they report themselves as married or separated on their income tax returns, and
- whether they tell other people they are separated or together.

---

[15] *Family Law Act*, R.S.O. 1990, c. F-3, s. 4(1); *Divorce Act*, R.S.C. 1985, c. 3 (2nd Supp.), 8(3); is similar in intent but contains different language.

John P. Schuman, C.S., Family Lawyer, Mediator and Arbitrator

There may be other factors, and none of these factors is determinative of the issue. A judge who has to decide the issue has to look at all of the circumstances to determine when the parties separated.

There have been cases where one spouse has questioned whether the other spouse had the mental capacity to decide to separate. Essentially, that spouse says, "She has to be crazy to want to leave me." However, the capacity to form the intention to live separate and apart is not a particularly demanding one. The mere fact of a mental illness is not enough for a court to find that a spouse cannot decide to separate. For a person to form the intention to separate, all that is required is that the intention must not be based on an irrational belief[16].

Molly told Desmond that she did not love him anymore and the relationship is over. However, things have been rough for her band, and she does not have enough money to rent an apartment. Desmond does not want to lose his role in parenting the children, so he does not want to leave either (more about this in Part 2). Molly moves into the guest bedroom. When Desmond says he is taking the kids out for dinner, Molly says she will take the kids out by herself on another day. Desmond and Molly stop doing housework for each other. Molly puts all the money she makes into a separate account and does not share it with Desmond. Even though Desmond and Molly are still living in the same house, Ontario Law would probably view them as separated.

What Happens After Separation? Is it Always Nasty?

Were you married or living common law or have children with someone? Are you now legally separated? What is next? What is the best path to follow to meet your (and your children's) needs? People who are going through a separation or divorce often have no idea what to expect. They want to know what is going to happen, and when, so that they can plan their lives and prepare for the future. It is difficult to predict how any particular separation or divorce will unfold. That depends largely on the couple who are separating or divorcing and the issues between them. Factors that affect how the separation or divorce will unfold include:

---

[16] *AB v. CD*, (2009) 66 R.F.L.(6th) 237 (B.C.C.A.) (leave to S.C.C. refused).

1. the bitterness of the parties;
2. the complexity of the financial issues;
3. whether there are any children and, if so, whether there are any concerns about those children;
4. whether one party wants to relocate; and
5. whether the parties are willing to cooperate with the process.

This being said, there is a general process by which things unfold.

Keeping it Simple: Negotiations and Separation Agreements

Once parties have separated, the first step is for them to determine whether they can sort out the issues on their own (usually with the help of lawyers), or whether they need to go to court or use another process, such as mediation or Collaborative Practice, to resolve the disputes. When the parties are negotiating, the goal is to arrive at a written separation agreement.

Separation agreements are a way that separated couples can set out how they have resolved all of the issues that arise from the breakdown of their relationship. They can include how children will be parented, whether spousal and child support will be paid and in what amounts and for how long, and how the couple's assets and liabilities will be divided. If the parties follow the rules for making a separation agreement, then they will have a legally binding document that resolves the issues between them and specifies how they will interact with each other in the future, if that is necessary[17].

The Ontario *Family Law Act* sets out many of the rules that apply to separation agreements. The basic rules are that the agreement must be in writing, must be signed by the parties, and those signatures must be witnessed[18]. The *Family Law Act* also sets out grounds on which a separation agreement can be set aside. Those provisions effectively create additional rules for making an enforceable separation agreement. Some of the additional rules are:

---

[17] Separated couples with children will probably have to interact with each other for the rest of their lives in relation to their children.

[18] Witnesses may be called upon later if there is a dispute as to whether the signature on the contract belongs to the person it says or whether someone fraudulently signed on for that person.

John P. Schuman, C.S., Family Lawyer, Mediator and Arbitrator

1. the parties must understand the agreement[19] (which the courts have said effectively means that each party must have had Independent Legal Advice from a separate lawyer and law firm from his or her spouse who has explained the legal significance of the terms of the agreement);
2. there must be full, complete, and accurate financial disclosure (at minimum each spouse must disclose his or her income, assets and liabilities and debts at the time of signing the agreement.[20] However, from when reviewing separations agreements, judges expect to see that information for both the date of separation and the date of marriage if it affects any of the legal issues in the agreement);
3. the contract must not violate the law of contract[21] (there are rules for separation agreements in both the *Family Law Act* – such as that they may not require chastity[22] – and under the common law – such as that parties must have the legal right to contract over any property in the agreement. Meeting this requirement is not usually a problem if each party has help from a separate lawyer);
4. the circumstances that result from the agreement must not be unconscionable.

In addition to the above considerations, the Supreme Court of Canada has stated that a domestic contract can be set aside where there were problems with the circumstances surrounding the negotiation of the agreement, such as where one of the parties did not have adequate legal (or accounting) advice. Additionally, a court may set it aside if one of the parties was oppressed, or was acting under duress, or where the calculations were made in haste[23]. An agreement can also be set aside if it is not in "substantial compliance" with the objectives of the Family Law legislation[24]. Finally, the agreement can be set aside if it results in consequences that the parties did not intend or contemplate[25]. The involvement of lawyers is necessary to ensure that any separation agreement is written in a way that addresses these considerations. Separated spouses who do not follow these "rules" may have the agreement they based their life around thrown out by a judge if the parties to the

---

[19] *Family Law Act*, R.S.O. 1990, c. F-3, s. 56(4)(b).
[20] *Family Law Act*, R.S.O. 1990. c. F-3, s. 56(4)(a).
[21] *Family Law Act*, R.S.O. 1990. c. F-3, s. 56(4)(c).
[22] *Family Law Act*, R.S.O. 1990. c. F-3, s. 56(2).
[23] *Miglin v. Miglin* (2003), 1 S.C.R. 303 at paragraph 81.
[24] *Miglin v. Miglin* (2003), 1 S.C.R. 303 at paragraph 84-85.
[25] *Carrier v. Carrier*, 2007 CarswellNB 155 at para 13 (N.B.C.A.).

John P. Schuman, C.S., Family Lawyer, Mediator and Arbitrator

agreement becomes unhappy with it. Separation agreements that do not follow the "rules" are only good for as long as both spouses voluntarily follow its terms.

Other sections of the *Family Law Act* state that the child support terms of a separation agreement must be in accordance with the *Child Support Guidelines*[26], unless some very specific requirements have been met. Further, courts are not bound by a separation agreement with respect to custody and access issues, because the courts must always make the order that it finds is in the best interests of the child. (However, courts give a lot of weight to what the two parents agree is in the best interests of their children, because the parents know their children better than the judge does). Finally, the *Divorce Act* states that when making a Divorce Order, a court must consider a separation agreement, but does not necessarily have to follow its terms. However, judges are very likely to incorporate the terms of a separation agreement into a Divorce Order unless the rules for making a separation agreement, as set out in the *Family Law Act*, are not followed.

If the parties are successful in negotiating a separation agreement, then there is no need for them to involve the courts unless they also need a divorce. If the parties cannot agree on terms for a separation agreement, or it is clear that the circumstances between the parties are not conducive to negotiating a separation agreement, then the parties will have to go to court to resolve all of the issues between them.

What is a Divorce? How Do I Get One? What Does It Mean?

If separated spouses were married, then they may need a divorce. All a divorce means is that the parties are legally free to remarry. Although parties usually wait until after hey have settled all of the issues between them to get a divorce (so that they can incorporate the settlement into the Divorce Order), it is not strictly necessary to do so.

The Ontario Superior Court of Justice will only grant a divorce if it satisfied that one of the following three grounds exists:

---

[26] The *Child Support Guidelines* are discussed below. They are both federal and provincial regulations that set out how much child support must be paid for children.

John P. Schuman, C.S., Family Lawyer, Mediator and Arbitrator

1. the parties have lived separate and apart for at least one year and there is no reasonable prospect that they will resume cohabitation;
2. one or both parties have committed adultery;
3. one party has treated the other party so cruelly as to make continued cohabitation impossible[27].

There is also the additional requirement, discussed below, that at least one of the spouses must have residing in Ontario for at least the year immediately preceding the divorce.[28]

In Ontario, almost everyone gets divorced on the ground that they have been separated from their spouse for a period of at least one year. To obtain a divorce on either of the other grounds, a person must prove to the court that their spouse committed adultery or acted cruelly towards them at a trial, or the other spouse must admit them under oath. In the case of adultery, the other participant in the adultery must also be a party to the proceedings and must also admit, in court, to having committed adultery with the spouse. Due to the other potential legal consequences of admitting adultery or cruelty, spouses do not usually admit to that type of behaviour.

If a spouse does not admit to being cruel or committing adultery, then those facts must be proven in court at a trial. It is extremely unlikely that the parties will be ready, or the court will be able to hear, a trial in less than a year. Once the parties have been separated for a year, they can automatically obtain a divorce as long as the other requirements, described below, have been met. This makes obtaining a divorce on the grounds of adultery or cruelty unnecessarily complicated and expensive.

In addition to having a ground for divorce, to obtain a divorce from the court, the spouses must meet four other requirements:

1. there must be adequate provisions in place for the financial support of any children of the marriage;
2. all religious barriers to remarriage that are within a spouse's control must be removed;
3. neither spouse must be unfairly prejudiced by the fact of the divorce; and

---

[27] *Divorce Act*, R.S.C. 1985, c.3 (2nd Supp.), s. 8(2).
[28] *Divorce Act*, R.S.C. 1985, c.3 (2nd Supp.), s. 3(1)

John P. Schuman, C.S., Family Lawyer, Mediator and Arbitrator

4. the parties must be getting divorced for legitimate reasons and not obtaining the divorce to perpetrate a fraud.

The requirements to get a divorce are not hard to meet if the spouses are acting reasonably. The judge who is being asked to grant the divorce will only want to see that the child support that is being paid is consistent with the *Child Support Guidelines* and that one of the spouses has sworn an affidavit that he or she is not conspiring with the other spouse to obtain a divorce to perpetrate a fraud. A spouse requesting a contested divorce may not be successful if he or she has not done what is in his or her power to allow both parties to remarry in their religion. In some instances, a judge may put off the granting of a divorce if there is prejudice to one of the spouses. An example of this would be where a spouse is dependent on the other spouse's health insurance for prescription medication, and the spouse's eligibility for those benefits will end when the parties are no longer married. However, with regard to this last requirement for divorce, the divorce will only be temporarily delayed and the judge would expect the parties to make alternative arrangements.

> *Desmond and Molly agreed that Desmond will pay for day care and the children's clothes and Molly will pay for their food until the move into separate homes. That arrangement will probably work while they are living together. However, to get a divorce, it may not. Desmond and Molly will have to show that the children are getting the same benefit as if Desmond and Molly were paying child support as set out in the Child Support Guidelines. That usually has one parent making monthly support payments to the other to pay the children's expenses.*

Obtaining a divorce with the consent of both spouses does not require a court appearance. A judge will decide whether to grant the divorce in chambers[29]. It usually takes about three months from the time the proper forms are submitted until a judge can look them over and grant the divorce. After a judge makes the Divorce Order, there is a 31-day period before the divorce takes effect and the parties can remarry. This additional time is to allow the opportunity for one of the spouses to appeal the divorce.

---

[29] The term "in chambers" means a judge deals with a matter in his or her office instead of in the courtroom, which is usually open to the public.

John P. Schuman, C.S., Family Lawyer, Mediator and Arbitrator

It may be possible to get a divorce processed more quickly after the parties have been separated for more than a year. Judges will sometimes allow a spouse to jump the line of waiting divorces, and also shorten the period before the divorce takes effect, if there is some sort of urgency and one of the spouses must remarry more quickly than would be possible with the usual timelines for obtaining a divorce. However, judges will only do this in exceptional circumstances.

Do I Need a Divorce if I Am Not Legally Married?

The only purpose of getting a divorce (as opposed to support, property division and other issues related to a separation) is so a person can be remarried. It is possible to get a support order, or divide property, or get a restraining order, or other court orders without ever getting divorced. So, a person who was never legally married has no need to get a divorce because he or she is free to go get a marriage licence.

A couple is considered legally married in Ontario if he or she was married by someone who is the government of Ontario has authorized to solemnize marriages in Ontario after the couple either obtains a marriage licence or has their church (or churches, where they attended different ones) publish banns, which are a formal written announcement of the wedding.[30] A couple who were properly married according to the laws of the jurisdiction where their wedding occurred are also considered legally married in Ontario.[31]

If someone was never legally married in Ontario or elsewhere, he or she cannot get divorced. That person would have the rights of a common law spouse, which are different from a married spouse, and are described in Part 2 of this book. However, if person genuinely believes he or she was legally married, but it turns out that was not the case, that person is still entitled to use the provisions of the *Family Law Act* to divide property as if he or she was married.[32] Those provisions do not apply to common law couples.

---

[30] *Marriage Act,* R.S.O. 1990, c. M-3, s. 4.
[31] *Family Law Act,* R.S.O. 1990. c. F-3, s. 1(1) and 1(2).
[32] *Family Law Act,* R.S.O. 1990. c. F-3, s. 1(1).

John P. Schuman, C.S., Family Lawyer, Mediator and Arbitrator

Can I Get Divorced in Ontario?

To get a divorce in Ontario, at least one of the parties must have lived primarily (the legal term is "ordinarily resident") in Ontario for at least the twelve months immediately before the divorce is applied for.[33] Even if one spouse left the other behind to come to Ontario "temporarily," the Ontario Superior Court will hear the divorce if that spouse has been in Ontario for at least a year. If one spouse is "ordinarily resident" in Ontario and the other spouse is "ordinarily resident" in another province or country, the divorce case will usually be heard, and the divorce granted, in the jurisdiction where court proceedings are started first.[34] However, there may be other factors that come into play as to which jurisdiction is the most appropriate one to deal with the divorce. To challenge the jurisdiction for a divorce, speak to lawyer in each jurisdiction involved.

Obtaining a divorce order, even an "uncontested divorce," technically requires starting a court proceeding. Starting a court proceeding means serving the other parties to the case, which means the other spouse in a simple divorce case. There are rules for serving court documents, and those rules are more complicated when serving the documents in other countries. For judges to recognize that documents have been properly served on people in most other countries, the spouse seeking the divorce must serve the court documents in accordance with the *Convention on the Service Abroad of Judicial and Extrajudicial Documents in Civil or Commercial Matters*.[35] It is always best to consult a lawyer to make sure the documents are served properly so the divorce can proceed.

The Usual Steps in Ontario Family Court Proceedings

The *Family Law Rules* set out a process for court cases. Some steps are optional; the parties do not have to follow them. Some steps won't apply in some cases, such as simple uncontested divorce cases. In addition, the parties can avoid many of the steps, and the associated costs, if they settle. In addition, under Rule 1(7.2), Family Court Judges have the ability to change the process to better suit the parties. However, the following chart sets out the usual steps in Family Court after which, this chapter will describe each step in more detail:

---

[33] *Divorce Act,* R.S.C. R.S.C., 1985, c. 3 (2nd Supp.), s. 3(1).
[34] *Divorce Act,* R.S.C. R.S.C., 1985, c. 3 (2nd Supp.), s. 3(2).
[35] 658 UNTS 163; 20 UST 361, available from:
https://www.hcch.net/en/instruments/conventions/full-text/?cid=17 .

Chart of the Usual Steps in Ontario Family Court Proceedings

Application Issued
- The "Applicant" must also file a financial statement and 3 years of CRA Notices of Assessment if the case involves money
- If the case involves a claim for child or spousal support, the Applicant must serve (but not file) the disclosure required by section 21(1) of the *Child Support Guidelines*, this includes complete copies of the Applicant's last 3 tax returns, last pay stub, business financial statements if the Applicant is self-employed or controls a corporation, benefits statements if the party receives government assistance, and information about any trust to which the Applicant is a beneficiary
- The Application must be accompanied by a Form 35.1 parenting affidavit if the case involves custody or access

Applicant has other parties served personally 30 days (60 days if other party is outside Canada or the United States)

Answer by Responding Spouse/Party(ies)
- The "Respondent" must serve & file a financial statement & 3 years of CRA Notices of Assessment if the case involves money
- If the case involves a claim for child or spousal support, the Respondent must serve (but not file) the disclosure required by section 21(1) of the *Child Support Guidelines*, this includes complete copies of the Applicant's last 3 tax returns, last pay stub, business financial statements if the Applicant is self-employed or controls a corporation, benefits statements if the party receives government assistance, information about any trust to which the Applicant is a beneficiary
- The Answer must be accompanied by a Form 35.1 parenting affidavit if the case involves custody or access

10 days

Reply (by Applicant)
- This document must only address issues in the Answer that he Applicant did not address in the Application
- If the Respondent added money or parenting issues to the case, then the Applicant must serve and file a financial statement and serve the disclosure set out above and a parenting affidavit where there are custody/access issues.

30 days

Parties exchange financial disclosure (in cases about money)
- In support cases, parties exchange any further information necessary to understand their respective incomes.
- In property division cases, parties provide disclosure about their assets and liabilities on the date of marriage and the date of separation, which include (as applicable) bank statements, pension valuation applications, MPAC assessments of properties, life insurance statements, business/corporate financial statements (where the business or corporation is controlled by the party), trust statements, valuations of other assets, mortgage statements, statements for other loans and other documents.
- If either party needs additional disclosure to understand the other party's financial situation, he or she makes a written request, and if it is not fulfilled, that party can bring a motion in writing to get the requested disclosure.
- Parties serve and file Form 13A Certificates of Financial Disclosure showing what disclosure each has provided

0-120 days (depending on Court's Schedule)

Case Conference
- Case conferences are less formal meetings with a judge to address procedural issues, timetable the next events and attempt to resolve matters on a temporary basis. Less complicated cases may be resolved completely at a case conference.
- Except in emergencies, no motions (except written motions for disclosure) can occur before a case conference. No motion can occur after a case conference if the judge does not permit motions.
- There can be repeated case conferences to address procedural issues or try to settle parts of the case and avoid motions.

Case continues (next page)

John P. Schuman, C.S., Family Lawyer, Mediator and Arbitrator

> Unless a judge orders deadlines, the following take place on the schedule of the parties:
>
> Parties retain any "experts" and get those experts to write reports
>
> **Motions** for temporary orders (if parties cannot agree)
>
> Parties can **question** each other under oath on their financial statements or on other matters if a judge allows.
>
> If a **custody/access assessment** is ordered, or the **Children's Lawyer** is doing an investigation, that process takes place.

Settlement Conference

- Parties should have case already organized for trial, and have all their expert reports completed. They present a synopsis of their case to the judge.
- Parties exchange offers to settle the entire case and present those offers to the judge. The judge helps the parties try to settle the case. The judge hearing the settlement conference cannot preside over the trial.
- If there is no settlement, the judge sets the case down for trial.

> 30-365 days (or more) as set by judge or parties
>
> Parties may prepare additional evidence or otherwise organize their cases in response to the settlement conference.
>
> The parties may exchange further offers to settle as a result of the judges comments.

Trial Management Conference

- A judge conducts a conference to ensure the trial is organized and proceeds in an orderly fashion. This includes setting out who the witnesses will be for each party, scheduling them, dealing with special arrangements needed for the trial, time tabling the exchange of documents that will be used for trial and similar matters.
- If the judge will not be the trial judge, and has time, he or she may try to further assist the parties with settlement.

> 10-120 days (depending on Court's Schedule)
>
> Generally, no further motions are allowed.
>
> Parties serve final expert's reports at least 90 days before trial.
>
> Responding expert's reports are due 60 days before trial.
>
> Any reply expert's reports are due 60 days before trial.
>
> Parties serve *Evidence Act* Notices 7 or 10 days before trial.
>
> Parties complete other trial preparations.
>
> Parties serve additional offers to settle.

Trial

- A different judge hears witnesses testify in court and reviews the documents that the witnesses present.
- The lawyers (or the parties if they do not have lawyers) tell the judge how each of them thinks the law applies to what the witnesses have said and the documents show.
- The judge decides the issues between the parties and makes a final order. The judge has 6 months to do this.

For each appearance before a judge, documents must be filed. These depend on the appearance and the particular court.

How to Start a Court Proceeding

If the parties cannot negotiate a separation agreement and resolve the issues between them on an amicable basis, then the most common method to reach a resolution of issues between them is to go to court. Going to court does not mean that the negotiations stop. To the contrary, more than 95 percent of all Family Law proceedings are resolved by way of a settlement between the parties, and not by a court's decision after a trial. Going to court is useful when court orders are necessary to make a party do what he or she is supposed to do under the law. For example, judges may make orders that parties have to provide financial disclosure, or that set a timeline for the parties to do various tasks, or make an order that one spouse pay the other an appropriate amount of support while the matters between them are being resolved. Going to court also allows the parties to get non-binding opinions from one or more judges as to what the appropriate resolution of the case should be. This can be especially helpful when the parties have very different views as to how they should finally resolve the issues between them.

If a party is going to court to enforce a Family Arbitration Award (there is more on Family Arbitration toward the end of this Part), then the process is a little different – and a lot more streamlined. That party starts the court proceeding using a "Request to Enforce a Family Arbitration Award" and not a standard "Application.[36] The parties then follow the special procedure for enforcing Arbitration Awards, which is described further below.

Applying for a Divorce (Pleadings)

The first step to get to court is to prepare the initial documents. Going to court requires the preparation of many documents. The first documents that must be put together for a court case are called the "pleadings." In addition, when a court case will address financial matters, the parties must prepare financial statements.

The pleadings are comprised of three documents: the Application, the Answer, and the Reply. These documents set out what each party wants from the court, the facts that the party says entitles him or her to that relief, and also a response to the other party's requests and facts.

---

[36] Rule 8(1.1) of the *Family Law Rules* (Ontario).

John P. Schuman, C.S., Family Lawyer, Mediator and Arbitrator

The party who starts the court proceeding files a document called an "Application". The Application sets out what orders that party wants the court to make, and the supporting facts.

The other party (or parties, as the case may be) files a document called an "Answer." The Answer sets out the facts that challenge the orders sought in the Application and any orders in the Application that you agree with. The Answer can also contain a request for the court to make orders in favour of the answering party and the facts on which a court would make those orders.

The party who initiated the proceedings is then permitted to file one last pleading, called a "Reply." The Reply is the first party's chance to respond to any new claims or allegations made in the "Answer."

Having properly drafted pleadings is important because, throughout the court proceedings, a judge cannot make an order that is not related to the relief sought in the pleadings, except in special circumstances where the court has to act on its own initiative to protect the children.

Parenting Affidavits Show that the Children Will Be Safe

Unfortunately, there have been a few cases where the Application, Answer and Reply did not provide the court with complete or accurate information upon which to base a custody or access order. The court, unknowingly, made an order placing children in the care of people who should not have been caring for children. There were incidents where some of those children died. As a result, in cases involving custody or access, the parties must file a Parenting Affidavit[37] to file an Application or Answer. The Parenting Affidavit is a court form that requires each party to provide specific sworn information. That information includes:

1. the party's proposed plan for the care and upbringing of the child(ren);
2. information about the party's involvement in any other Family Court proceedings, any child protection proceeding (court cases brought by a children's aid society) and any criminal proceedings;
3. details of any special needs that the child or children in the proceedings may have;

---

[37] The Parenting Affidavit is sometimes referred to as the Form 35.1. Both terms mean the same thing.

John P. Schuman, C.S., Family Lawyer, Mediator and Arbitrator

4. details of the parenting arrangements that person may have in respect to other children[38].
5. If the person claiming custody or access is not the biological or adoptive parent of the child, the affidavit also requires that person include the following additional facts in the sworn affidavit:
6. the details of any other court cases involving the child or children in the court proceeding[39];
7. a completed recent police records check[40];
8. a list of all the places where the parent has lived since the party turned 18 years old or became a parent (whichever is earlier); and
9. authorization for the court to obtain a report from every children's aid society where the party has lived regarding any involvement that the party has had with those children's aid societies[41].

Financial Statements – The Most Basic Way to Show What You Have

In cases involving financial issues, the parties must also file financial statements. There are two different financial statement forms in Ontario. Which form the parties have to fill out depends on whether the case deals only with support or whether there are issues that relate to property. Each party's financial statement sets out his or her personal income, expenses, assets and liabilities. Financial statements are sworn documents, like affidavits. The parties are allowed to cross-examine each other (by having their lawyers ask the questions) about the financial statements at any point in the proceedings. It is very important that each party ensures that his or her financial statement is accurate. It is easier to show that a party is lying, or not being careful, with regard to specific financial details, than it is on issues where it is possible for the parties to have different views on what is the truth. A party who has been shown to have been untruthful, misleading or inaccurate on his or her financial statement will have difficulty convincing the court that he or she is being truthful on other matters.

---

[38] *Children's Law Reform Act*, R.S.O. 1990, c. C-12, s. 21(2), as amended.
[39] *Children's Law Reform Act*, R.S.O. 1990, c. C-12, s. 21.3.
[40] *Children's Law Reform Act*, R.S.O. 1990, c. C-12, s. 21.1.
[41] *Children's Law Reform Act*, R. S.O. 1990, c. C-12, s. 21.2.

To start a court case that involves any form of financial matter (for example, child support, spousal support or property division), a party must file a fully completed financial statement. Many people find completing their financial statement like completing their income tax return. Even though the financial statement is much easier to complete, people put off the task of finishing it. It is best to start working on the financial statement right away so that there is no delay in going to court.

Part of completing a financial statement involves attaching the party's Notices of Assessment from the Canada Revenue Agency for the three years preceding the date of the financial statement. The court will not accept the financial statement (or the Application or Answer that accompanies the financial statement) without those Notices of Assessment. If a person does not have his Notices of Assessment, the fastest way to get them is to use the on-line My Account service on the Canada Revenue Agency's website. The web address for My Account is: http://www.cra-arc.gc.ca/myaccount/. However, ordering the Notices of Assessment does not satisfy the court. The copies of the Notices of Assessment must be attached for the court to accept the financial statement and related documents.

Molly thinks that things are not going fast enough. She sees a lawyer. The lawyer gives her several documents that she must fill out before she goes to court. There is a financial statement, with several pages of instructions, and hundreds of spots to fill in the values of her income, her expenses, her assets and her liabilities. Since there are kids involved, she also has to fill out an affidavit with the basic information about the kids, such as their ages, their schools and their special needs. Molly's lawyer also asks her to write out the history of her marriage, so the lawyer can start writing the application.

Financial Disclosure – The Foundation for Court Cases Involving Money

In cases involving any form of financial issue, be it support, property division or any other claims regarding property, separated spouses or parents must be able to clearly understand each other's financial situation. Parties cannot make arguments to a court about financial matters if they don't have a clear picture of the case's 'financial landscape.' Similarly, a party can only understand if a proposal or an agreement is fair or if they know what the other party has and what they could be entitled to. Parties cannot calculate how much child support or spousal support they may owe (or are owed) if they don't

John P. Schuman, C.S., Family Lawyer, Mediator and Arbitrator

know how much the other spouse earns, and they can't calculate a fair equalization of their net family properties without having a clear picture of each other's assets and liabilities.

Since financial disclosure is crucial to have productive discussions about any financial issue in a case, the *Family Law Rules* require that it be provided at the start of any Family Court Case. One of the most guaranteed ways to annoy judges is to refuse providing the basic financial disclosure early in the case. If parties are not prompt in providing disclosure, the other party may ask the Court to order you to provide it and get costs against you for having to do so.

Within 30 days of serving his or her Application or Answer, each party must provide to the other party all the financial disclosure that to understand each party's financial situation.[42] The *Child Support Guidelines* and the *Family Law Rules* list what some of these documents are. The overall list is extensive and includes, among other documents:

- Income tax returns (T1 General Returns), with all schedules and attachments, and Notices of Assessment (the document that comes back from the Canada Revenue Agency) for the three most recent years;
- The party's most recent paystub;
- A statement of performance-related pay (a statement of tips, profit sharing plans, or other incentive structures);
- If the party recently lost a job, a copy of the Record of Employment and information related to any severance package;
- For self-employed persons - three years of their business' financial statements or statements of business and professional activities, and the details of any payments made to non-arms-length individuals;
- For people receiving Employment Insurance, Ontario Works, Ontario Disability Support Program benefits, Workplace Safety and Insurance Board benefits, CPP benefits, or private pension plan benefits, statements showing the benefits paid to date and being paid;

---

[42] Rules 13(3.1), (3.3) and (3.4) of the *Family Law Rules* (Ontario).

John P. Schuman, C.S., Family Lawyer, Mediator and Arbitrator

- Municipal Property Assessment Corporation ("MPAC") assessments for all real estate owned by the party;
- Copies of statements for all bank, RRSP, and investment accounts showing the balance on the date of separation and, where available, the date of marriage;
- A statement of the number and types of shares owned by a party in any publicly-held corporation;
- For beneficiaries of a trust, the trust financial statements and trust settlement agreement;
- Mortgage statements showing the balance on the date of separation and, where available, the date of marriage;
- Statements for any lines of credit showing the balance on the date of separation and, where available, the date of marriage;
- Statements for all credit cards and other credit facilities showing the balance owing on the date of separation and, where available, the date of marriage;
- Any documents proving the giving or taking of a private loan.

The above is not a complete list of the disclosure that may be required to understand a party's financial situation. The disclosure that is necessary depends on the specific circumstance of the family. For example, where a party has valuable jewellery or artwork, he or she will also have to provide appraisals of those items. In addition, determining the 'income for support purposes' is much harder for a self-employed person who can control how and when they get paid, than for an employee who is paid by an arm's-length employer. This is why self-employed persons are not presently allowed to use the Ontario Government's newly introduced Administrative Calculation and Recalculation of Child Support service.[43]

When, after reviewing the initial disclosure, a party does not adequately understand the other party's financial situation, there is a procedure to get more disclosure:

---

[43] O.Reg. 190/15, s. 2.

John P. Schuman, C.S., Family Lawyer, Mediator and Arbitrator

1. The first step is to send a written request (letter or email) to the party, or their lawyer, for the additional documentation or information necessary to understand the other party's financial situation. The expectation is that anyone who receives such a request (if it is reasonable) will answer it within seven days.[44]
2. If the answer is inadequate, the party requesting the additional disclosure may bring a motion in writing for a court order requiring the other party to produce the required disclosure.[45] The disclosing party can challenge the necessity or relevance of the disclosure by responding to that motion. The expectation is that if such motions are necessary, the parties will bring them *before* the case conference with the intent of having the motion decided and the disclosure provided *before* the case conference. Judges' time is valuable and conferences in family court can be spent resolving many, if not all, parts of a case if the time doesn't have to be spent arguing about who has to provide what disclosure.

Practical Tip: Disclosure

People in family court, especially self-employed people, often feel that their spouse is demanding excessive disclosure just as a tactic to wear them down and drive up their lawyer's fees. Unfortunately, that is a tactic that some lawyers use. However, it is also often the case that a lot of information is needed to understand a person's financial situation - especially where it is complex. Every Family Court Judge has encountered countless bitter and dishonest parents or ex-spouses who try to hide large sums of money through organizing their finances in complex, but otherwise legitimate, ways. While former spouses who trust each other may be able to avoid extensive disclosure, former spouses who are suspicious of each other often need extensive disclosure to be sure that the other party is not hiding money.

In most cases, it is faster and less expensive to just provide all the requested disclosure than it is to fight about it. Judges like to see parties that do not spend their time arguing about disclosure, and who don't lose focus of the real issues in the case chasing disclosure.

---

[44] Rule 13(11)(a) of the *Family Law Rules* (Ontario).
[45] Rules 13(11)(b) and 13(11.1) of the *Family Law Rules* (Ontario).

Parties can use approach disclosure strategically. In cases where parties are suspicious of one another and may be trying to run up each other's litigation costs, providing large amounts of requested disclosure often forces the requesting party to expend large amounts of money having their lawyer (or accountant) review the disclosure to look for any clue of hidden money, only to find nothing. In cases where one party is seeking extensive disclosure as a tactic to annoy or frustrate the other party, it can also be quite disheartening when the party simply hands over disclosure without a fight because and shows that the requesting spouse is not "getting to them."

Not letting a former spouse get under your skin is one of the best tricks for succeeding in Family Court.

What If I Ignore a Family Court Application Against Me?

Every Family Court Application starts with a warning to the Respondent that he or she has 30 days to file an Answer[46]. (If the Respondent is served outside Canada or the United States, he or she has 60 days to respond[47]. In adoption cases, the timelines are shorter [48]). In addition to an Answer, the Respondent must also file a financial statement and parenting affidavit, as required, within 30 (or 60) days after being served with the Application. If the Respondent does not file the required documents before the deadline, then the court can continue the case without allowing the Respondent to participate at all. A Respondent who does not file an Answer may not receive notice of any further steps in the case[49]. If the deadline passes for filing an Answer, the Respondent needs the consent of the other parties, or a court order, to file an Answer or participate in the case[50].

When a Respondent has not filed an Answer on time, he or she is not permitted to participate in the case. The Applicant can move the case to an Uncontested Trial without taking any other steps[51]. Uncontested Trials can be heard either by way of affidavit or live evidence[52]. However, the Respondent is not permitted to be present and cannot challenge the Applicant's evidence.

---

[46] Rule 10(1) of the *Family Law Rules* (Ontario).
[47] Rule 10(2) of the *Family Law Rules* (Ontario).
[48] Rule 10(2.1) of the *Family Law Rules* (Ontario).
[49] Rule 10(5) of the *Family Law Rules* (Ontario).
[50] Rules 4(6) and 4(7) of the *Family Law Rules* (Ontario).
[51] Rule 10(5)(d) of the *Family Law Rules* (Ontario).
[52] Rule 23(22) of the *Family Law Rules* (Ontario), as amended.

John P. Schuman, C.S., Family Lawyer, Mediator and Arbitrator

Sometimes the presiding judge only reads the Applicant's affidavit in chambers and there is no court appearance. The judge at the uncontested trial cannot make an order for more than the Applicant asked for in the Application. However, the judge can order everything that the Applicant asked for in the Application. Therefore, it can be very dangerous for a Respondent not to file responding material on time.

Sometimes Respondents do not file an Answer intentionally. That occurs when the Respondent agrees with the Applicant getting the orders requested in the Application. Most commonly, this is how spouses get an Uncontested Divorce. One spouse asks only for a divorce in the Application. The other spouse does not file an Answer, which allows the Applicant to ask a judge to grant the divorce after 30 (or 60) days have passed. Sometimes the parties agree on the order that they want the court to make before either of them starts the court proceeding. If the Application only asks for an order that reflects the agreement, then the Respondent may not want to file an Answer, to allow the court to make the order more quickly.

If the parties do not agree on the orders that the court should make, then the Respondent must file an Answer before the deadline. Then the parties attend court to resolve the issues between them and have the court make orders.

After a year, Molly decides she wants to remarry. Desmond also wants a divorce. Molly starts the Court Application asking only for the divorce. She has a process server serve the Application on Desmond. Since Desmond does not object to the Divorce order that Molly is seeking, he does nothing. Molly waits 30 days, and then files an affidavit about the divorce, together with her marriage certificate, with the court. She also pays the required court fees. About two months later, Molly gets the Divorce order in the mail.

Your First Time in the Court House: The Mandatory Information Program

The parties' first court appointment will not be with a judge unless they find themselves in some sort of emergency. That emergency has to be a true emergency, such as a parent trying to abduct a child, a one spouse threatening to kill the other, or similar circumstances. In most circumstances, the first time the parties go to court will be for the Mandatory Information Program, or "MIP". The parties are required to go to the MIP within 45 days of the start of the case. The usual first court date before a judge or judicial official, the

Case Conference, is commonly at least six weeks after the start of the case. Each party goes to their MIP on a different day. There are separate MIP days for Applicants and Respondents. The sessions are often in the early evening and usually last about two hours. As the name implies, these sessions are mandatory; neither party can take any step before the court until they attended their MIP.

The MIP is required to provide information to parties on three topics:

1. the options available for resolving differences, including alternatives to going to court;
2. the impact the separation of parents has on children; and
3. the resources available to deal with problems arising from the separation[53].

Most people find the MIP session helpful because they know nothing about family law, the family court process, or the alternatives to court. However, the MIP session has been criticized because separated spouses do not attend until one of them has started a court proceeding. At that point, the parties may be committed to having a fight in court and the door is already closed on using Collaborative Law or Collaborative Practice to resolve their disputes. However, parties can still use negotiation, mediation or arbitration to resolve matters between them after starting a court case. They just put the court case on hold while trying those options.

First Meeting with a Judge: The Case Conference

In Family Law proceedings in Ontario, the first court appearance before a judge is supposed to be a Case Conference. The Case Conference is a less formal meeting between the parties, their lawyers and the judge. In a few court locations, when both parties have lawyers, the judge holds the Case Conference in chambers, or in a meeting room, rather than in open court. This is because, unlike other court appearances, conferences are not supposed to be adversarial. The idea behind Case Conferences is to allow the parties to have an open exchange of their positions on the issues with a judge present who can give non-binding opinions about each party's position. The focus of the Case

---

[53] *Practice Direction: Mandatory Information Program in the Superior Court of Justice in Brampton and Milton* (Attorney General of Ontario), available at: http://www.attorneygeneral.jus.gov.on.ca/english/family/family_justice_services.asp. Similar programs exist in all courts in Ontario.

John P. Schuman, C.S., Family Lawyer, Mediator and Arbitrator

Conference is usually on setting up the procedures necessary for the parties to move towards a resolution. That usually involves setting timetables, addressing any outstanding disclosure issues, and making other procedural orders to allow the case to proceed to trial in an orderly fashion. A Case Conference Judge can make any procedural order that is necessary to move the case forward. However, they cannot make any substantive orders (such as orders regarding support, custody, access or property issues) unless the parties agree on the order.

To make Case Conferences a productive discussion of the issues, the *Family Law Rules* require the parties to be present in court and prepared for all conferences.

After the Case Conference, the only other mandatory steps in a Family Law court case are the Settlement Conference, the Trial Management Conference, and the trial. However, Family Law proceedings frequently have additional steps along the way.

> *Desmond decides he does not agree with the orders that Molly is asking the court to make. He files an Answer and his own financial statement and affidavit regarding the children. About two months later, the first court appearance, the Case Conference, arrives. Molly and Desmond and their lawyers sit in a room with the judge. The judge talks to everyone about the case and tells them about the court process. After that, the judge tries to get the parties to agree on some of the issues to make the process easier.*

Having a Judge Decide Matters Temporarily: Motions

Frequently, the parties will need to have certain issues resolved on a temporary basis until they are resolved finally at trial. While a trial is necessary for a judge to make a final order on a contested issue, where a decision cannot wait until trial, judges can make temporary orders on that issue that last until the trial or the parties reach a final settlement. To have a judge make such a decision, a party must bring a motion. The type of issues that are frequently decided on motions are: how much temporary support will be paid, where the children will live until the trial, what access a child will have to each parent, and what travel arrangements will be permitted until the trial is heard. Judges expect that the parties will have discussed these issues and tried to resolve them before bringing a motion. In Ontario, there is a rule that, except in exceptional circumstances, the parties must discuss an issue at a Case Conference before they are allowed to bring motions about them[54].

Where one of the parties is being very uncooperative or behaving poorly, it is possible to bring a motion before a Case Conference. However, judges will only hear a motion before a Case Conference if there is urgency[55]. "Urgency" means that one of the parties, or a child, will be irreparably harmed if the parties are forced to wait to discuss things at a Case Conference before bringing a motion. Since motions are adversarial and often involve the parties filing material attacking the other, judges have set a high threshold for hearing a motion before a Case Conference, which is supposed to be less adversarial. It is common to hear judges say that before they will hear a motion before a Case Conference there must be "no money left for food" or "the plane must be on the tarmac to take the child away".

The preparation for a motion is quite labour intensive - much more so than the preparation necessary for a conference. There must be Notices of Motion that set out exactly what order a party wants the court to make. In addition, since the parties do not testify in the witness box at a motion, their evidence is put before the court in written affidavits[56]. Affidavits are also sworn documents. Judges expect parties to make sure that their affidavits are 100 percent accurate. A party who lies in an affidavit, in addition to losing all credibility before the court, can also be prosecuted for perjury. Since a judge hearing a motion will be imposing a decision on the parties, it is very important that the affidavits be carefully drafted to tell the judge all the facts that he or she needs to know in a persuasive manner. For these reasons, the preparation of affidavits for a motion is a very large and time-consuming job.

In addition, many courts in Ontario either require each of the parties to file a factum, or strongly encourage parties to do so. A factum is a written summary of the important facts, the relevant legal principles, and the party's argument as to why it should be successful on the motion. A proper factum is a complex and technical legal document. Finding exactly the right precedent cases to support a client's position, and applying those cases' principles to the particular facts of the case is often a very time-consuming process for lawyers. It is very important that a factum be written in a persuasive way to help the judge see the law and the case from one side's perspective. For these reasons,

---

[54] Rule 14(4) of the *Family Law Rules* (Ontario), as amended.
[55] Rule 14(4.2) of the *Family Law Rules* (Ontario), as amended.
[56] Rule 14(9) of the *Family Law Rules* (Ontario), as amended.

John P. Schuman, C.S., Family Lawyer, Mediator and Arbitrator

the drafting of a factum is a very labour intensive process and, like the careful drafting of affidavits, is one other reason why motions are a very expensive undertaking. Each party should expect to spend $5,000 to $10,000 per motion.

At the end of a motion, the Motions Judge will make a decision, and that decision will be turned into a court order, which the parties must obey. When making a decision on a motion, the Judge must strictly apply the law. Judges cannot come up with creative solutions that the parties would have been free to create if they had been able to agree. For this reason, motions should only be brought when one or both parties have needs that are not being met and they cannot reach an agreement as to how to meet those needs.

Finding Out Your Spouse's Position: Disclosure and Questioning

As noted above, resolving Family Law matters requires that the parties make complete disclosure regarding their affairs to each other. Judges expect that each party will disclose all of the documents that could be in any way linked to any of the issues between the parties. This is why parties have to start their court proceedings with disclosing all of their financial disclosure. While the *Family Law Rules* do not set the same strict timelines for the disclosure of documents related to parenting, judges still expect that the parties will promptly exchange disclosure in relation to the custody access issues. In addition to each party providing all the documents that he or she has, through the course of the proceedings a party may also have to disclose documents in the possession of third parties that are in any way related to their income, expenses, assets, liabilities, or the parenting of the children. Generally, if there is any doubt as to whether a document can be in any way linked to an issue in the case, then that document must be disclosed.

Judges expect that parties will provide their disclosure quickly and will not conceal anything. Concealing a relevant document for any period of time can result in the court imposing sanctions against the concealing party[57]. A party who plays games with regard to disclosure is sure to acquire a bad reputation with the court that can work against them if they ever need relief from the court[58]. For this reason, it is important that parties to a Family Law

---

[57] Rule 19(10) of the *Family Law Rules* (Ontario), as amended.
[58] In 1978, Galligan J. commented on the expectations of parties in Family Law proceedings to make disclosure. In *Siverstein v. Silverstein* (1978), 20 O.R. (2d) 185 (H.C.J.) at page 3, he wrote:

John P. Schuman, C.S., Family Lawyer, Mediator and Arbitrator

proceeding give their lawyers every document that they think could possibly be relevant to the issues in that proceeding as soon as possible and ask their lawyer if they are unsure as to whether they need to produce something. The obligation to provide disclosure is an ongoing one. This means that each party has to keep the documents that are relevant as they come into existence, and provide them to the other party, during the course of the proceeding[59]. For example, in support cases, the parties must continue to provide their tax returns, every year, during the proceedings[60]. They will probably also have to disclose updated banking records, proof of expenses relating to the children, and other documents as those documents are created through the course of the proceeding.

In addition to the disclosure of documents, it is commonplace in Family Law proceedings to have Questioning. Questioning is another type of disclosure. It involves a party going to a court reporter's office to answer questions posed by the other party's lawyer. The questions are asked under oath in the same way that a witness swears to tell the truth at a trial[61]. There is a court reporter present who records all the answers. Usually, the court reporter prepares a transcript of the questions and the answers[62]. That transcript can then be filed with the court and used by a party in the same way as an affidavit. Because of this, it is very important that a party's answers at the Questioning be truthful and accurate. Parties should expect to spend time preparing for Questioning to make sure they know the facts of his or her case

---

It seems to me that any party who does not comply with the letter and the spirit of ss.5 and 23, must realize that a Court might very well draw unfavourable inferences against that party if a statement under those sections is less than frank and complete. Any unnecessary prolonging of process because of the failure of such statement to be full, frank and complete ought to be at the cost of the person whose statement or statements are deficient. It is desirable that litigation relating to property and/or support ought not to be prolonged by extensive inquiry into a party's assets, means, income or needs. All of these matters ought to be capable of a speedy resolution based on full, complete, frank and early disclosure. I think a Court should look with great disfavour upon a party who neglects to give that kind of disclosure in the statements required under ss. 5 and 23.

[59] Rule 19(8) of the *Family Law Rules* (Ontario), as amended.
[60] Section 25(1) of the *Child Support Guidelines* (Canada and Ontario).
[61] Rule 20(1) of the *Family Law Rules* (Ontario).
[62] Rule 20(23) of the *Family Law Rules* (Ontario).

John P. Schuman, C.S., Family Lawyer, Mediator and Arbitrator

and do not contradict what he or she said in the pleadings, affidavits, or financial statements.

Frequently while being questioned, a party will be asked questions where they aren't sure of the answer, or that relate to documents that have not been disclosed. In either case, the party, or his or her lawyer, may give an Undertaking to either answer the question more fully later, provide undisclosed documents, or make inquiries as to whether a certain document exists. If a party undertakes to provide a document, that undertaking has the same force in law as a court order. Judges expect parties to fulfill their Undertakings completely and quickly. Failure of a party to do so can also result in serious sanctions by the court.

> *Desmond and Molly are both self-employed, so their divorce is much more complicated. Desmond's store is incorporated. In addition to his own tax returns, Desmond must produce his corporate tax returns and his corporation's financial statements. Molly also asked for his General Ledger because she wants to see if in addition to his "salary", Desmond is "writing off" some of his personal expenses through the corporation. If Desmond does that, it affects both the value of the corporation and the income he has to pay support.*
>
> *Molly is not incorporated. However, she does write off "business expenses" on her tax return. Desmond wants to see whether the expenses are legitimate.*
>
> *Both Desmond and Molly are confused by the documents that they have given to each other. They decide to do "Questioning" to help each of them understand the other's finances.*

In addition to facilitating disclosure and allowing each party to understand the other party's positions, Questioning serves the important function of letting the opposing party and his or her lawyer see how a party testifies. If a party at Questioning presents as a good and credible witness, then that same party will likely be a good and credible witness at trial which may result in the Trial Judge making an order in that party's favour. If a party testifies poorly at Questioning, then the opposing lawyer may form the opinion that it is worth going to trial. It is common for cases to settle after Questioning. This is because if a party testifies well, then the other party will want to avoid the trial. If a party testifies poorly, then that party's lawyer will feel that a better result could be reached by settling than taking the issues to trial.

John P. Schuman, C.S., Family Lawyer, Mediator and Arbitrator

Stuck in an Impasse: Settlement Conferences and Moving to Trial

After both parties have completed all of their disclosure, and finished the process of Questioning (if Questioning was held), the parties should each have enough information to know what an appropriate way to resolve the case should be or what the range of possible results at trial could be. It is at that point that the parties go back to meet with a judge for a Settlement Conference. This is another less formal attendance, like a Case Conference. The parties present their positions to the court and the reasons why he or she believes that his or her position will succeed at trial, based on the disclosure and other evidence he or she has received up to that point. Both parties are also required to make Offers to Settle at the Settlement Conference. The Settlement Conference Judge's mandate is to look at the parties' positions and the facts that they present, and try to help the parties reach a settlement either by commenting on the strengths and weaknesses of their respective cases or by providing an opinion as to how that Judge would decide the issues at trial[63]. It is hoped that at that point, the parties will be able to reach a settlement, or shortly thereafter.

It is important to note that the Settlement Conference Judge will *not* be the Trial Judge[64]. And the opinion that the Settlement Conference Judge gives is not binding on the Trial Judge. Further, the Settlement Conference Judge does not tell the Trial Judge what happened in the Settlement Conference, what the positions of the parties were, or what the Settlement Conference Judge recommended. In fact, what happens at a Settlement Conference is confidential and neither party is permitted to tell another judge what anyone said at the Settlement Conference[65]. The confidential nature of Settlement Conferences is designed to allow parties to speak candidly about what they want at the end of the proceedings, without compromising their positions if the matter proceeds to trial. If the parties are not able to settle, the Settlement Conference Judge can either adjourn the proceeding to another Settlement Conference if the parties are working toward settlement, or, if it appears that settlement is unlikely, the Settlement Conference Judge can adjourn the proceedings to a Trial Management Conference[66].

---

[63] Rule 17(5) of the *Family Law Rules* (Ontario), as amended.
[64] Rule 17(24) of the *Family Law Rules* (Ontario), as amended.
[65] Rule 17(23) of the *Family Law Rules* (Ontario), as amended.
[66] Rule 17(10) of the *Family Law Rules* (Ontario), as amended.

John P. Schuman, C.S., Family Lawyer, Mediator and Arbitrator

Planning an Orderly Trial at Trial Management Conferences

The last step before trial is usually a Trial Management Conference. In some jurisdictions, the Trial Judge conducts the Trial Management Conference. In others, another judge, usually a judge who has heard one of the previous conferences, conducts them. The purpose of the Trial Management Conference is only procedural. It is to help the parties, and the judge, organize the trial. There is a discussion of how many witnesses will be called, how long those witnesses will take to testify, how the witnesses will give evidence (in person or by way of affidavit), any scheduling issues and whether the Trial Judge must hear any motions at the outset of trial[67]. The Trial Management Conference Briefs also include opening statements to give the Trial Management Conference Judge an idea what the trial is about. This allows the Judge to be of greater assistance in organizing the trial. If the Trial Judge does not conduct the Trial Management Conference, then the parties' Trial Management Conference Briefs, the opening statements, and the Trial Management Conference Judge's Endorsement (that Judge's comments and directions regarding the trial) go to the Trial Judge for review.

The Trial Management Conference is not another attempt to settle the case, although the Trial Management Conference Judge may direct another Settlement Conference if that Judge believes a settlement is possible[68]. The Trial Judge will not try to mediate or otherwise assist the parties in reaching a settlement. The Trial Judge's only job is to hear the trial and come to a decision. In most jurisdictions, if a case has made it to the Trial Management Conference, then the Settlement Conference Judge has previously reached the decision that it is not possible for the parties to settle.

Preparing for Trial is a Big, Difficult Job

Trials are very formal proceedings. The lawyers and the parties must complete many procedural steps in preparation for the trial. One of these steps is the preparation of the trial record, which is a bound volume containing the pleadings, financial statements, court orders and other important documents[69]. The trial judge does not get the whole court file for the proceeding but instead gets the trial record with the essential documents.

---

[67] Rule 17(6) of the *Family Law Rules* (Ontario), as amended.
[68] Rule 17(6)(a) of the *Family Law Rules* (Ontario), as amended.
[69] Rule 23(1) of the *Family Law Rules* (Ontario), as amended.

In preparation for trial, the parties must also exchange various formal notices to rely on business records or expert opinions at trial. They may also exchange witness statements, and binders (or computer DVDs) that contain all documents that each party wants the judge to see at trial. In addition, each side must prepare its own witnesses and also prepare the cross examinations of the other side's witnesses. Each side also prepares any objections that it anticipates to the other party's evidence, which can include legal research on complex areas of evidence law and preparing oral or written arguments. Usually, both sides also prepare written opening and closing statements that contain their interpretations of the law that applies to the issues in the trial. Trial preparation is a very labour intensive and time consuming process. It often involves several lawyers and law clerks, together with their assistants, working very hard to get all of the work completed that has to be done for trial.

During the trial preparation, both sides become very familiar with both his or her case and the case that the other side will likely present. In addition, each party will look at the strengths and weakness of her case to determine her strategies for trial. After all of this analysis, both sides usually have a fairly realistic idea of what the likely outcome at trial should be. It is at this stage that not only is there a lot of work being done preparing for the trial itself, but there is also a lot of work being done exchanging Offers to Settle.

One Last Attempt to Avoid the Big Battle: the Pre-Trial

In some jurisdictions, the court will schedule an Exit Pre-Trial[70] shortly before the trial is scheduled to begin. The purpose of these pre-trial is to give the parties, who should have been exchanging offers, one last chance meet with another judge to try to settle the case. At this point, each party should know the range of possible outcomes at trial, the strengths and weaknesses of their case, and what the cost will be if the matter goes to a full trial. Having one or two lawyers spend all day at court for several days, and then spend the evenings doing additional preparation, while the law clerks also work during the day on issues that arise during the trial, is very expensive. In addition, the trial, which is essentially an all out war between the parties, can be emotionally draining on the parties and very damaging to any rapport that they may have left with each other. This is why, even at this late stage, judges may want to hold a Pre-Trial to resolve the case without a full trial.

---

[70] So called because the parties are exiting the court's case management system designed to facilitate settlement.

John P. Schuman, C.S., Family Lawyer, Mediator and Arbitrator

In jurisdictions that do not have Pre-Trials, if the lawyers, or the Trial Judge, think it is possible to reach a settlement, then the Trial Judge may refer the parties to meet with another judge to try to mediate a settlement. This can happen anytime before trial, and can also take place in the middle of a trial in an attempt to come to a settlement. While cases can settle after a judge hears the trial but before that judge renders the decision, it is very uncommon for another judge to step in at that point to try to mediate a solution.

Being Reasonable Helps: The Advantage of Offers to Settle

Offers to Settle are almost always exchanged before trial and before motions, and often before other steps in a court proceeding. It is critical for the parties in a court proceeding to understand the rules regarding Offers to Settle[71].

In Family Law matters, Offers to Settle must be in writing, must be signed by the party making the offer, and the party's signature must be witnessed. These rules should be familiar as they are the rules that must be followed to have an enforceable separation agreement. If a party makes an Offer to Settle, and the other party accepts it, which must also be done in writing, the Offer to Settle becomes a separation agreement and is enforceable as such[72]. When making an Offer to Settle, the party making it must understand that if the other side accepts the Offer, it becomes a binding contract.

Offers to Settle have a profound impact on the awarding of costs if the parties do not settle their case. In Canada, there is a "loser pays" court system. What this means is that at each step in a case, the party that loses can expect to pay some or all of the legal fees incurred by the winning party[73]. The exception to the general rule that costs will be ordered at every court date is conferences. At Settlement and Trial Management Conferences, costs are usually only awarded against a party if that party is unprepared for the conference or has otherwise caused the conference to be less productive than it should have been[74]. However, a party who does not get what he or she wants at a motion or trial should expect to pay some or all of the other party's legal fees.

---

[71] These are found in Rule 18 and Rules 24(5) and (11) of the *Family Law Rules*.
[72] Rule 18(13) of the *Family Law Rules* (Ontario).
[73] Rules 24(1) and (10) of the *Family Law Rules* (Ontario).
[74] Rules 17(18) and 24(7) of the *Family Law Rules* (Ontario).

John P. Schuman, C.S., Family Lawyer, Mediator and Arbitrator

One of the most important factors for a judge in determining how much a party pays for costs is the Offers to Settle exchanged by the parties. It is very important for parties to understand that if they refuse to accept an Offer made by the other side, and the judge's decision in that step of the case is as favourable or more favourable to the party that made the offer, as a general rule, the judge must order that the party who did not accept the Offer pay all of the other sides legal fees from the date of the Offer until the hearing of that step in the case[75].

> *Molly brought a motion seeking a payment of $10,000 from Desmond. She served the motion materials on Desmond on June 30. On August 15, Desmond offered to settle the motion for $5,000. Molly did not accept that offer. After serving the Offer to Settle, Despond spent $10,000 on legal fees related to the motion. The judge heard the motion on September 1. After hearing the motion, the Judge ordered Desmond to pay Molly $4.500.00. Desmond asked the Judge for his costs in relation to the motion. He argued that had Molly accepted his offer, she would have received more money and he would not have incurred any legal fees. As a general rule, if Desmond spent $10,000.00 on the motion after making the Offer to Settle, Molly would get the $4,500.00, but would also have to pay Desmond $10,000 to cover his legal fees. Molly ended up paying Desmond $5,500.*

Judges consider other factors when deciding the issue of costs[76]. However, the most important factor is often the Offers to Settle that the parties have made. If a party has not made an Offer to Settle, the judge may view that party as unreasonably litigious. A party who does not make an Offer

---

[75] Rule 18(14) of the *Family Law Rules* (Ontario).
[76] Rules 24(8) and (11) of the *Family Law Rules* (Ontario) state that these factors are:
   a) whether a party acted in bad faith;
   b) the importance, complexity or difficulty of the issues;
   c) the reasonableness or unreasonableness of each party's behaviour;
   d) the lawyer's rates;
   e) the time properly spent on the case, including conversations between the lawyer and the party or witnesses, drafting documents and correspondence, attempts to settle, preparation, hearing, argument and preparation and signature of the order;
   f) expenses properly paid or payable; and,
   g) any other relevant matter.

John P. Schuman, C.S., Family Lawyer, Mediator and Arbitrator

appears to prefer fighting over negotiating. That gives the judge a negative view of that party, which may also influence the awarding of costs. Offers to Settle are very important in relation to trials and other expensive steps in court proceedings. When the parties are spending significant sums on legal fees, who is going to be responsible for paying those fees at the end can be a very important consideration. An award of costs can significantly increase or decrease how much a party receives at the conclusion of the motion or trial.

Trial: The Big Show Down

Where the parties have genuine issues that they cannot settle, the way those issues are resolved is by way of a trial. As a general rule, when the issues are important, there is no quicker or less expensive way to have the issues determined on a final basis. The trial is the "party's day in court" and a judge will not deprive a party of his or her day in court unless that party has behaved particularly badly throughout the court proceedings.

Trials usually start with the lawyers giving a speech to the judge, called an opening statement, about what they anticipate the evidence will be and how the law applies to that evidence. After that, the court hears from witnesses. Each witness goes into the witness box, swears or affirms to tell the truth, and then answers questions first posed by the lawyer who calls the witness and then cross-examination questions posed by the opposing lawyer (or lawyers where there are more than two parties). The Applicant in the court proceedings calls all of his or her witnesses first. Then the Respondent calls all of his or her witnesses. After that, the Applicant then has the opportunity to call witnesses to reply to the Respondent's witnesses, but only about issues that the Applicant's witnesses did not already address.

Trials have very strict rules of evidence. Some important rules include the following:

1. The lawyer who calls the witness cannot ask "leading questions". Leading questions are questions that suggest the answer and usually have yes or no as the answer. Witnesses must be able to tell their story on their own without being told by the lawyer what to say.
2. During cross-examination, the cross-examining lawyer can ask any question, including leading questions, provided that the question is somehow connected to the issues in the case and is not insulting or abusive and is somehow connected to the issues in the case.

John P. Schuman, C.S., Family Lawyer, Mediator and Arbitrator

2. Witnesses are only allowed to testify about what they actually saw, heard or did. They cannot testify about something that someone else told them. If a party wants to put what another person saw or heard before the court, the party must call that person as a witness. All witnesses must actually come to court and give their evidence in the witness box and be cross-examined. Judges will normally not allow parties to use letters, written statements, or audio or video recordings as a substitute for live testimony. The exceptions to this rule are very limited.
3. Every fact must be proven at trial, including ones that a party may think are obvious. Judges are not allowed to take anything for granted. They can assume very basic facts that are common knowledge and not contested, such as 1+1=2. However, each party must prove every fact, even the most basic ones, with which the other party does not agree. In addition, the law requires the parties to prove specific facts to allow a judge to make an order. By way of example, in a divorce proceeding, the parties must prove they were married, that they separated, that there is no chance of reconciliation and the divorce is not an attempt to perpetrate a fraud. If they do not prove these facts, the parties cannot be divorced.
4. Witnesses can only give evidence about facts, which are their recollections of things that they actually saw, heard, or otherwise experienced. Witnesses cannot give their opinions about anything unless they have been qualified as an expert. To be an expert, the witness must have special skills or training, which the Trial Judge does not have, such that hearing that person's opinion would be helpful to the Judge.

If one side tries to lead evidence at trial that is contrary to the rules of evidence, such as breaking one of the rules described above, that is when the opposing party, or more often that party's lawyer, raises an "objection". In Canada, that does not involving banging the table and yelling 'objection'. Instead, it involves standing up, and politely getting the judge's attention. If the judge does not notice you stand up (which is unlikely because judges hear a lot of trials and can anticipate when someone will want to object) simply saying "Justice"[77] to get the judge's attention. The objection should be made before the evidence is given in court, not after. So, as soon as there is a question, or

---

[77] In Ontario, the proper way to address a judge is using by calling him or her "Justice." Old terms like "Your Honour" or "My Lord" are no longer considered proper, although many older lawyers still use them.

John P. Schuman, C.S., Family Lawyer, Mediator and Arbitrator

the start of a comment by a witness that is improper, it is important to object immediately. The party will be expected to explain why the question or answer is improper, and the other side will have the opportunity to explain why it isn't improper or withdraw the question. Parties will reference the facts of the case, the relevant Rules of the *Family Law Rules,* and the rules of evidence after which the judge makes a decision on whether to hear the evidence. Many judges feel that parties do not object enough and allow too much inadmissible evidence to be given to the court at trial – often to the detriment of the party who did not object. However, parties that object too often without reason will be seen as disruptive and, in extreme cases, be prevented from making further objections.

After the Trial Judge has heard from all the witnesses, the lawyers give another speech to the Judge. That speech is called a closing statement. In it each lawyer argues why the evidence entitles her client to the relief that her client is seeking at the trial. A closing statement involves summarizing the evidence and applying the applicable legislation and court decisions (such as the ones referenced in the footnotes throughout this book) to demonstrate to the judge how the law and facts require that the judge make the orders the party has asked for. In many trials, the parties either do not agree on the facts, or do not agree on how the law applies to the facts, and their closing submissions reflect that. It is very important that the closing submissions are carefully and persuasively written, as they are they are often what the judge is thinking about when writing their decision.

Trial Judges almost never give their decisions immediately after the lawyers finish their submissions. Judges like to carefully review the evidence, the law and arguments made by the lawyers, and the Judge's own notes made during the trial. Judges must write up reasons that carefully explain the Judge's basis for decision after the trial. In most cases, judges will release their decision and the reasons behind it simultaneously. In some cases, such as where it is important that final arrangements for children be imposed without delay, the judge will (if possible) give their decision immediately after the trial and release their supporting reasons later. The Court of Appeal has held that Trial Judges are required to give full and complete reasons for their decisions[78]. It usually takes a judge some time to write a trial decision. The Judge may take up to a year to write his or her reasons. Judges usually deliver their decisions to the parties by sending it by fax to their lawyers. Trial decisions are public

---

[78] *Lawson v. Lawson* (2006), 81 O.R. (3d) 321 at para 9 (C.A.).

documents and are often published on a number of websites, such as CanLII,[79] for lawyers, parties and judges to rely on and reference in future cases.

How to Get a Formal Court Order

It is only in exceptional circumstances where a judge, or the court staff, writes up the court order arising from a judge's decision after a motion or trial. In almost every case, the judge only provides his or her reasons for decision, called an Endorsement, which sets out, in a general way, what the decision is. It is up to the winning lawyer to convert that decision into a formal court order, with precise terms[80]. The winning lawyer then has to send the court order to the other party's lawyer to verify that the order, as drafted, reflects the judge's decision[81]. There is a process by which the lawyers can go back to court if they do not agree on exactly what the terms of the formal order should be[82]. However, that is a relatively rare occurrence. When the lawyers are drafting up the order, they have a duty to the court to make the order accurately reflect the judge's intentions. The lawyer's duty is not to make sure the order says what his client wants it to say. For that reason, the drafting of the formal order is a process that has little client involvement.

After the lawyers have agreed on what the terms of the formal order should be, one lawyer sends a typed coped order on the court's form to the court office. The court staff reviews and signs the order, places the court seal on it, and puts a copy of it in the court file. This is called "issuing and entering" the order. The parties should accept that, except in emergencies, the process of getting the formal order issued and entered could take a few weeks.

What Do You Do If You Did Not Like The Decision? Appeal

If a party believes that a judge's decision was clearly wrong, then it is possible to appeal. The process for appealing a judge's decision is different depending on whether the order is temporary or final. Temporary orders are orders made after a motion or conference. Final orders are orders made after a trial or a summary judgment motion[83]. Temporary orders made by the Ontario

---

[79] http://www.canlii.org
[80] Rule 25(2) of the *Family Law Rules* (Ontario).
[81] Rule 25(4) of the *Family Law Rules* (Ontario).
[82] Rules 25(4)-(7) of the *Family Law Rules* (Ontario).
[83] A summary judgment motion is a special motion where one party tries to convince the judge that there is no genuine issue for trial, so it is safe for the judge to make a final order without hearing from witnesses.

Superior Court of Justice require leave to appeal. That means that to appeal a temporary order, the Appellant (the party bringing the appeal) must obtain a judge's permission to have the appeal proceed. For temporary orders, not only must the motions or conference judge's decision be clearly wrong and contradict other court decisions on the same topic, but the issue under appeal must be of some importance and have an impact on other cases[84]. This is a very hard test to meet and it is only in exceptional circumstances that a party can get the court's permission to appeal a temporary order. Even if a party gets permission to appeal a temporary order, there is no guarantee that the appeal will succeed.

Judges who hear trials make findings of fact. That means the Trial Judge decides whose version of the events is the correct one. The Trial Judge then applies the law to the version of the facts that the Judge believes to be correct. It is only in the most exceptional of cases that an appeal court will consider changing the Trial Judges findings of facts. The appeal court does not get to see the witnesses testify or see the documents or exhibits presented in context. Therefore, it is impossible for the appeal court to decide who the more believable witness was and which facts seem more likely to be correct. If the appeal court thinks that the Trial Judge was clearly wrong in making a finding of fact, then the appeal court will usually orders a new trial and will not make a decision on the factual issue.[85]

The usual ground for an appeal is that a judge got the law wrong. Appeal courts will consider whether a judge correctly interpreted and applied the law and, if they decide the judge got it wrong, they will substitute their decision for the trial judge's decision without a new trial.

Appeals are very labour intensive and involve a lot of paper work. If there was a trial, the Appellant must get copies of the transcripts and deliver them to the other party and to the appeal court[86] (transcripts are very expensive). Appeal courts also have very strict rules about how all the other documents they receive must be presented. They require several different types of briefs, which are bound books containing various documents. Appeal courts

---

[84] Rule 62.02(4) of the *Rules of Civil Procedure* (Ontario).
[85] The parties will be responsible for paying for that new trial just as they paid for the original trial
[86] Rule 38(12) of the *Family Law Rules* (Ontario).

also require elaborate written legal argument[87]. Since appeals are very labour intensive, they are also quite expensive. As with other court appearances, the loser in the appeal pays for some or all of the legal costs incurred by the winner. Again, Offers to Settle are one of the most important considerations for the appeal courts in making costs awards.

Appeal courts have the power to change or set aside the decision of the original judge who heard the matter. If a judge did make a decision that was clearly wrong, then a party should discuss with his or her lawyer whether an appeal would be worthwhile.

People Are Often Unhappy in Court – The Reasons to Consider Alternatives

Many people express that they were not satisfied with the results that they obtained by going to court. There are several reasons for this, which are also reasons to give serious considerations to the alternatives to court.

Court Takes the Decision Making Away from the Separated Spouses or Parents

Going to court takes all of the decision making power out of the hands of the spouses or parents. A stranger to the family, the judge, who has only a little time to get to know the parties and the children, makes decisions that can change the family forever. That may be a good thing when the spouses or parents cannot make good decisions. However, often the issue is not that the spouses or parents are making bad decisions, but that they do not agree which acceptable choice is the best. So, they turn over that decision making to the judge. Each judge applies the law as he or she sees it. A particular judge's values may differ from the ones that the parties used to make decisions when they were together. The judge's values can be different from the values that the parties want to use when making decisions now. However, if the parties cannot agree on anything, and they have to turn over decision-making to the court, they lose the power to shape their family the way they want.

---

[87] Rules 61.09-61.12 and 62.01 of the *Rules of Civil Procedure* (Ontario) and Rules 38(17)-(20) of the *Family Law Rules* (Ontario).

John P. Schuman, C.S., Family Lawyer, Mediator and Arbitrator

Court Resources Are Limited and Limit the Judge's Knowledge of the Family

It can be really helpful to have someone who knows the family and its situation either make the decisions or help the separated spouses or parents try to settle. The number of judges available to hear family court matters varies from place to place. However, it is only in exceptional circumstances, or with an exceptional judge, that a judge can really get to know a family and find creative solutions to problems. It is not uncommon for a judge to have more than twenty families on her list for one day, which allows that judge to spend ten minutes on each family's problems. One of the advantages of the alternatives to court is that the professionals are being paid to get to know the family well enough to create solutions tailored for the family.

Courts Can Only Deal With Legal Issues – Not Emotions or Feelings

Feelings do not matter in court. Judges are lawyers by training. Their job is to apply the law. It is not their job to listen about how separated spouses feel, or do things to make them feel better. The law says that a spouse having an affair does not matter[88] unless the children are somehow involved[89]. A judge is not going to say that one spouse was bad for having an affair. Further, judges do not want to hear about how a spouse was hurt by the other's infidelity. It is quite the opposite: judges will not like people who act on, or talk about their hurt feelings. Judges expect separated spouses to behave reasonably, no matter how hurt they feel. A spouse who acts on hurt feelings may find that those actions seriously hurt their case. Spouses have to keep their feelings "bottled up" in the court process and find other ways to deal with their emotions.

Court Will Make Disagreements Worse Before Anything Is Resolved

By its nature, court is adversarial. It forces the parties to take positions and argue for their rights. That focus can actually ignore what the family, or its members, need or want. When there is a contested motion, trial, or other hearing at court, the parties attack each other's credibility and truthfulness. These attacks can leave long-lasting scars that hurt both parties, and to their ability to work together in the future for the benefit of their children.

---

[88] *Divorce Act*, R.S.C. 1985, c.3 (2nd Supp), s. 15.2(5); *Family Law Act*, R.S.O. 1990, c.F-3, s.5(6), 33(10)
[89] *Children's Law Reform Act*, R.S.O. c.C-12, S.24(2)(g), as amended.

John P. Schuman, C.S., Family Lawyer, Mediator and Arbitrator

Court is Expensive and Time Consuming

In addition, the court process is very formal. There is a lot of paperwork that has to be filed at each step and many rules about how that paperwork must be filed. Court documents must be properly served. Proper service often requires that the court documents be delivered to the other party or the other party's lawyer using a process server, which results in additional expense. In addition, the courts usually function by way of in-person appearances that must be scheduled when judges are available. It is only in exceptional circumstances that a judge will hear a matter before or after business hours or on weekends. That can mean lengthy waiting times before a judge is available to hear a particular matter. In addition, going to court often involves the lawyers having to sit and wait for the court to call the matter on which they are appearing. It is difficult for lawyers to do work for other clients while they are at court waiting. This means that the clients have to pay for the lawyers to wait.

As a result of all of the above, the court process is expensive. Even Case Conferences are likely to cost more than $2,000. Motions almost always cost more than $5,000, and it is not uncommon for them to cost $15,000 or more for each side. The intensive preparation and time required in court for trials means that they are very expensive. Trials can easily cost more than $50,000 per week of actual trial, which does not include the preparation costs incurred prior to trial. However, if the issues at a trial are complex, the cost to each party may be much higher, and may amount to hundreds of thousands of dollars. Trials over child custody issues are almost always long and complex. These figures do not include the costs of the steps required to get a case to trial.

Court is Public: Everyone Can See Your Dirty Laundry

Family court, except for child protection proceedings, is open to the public. Not only can the public go and sit and watch court hearings, but also anyone can walk off the street and read court documents. That can be a problem in many circumstances. Spouses in court over any sort of financial issue have to file their tax returns with the court. Anyone can go look at those tax returns. Anyone can go and read all the allegations in the parties' affidavits and learn the details of the family's problems. The situation can be particularly problematic if one or both spouses have filed tax returns that are not entirely accurate. If a party admits to problems with his tax return, or the other party proves inaccuracies in those returns in court, the taxman can go into the court, read the file, and then go after the party with the problematic tax returns. Creditors who are owed money can read the financial statements and find out where the money is or is not. Many people like the alternatives to court because their private affairs stay private.

John P. Schuman, C.S., Family Lawyer, Mediator and Arbitrator

But Sometimes You Have to Go to Court...

Nobody can force an angry or bitter or mentally ill or personality disordered former spouse to be reasonable. In the same way, nobody can force such a person to agree to an alternative to court. Where one of the spouses is out of control, only the Court has the enforcement powers necessary to control him. All of the alternatives to court require that both parties agree to use the alternative process. If one spouse just will not agree to anything, then she will likely not agree to an easy or streamlined out-of-court process. Court is the only process that one spouse can force the other spouse to use.

Ways to Avoid Big Nasty Fights: Alternative Dispute Resolution (Mediation and Arbitration) and the Online Child Support Calculation Service

Many Family Law parties want to get results faster than is usually possible in court. They also want to get a result without the costs involved with the formal court process. In Family Law matters, alternative dispute resolution (or "ADR") and Collaborative Practice are increasingly popular alternatives to court. To further assist parents to stay out of court where the only issue in dispute is child support, the Ontario Government has instituted an On-Line Child Support Calculation Service that can help parents set up or update child support obligations through an online portal rather than going to court.

Alternative dispute resolution or ADR consists of three types of processes: mediation, arbitration and mediation/arbitration.

Choosing ADR and Screening the Parties Before the Process

Alternative dispute resolution processes are voluntary. Both parties must agree to use the alternative dispute resolution process. They must also agree on who the mediator or arbitrator will be and some rules that govern the process. To ensure that the ADR process is voluntary, the mediator or arbitrator must screen the parties for power imbalances or domestic violence issues that might allow one party to coerce the other[90]. If the parties cannot agree on the ADR process or with whom they will mediate/arbitrate, or if there is a power imbalance such that one of the parties is not entering the process freely, then the parties must resolve their affairs through court. However, once the parties have both agreed to use an ADR process, and they have signed the required written agreement to use that process, they must use that process.

---

[90] *Arbitration Act*, S.O. 1991, c-17, s.58, as amended, O.Reg 134/07 s.2.

John P. Schuman, C.S., Family Lawyer, Mediator and Arbitrator

Neither party can go to court until either the mediation, or the arbitration, is finished. In the case of arbitration, parties can only go to court afterwards for the purpose of enforcing, appealing or setting aside the arbitration award.

Mediation

Mediation is a process whereby the parties meet with a mediator to try to resolve the issues between them. The mediator does not render a decision like a judge would. Instead, the mediator tries to help the parties come to an agreement. In mediation, the parties remain in control of the process. The parties work to come up with their own agreement that reflects their own values and what they want for their family. If the parties reach an agreement at mediation, that agreement is reduced to writing in a way that meets the rules for separation agreements. The parties are bound by their agreement. If the parties do not reach an agreement, then they are not bound by anything that anyone said during the mediation process.

Parties are usually more accepting of an agreement that they work out on their own, based on what they want, than they are of a decision that is imposed upon them. Court decisions often result in one or both sides being upset. The party that is upset may not follow the terms, which can lead to problems[91]. A successful mediation results in an agreement that both parties like, or can at least live with. When parties have a hand in making an agreement, they are more likely to follow it.

There are two types of mediation: open and closed. In open mediation, the mediator provides a report to a court, or an arbitrator, about what transpired at the mediation. In reading that report, the judge or arbitrator is able to determine what the issues were between the parties, what the obstacles to settlement were, and whether the parties were behaving unreasonably. In closed mediation, there is no report to an arbitrator or judge unless the parties reach a settlement agreement. If there is a settlement, the mediator reports the terms of that settlement[92].

Mediators are often Family Lawyers, retired judges, or mental health professionals such as psychologists or social workers. Psychologists and social workers are usually involved in mediations that only involve parenting issues.

---

[91] Part 3 of this guide includes a discussion of what to do when a party does not follow an order.
[92] *Children's Law Reform Act*, R.S.O. 1990, c.C-12, s.31(4); *Family Law Act*, R.S.O. 1990, c.F-3, s.3(4).

John P. Schuman, C.S., Family Lawyer, Mediator and Arbitrator

Lawyers or retired judges commonly mediate financial issues and often do mediation of parenting issues as well.

It is possible to go to mediation with or without a lawyer. However, it is not possible to finalize an agreement reached at mediation without a lawyer. Separated spouses will still have to go find independent lawyers to help them convert their agreement into an enforceable separation agreement. However, it can be very helpful to speak to a lawyer before going to mediation. A good family law lawyer can help streamline the mediation process to cut down on the time it takes to resolve the issues and the time it takes to finalize a separation agreement. Some mediators even require the parties to have lawyers for that reason. However, it in many cases, it is possible to get advice from a lawyer and then go to mediation, prepared with some understanding of how the law applies to the case and, consequently, what the range is for reasonable settlements. This can prevent second thinking a settlement later.

When parents are mediating with a social worker or psychologist, it is common for them to go to mediation without their lawyers. However, lawyers can be involved in those mediations as well, especially when the parties must deal with legal issues. Lawyers are sometimes not present at mediations where:

1. there is no power imbalance between the parties; and
2. the issues to be mediated are purely logistics, communication, or relationship issues and not legal issues.

Lawyers are usually present at mediations over financial matters. Financial matters are complex, because the law regarding financial matters (which includes family law, tax law, and in some cases trust and estate law) can be complex and parties may require some assistance in understanding how those laws will impact any settlement they reach. The parties may also need advice and guidance regarding how to come to a settlement and what a fair settlement would be.

When Going to Mediation, You Need to Speak to a Lawyer First

Even when you are proceeding with mediation, which is an excellent choice for most people, you should see a lawyer first and strongly consider having a lawyer's assistance throughout the process. There are three main reasons why:

John P. Schuman, C.S., Family Lawyer, Mediator and Arbitrator

1. Speaking to a lawyer helps the parties reach a good settlement at mediation. If you are reading this book, chances are you do not know much about the specifics of family law. You still may not know how family law principles apply to your situation. Most people fall into these categories and, consequently, can make costly mistakes. For mediation to work well, each party must go into the mediation knowing how the law applies to him or her and what is the best outcome and worst outcome if he or she went to court or arbitration instead. If a party know this, he or she knows the "settlement range." A person who knows his or her settlement range can confidently make informed decisions about what terms to accept for a separation agreement. Parties who wait until after mediation to see a lawyer may find out then that they made a "bad deal", that they got too little, or gave too much. In many of these cases, one party no longer wants to follow through on the agreement and the parties are back at square one. Making informed decisions through mediation leads to better and more lasting results. Even if a party does not hire a lawyer to go to mediation, he or she should still arrange to have a lawyer available by phone to get ongoing advice on the discussions at mediation.
2. Section 56(4) of Ontario's *Family Law Act* says that the Family Courts can ignore or completely discard a separation agreement if either party does not "understand it." Family Court decisions have also said that almost everyone needs to see a lawyer to fully understand a legal contract - especially complicated ones. So whenever judges are asked to rule on separation agreements, including ones for people who went to mediation, they always look first to see whether the parties each had independent legal advice.
3. When you are hire a mediator, you are hiring that person to get you and your spouse to reach a settlement - not to give you legal advice or to get the best settlement for you. Some people are unreasonable and they will only settle if they "get everything". In these cases, a mediator may only be able to get the parties to a settlement that is fair to only one party. There may be a big difference between what you should get under the law and the possible settlements at mediation. There are many different outcomes to mediation and you need the advice of a lawyer to know how to get what is best for you.

John P. Schuman, C.S., Family Lawyer, Mediator and Arbitrator

4. When both parties have lawyers, the mediation can often be finished much faster than if they do not. When the parties do not have lawyers, the mediation will usually take several sessions, often scheduled weeks apart. The mediator starts with helping the parties gather the information they need to understand each other's situation and financial circumstances. It can take several sessions for the mediator to gather all the information and then more sessions for the mediator to understand each party's position based on that information. In situations where a party takes a position that is not consistent with the law, it can take some time to draw that person away from that position as mediators are not allowed to give legal advice.

With lawyers attending at mediation, all the issues are often resolved in one or two mediation sessions. Most lawyers do not like to waste time (or their client's money) at mediation. So they get everything that the mediator and the parties need to settle the case together before the mediation - such as financial disclosure and briefs clearly outlining their client's position and goals at mediation. With briefs and all the disclosure exchanged, the parties and the mediator have all the information necessary to make a deal before the session even starts. With lawyers there to keep their clients informed and comfortable with the direction of the negotiations, matters are likely to resolve quickly – often in a matter of hours rather than weeks or months.

> *Molly and Desmond decided to take the issues between them out of court and try to resolve them at mediation. Their lawyers helped them find a mediator who would work well with both of them. Then their lawyers, exchanged Molly and Desmond's sworn financial statements and disclosure and addressed questions arising from that disclosure. About a week before the mediation date, the lawyers wrote "mediation briefs" which allowed the parties and the mediator to see each side's position and helped to narrow the issues to be mediated. The briefs helped Molly and Desmond recognize that there were some issues that they actually agreed on. They went into the mediation session knowing specifically what issues remained outstanding and each party knew his or her settlement range. The mediator focussed on those issues and after about six and half hours, Molly and Desmond had reached an agreement on all the issues between them. Their lawyers then started working on drafting the separation agreement based on the agreement reached at mediation.*

John P. Schuman, C.S., Family Lawyer, Mediator and Arbitrator

Family Arbitration

Family arbitrations are like a private court process. The parties pick the judge in that they pick the arbitrator. The parties cannot pick what law they want the arbitrator to follow. The arbitrator must apply the law of Ontario or of another Canadian jurisdiction and not religious laws or the laws of foreign countries (except where doing so is permitted by the law of Ontario)[93]. They are also able to pick what type of procedures the arbitration may follow and what procedural steps will be taken in the arbitration. Thus, the parties are able to tailor many of the formal court procedures to make their arbitration process less time-consuming or less costly. The hope is the modified process will assist the parties to come to a quick and friendly resolution.

Ontario Courts have constantly encouraged people to choose the family arbitration process to resolve disputes arising from their separation, because the arbitration "process can be less costly, more efficient and speedier than court proceedings"[94]. Another advantage of arbitration is that the parties can literally "pick their judge." They can select an arbitrator whose credentials, values and priorities match the need of the separating family. Because arbitrators are being paid to do so, they have the ability to spend more time getting to know the family and its needs priorities and to create an arbitration award that is tailored specifically to the needs of that family. Judges, especially in busy jurisdictions, have difficulty making the same "connection" with the family to arrive at a decision that fits "perfect" for the family.

Separated couples who want to resolve matters between them through arbitration must be represented by lawyers. For an arbitration process to be binding on the parties, they must sign an arbitration agreement that sets out the power of the arbitrator to make binding decisions, the issues on which the arbitrator can make decisions, the process that the arbitrator is to follow, and the rights that the parties have to appeal the arbitrator's decision. For arbitration on family law issues, neither the arbitration agreement, nor any awards that the arbitrator makes, are binding unless both parties had independent legal advice before signing the arbitration agreement.[95]

---

[93] *Family Law Act*, R.S.O. 1990, c.F-3, s.3(4), s.59.6 and *Arbitration Act*, S.O. 1991, c.17, s.2.1
[94] *Kroupis-Yanovski v. Yanovski*, 2012 ONSC 5312 at para 74
[95] *Family Law Act*, R.S.O. 1990, c.F-3, s.3(4), s.59.6(1)(b).

John P. Schuman, C.S., Family Lawyer, Mediator and Arbitrator

The parties can often move through an arbitration process much more quickly than they can move through a court process. The final step in the arbitration process is some form of arbitration hearing. Unlike with court where the final hearing has to be a full trial with sworn witnesses, a court reporter and strict rules of procedure and evidence, parties to an arbitration can agree to use a less formal type of hearing. The less formal type of hearing may involve the exchange of unsworn documents and written arguments rather live witnesses. The only rules for how an arbitration hearing must be conducted are:

1. the parties must be treated equally and fairly;
2. each party must have the opportunity to present a case and respond to the case of the other party; and
3. the arbitrator's decision must be based on the law of Ontario and Canada, and no other law.[96]

However, a more formal hearings may be necessary to decide children's issues as the arbitrator must have complete access to the all information necessary to decide those cases and have it available in a reliable way, or in a way where the arbitrator can assess the reliability of the evidence.

Even if the parties agree to use a very formal, court-like process in their arbitration, it may still be cheaper as the parties and the arbitrator are usually able to book the hearings in a more efficient manner than is possible in court.[97]

> *Desmond and Molly cannot agree on the value of Desmond's retail fruit business. Their lawyers help them pick an arbitrator to decide the issue. Desmond wants the arbitrator to flip a coin to decide whose value to use for the business. Molly wants a hearing that looks like a full trial in court. After negotiations, they agree that the arbitrator will receive written arguments from their lawyers with the documents that support those arguments. The arbitrator will make a decision based on only those documents. Molly and Desmond also agree that neither of them can appeal the decision to court as they both want the matter finished.*

---

[96] *Kroupis-Yanovski v. Yanovski*, 2012 ONSC 5312 at para 75, 86.
[97] By way of example, arbitrations can start early in the morning and end later in the evenings so that the process gets finished more quickly. In addition, the lawyers and arbitrator can schedule arbitration hearings in a manner that is more flexible than the court can be so that they lawyer can schedule the hearing around the availability of the witnesses, the parties and the lawyers.

After appeal period for an arbitration award expires, the arbitration award a party can filed it with a court and enforce it like a court order. Appeals of arbitration awards are to the Ontario Superior Court of Justice. The appeal is very similar to the appeal of a judge's order as described above.

Mediation/Arbitration

Mediation/arbitration is a hybrid ADR approach. As tits name implies, it is a combination of mediation and arbitration. In this process, all of the earlier procedural steps that are found in a court case (Case Conferences, Settlement Conferences, etc.), are replaced by mediation. If the parties are unable to reach a resolution at mediation, then the same person who was the mediator becomes the arbitrator. When the parties decide that a mediated result is not possible, the arbitrator makes a binding decision on the issues. However, the mediator/arbitrator cannot base his or her decision on what occurred at mediation. There must still be a distinct arbitration hearing or, for temporary matters, motions. The process for hearing those motions and the final arbitration is exactly the same as if the parties had just gone to arbitration.

Desmond and Molly cannot agree on support. However, they both think that court is taking too long and costing too much money. They agree to have a one-day mediation with Mr. Smith, a lawyer. If they cannot settle, then they agree Mr. Smith will arbitrate the issue.

On the first day, Desmond, Molly, their lawyers and Mr. Smith meet at Mr. Smith's office around the boardroom table. Mr. Smith speaks to Desmond and Molly separately about power imbalances and domestic violence. Since those are not issues, Mr. Smith tries to mediate the support issue. During the mediation, Mr. Smith talks to Desmond and Molly about their respective positions and gives ideas about how to settle. Unfortunately, Desmond and Molly do not settle.

Desmond and Molly go back to Mr. Smith's office for a second day. This time, the room has several tables and looks a little like a courtroom. There is a court reporter there. Desmond and Molly testify. They each answer questions asked by both lawyers. Then each lawyer tells Mr. Smith why his or her respective client should win.

A few days later, Mr. Smith gives a decision in writing. The decision is based on what Desmond and Molly said on the second day. It does not make any mention of what anybody said that the mediation. The decision is different from anything that Mr. Smith said at the mediation. Unless Desmond or Molly appeals, the matter of support is now determined.

John P. Schuman, C.S., Family Lawyer, Mediator and Arbitrator

Parenting Coordination is ADR for Difficult Situations

A special kind of mediation/arbitration that is often used in high conflict separations with children is "Parenting Coordination." Parenting Coordination is a type of mediation/arbitration for parents after they have a final parenting agreement or a final parenting order from the court. The purpose of Parenting Coordination is to aid in the implementation of the parenting plan in that agreement or court order. Parenting Coordination does not create a parenting plan – that is done through court, negotiation or through parenting mediation (or parenting mediation/arbitration), which follows the process for other mediations and arbitrations set out above. A Parenting Coordinator uses the parenting plan as the rules that the parents must follow, helps them implement them and resolves any dispute between the parents according to the parenting plan.

Parenting coordinators are most often social workers or psychologists. A big part of their role with the family is to improve communication and collaboration between parents. They not only mediate disputes between parents, but also try to teach the parents the skills to avoid future disputes, or at least resolve them on their own. However, when the parents cannot resolve the issues between them, the parenting coordination agreement give the parenting coordinator the power to arbitrate those disputes. The *Family Law Act* allows parenting coordinators to conduct especially quick arbitrations, based on as little as emails or phone calls, and without the need for an arbitration agreement for each specific dispute,[98] in order to facilitate the quick resolution of disputes. While this allows issues related to children to be resolved quickly, inexpensively, and with minimal impact on the children, it can also give parents who want to fight easy access to a forum to have those fights.

Family Arbitration Awards Are Binding on the Parties

All of the time and money that parties save using a family arbitration process would be wasted if the arbitration awards were not enforceable – or not easily enforceable. The parties would lose the benefits of a simplified procedure if they had to go through the entire court process whenever one party didn't follow the arbitration award. Fortunately, the *Family Court Rules* recognize this and Rule 32.1 allows for parties to head straight to a hearing before a judge once a party files:

---

[98] *Family Law Act*, R.S.O. 1990, c. F-3, s. 59.7.

John P. Schuman, C.S., Family Lawyer, Mediator and Arbitrator

1. A Request to Enforce a Family Arbitration Award (Form 32.1) or a Notice of Motion if there is already an ongoing court proceeding between the parties;
2. Copies of the certificates of independent legal advice showing the parties had "ILA" before signing the arbitration agreement;
3. A copy of the arbitration agreement;
4. The original award signed by the arbitrator or a Certified Copy[99]

If a party follows the above procedure, then the *Family Law Act* makes it mandatory for the judge to make an order on the same terms as the arbitration award (the judge cannot refuse to make the order) unless the time to appeal the award has not ended, there is an appeal in progress, or a judge has declared the arbitration to be invalid.[100] So, unless an arbitration award is successfully appealed, it will have the same legal effect as a court order and can even become a court order.

What to do if the Arbitrator "Got it Wrong"

Just as a party can disagree with a judge's decision and seek to appeal it to a higher court, there are also ways to have an arbitrator's decision reviewed by a judge in court. However, since parties make a legal agreement to get out of court by signing their arbitration agreement, going to court to get out of an arbitration award can be much harder than it seems - even before considering that the case law tells judges to be very reluctant to set aside the decision of an arbitrator[101].

There are three ways to get out of arbitration award:

1. Appeal the award;
2. Ask to have the award set aside because the arbitration process was improper;
3. Ask to have the arbitrator removed;

How difficult it is to appeal an award depends on what the arbitration agreement between the parties says. To have an enforceable family arbitration award, the parties must have gotten independent legal advice before signing the arbitration agreement[102] and advice on how and when a party could appeal is

---

[99] Rules 32.1(1),(2) and (4) of the *Family Law Rules* (Ontario).
[100] *Family Law Act*, R.S.O. 1990, c. F-3, s. 59.8(4).
[101] *Costa v Costa,* [2008] O.J. No. 930 (S.C.J.) at para 39
[102] *Family Law Act*, R.S.O. 1990, c. F-3, s59.6(1)(b).

John P. Schuman, C.S., Family Lawyer, Mediator and Arbitrator

assumed to be included in that advice. For that reason, the ability to appeal an arbitration award range from being difficult to appeal to being almost impossible. If the arbitration agreement does not set out the appeal rights, then the most limited rights apply: an award can only be appealed with a judge's permission and only on a question of law. The court will only grant permission for the appeal if the appeal is important beyond that specific case and the arbitration award significantly affects the rights of the parties. It is difficult to prove that both those conditions exist and convince a judge to give permission for the appeal to proceed. However, even if the appeal proceeds, the party appealing has to show that the arbitrator made a error law - this doesn't mean that the arbitrator got a fact wrong or even that the decision is unfair or unreasonable - the arbitrator must have applied the law incorrectly.

Setting aside an arbitrator's award is different than appealing it. There are a limited number of circumstances in which a court will set aside an arbitrator's award. These circumstances are found in section 46(1) of the *Arbitration Act, 1991*.[103] They are unusual and exceptional circumstances such as the arbitrator deciding issues not included in the arbitration agreement or the arbitrator committing a corrupt or fraudulent act. Perhaps the most common is that the arbitrator did not treat the parties equally and fairly or did not allow one side to present his or her case. However, an arbitrator can treat a party fairly and make a decision that is not favourable to a party. Before setting an award aside, a judge must decide that an objective observer would conclude that the arbitrator could not decide the matter fairly.[104] That means the process, not just the decision, must give an unfair advantage to one party over the other.

Similarly, the circumstances in which a judge will remove an arbitrator are very limited. Those circumstances only exist where there is a clear apprehension of bias, the arbitrator is unable to conduct the arbitration, the arbitrator commits a corrupt or fraudulent act or there have been undue delays in the arbitration.[105] Where there is an allegation that the arbitrator has acted inappropriately, the arbitrator is also a party to the court hearing and must be served[106] and allowed to participate to defend themself.[107]

---

[103] *Arbitration Act*, 1991, S.O. 1991, c. 17, s. 46(1) as amended.
[104] *Mclintock v Karam*, 2015 ONSC 1024.
[105] *Arbitration Act*, 1991, S.O. 1991, c. 17, s. 13(6) and 1s. 5(1) as amended.
[106] *Arbitration Act*, 1991, S.O. 1991, c. 17, s. 47(1) as amended
[107] *Arbitration Act*, 1991, S.O. 1991, c. 17, s. 15(2) as amended.

John P. Schuman, C.S., Family Lawyer, Mediator and Arbitrator

Further, if the parties agree on a specific process for the arbitration, which process may be very different from what happens in court, a party cannot later seek to have an award set aside, or an arbitrator removed, because the arbitration used the agreed-upon process.[108]

A party only has 30 days from the date of an arbitration award to bring an appeal of that award or to ask a Court to set aside the award.[109] There is no legal authority to extend that period - once it is passed, the right to appeal or have the award set aside is gone.[110]

> *Desmond and Molly decide to use family arbitration to resolve the issues on which they just cannot reach agreement. They chose an arbitrator together and agree on a simplified process for the arbitration. When Desmond gets the arbitrator's award, he does not like the result. He knows that the arbitrator's decision does not contradict any laws so, as his arbitration agreement does not give any special appeal rights, he cannot appeal. But, he still feels the decision was unfair to him. He asks a judge to set aside the award on the basis that the arbitrator did not treat him "equally and fairly." The judge refuses to do so as the arbitrator allowed Desmond to present his side of the story and listened to what he had to say. As is the case in most arbitrations, the arbitrator was careful to treat Desmond fairly and just disagreed with Desmond's position.*

Parties cannot get out of arbitration awards just because they do not like them. To the contrary, it is the finality of the arbitration process that makes it so attractive to many people involved in family law disputes.

Collaborative Practice – "Divorcing Without Wrecking the Kids"

Another very effective form of resolving issues through the negotiation of a separation agreement is called Collaborative Family Law, or Collaborative Practice. The clients, lawyers, and sometimes other professionals (such as divorce coaches, psychologists, child experts or financial advisors) work as a team in a fair and respectful process[111]. The goal is to reach solutions for the

---

[108] *Kroupis-Yanovski v. Yanovski*, 2012 ONSC 5312 at para 108.
[109] *Arbitration Act*, 1991, S.O. 1991, c. 17, s. 47(1) as amended
[110] *R & G Draper Farms (Keswick) Ltd. v. 1758691 Ontario Inc.*, 2014 ONCA 278 at para 19
[111] When only the parties and their lawyers are involved, the process is known as Collaborative Law rather than Collaborative practice.

clients which are mutually acceptable, constructive, and which allow them to move forward with their new lives.

An essential principle of Collaborative negotiations is that the parties want to settle without going to court or even threatening court. Before negotiations can begin, both parties and their lawyers sign a Participation Agreement that commits them to this principle. If one party does decide to go to court, both lawyers must resign from the case. This agreement ensures that everyone works hard to reach a settlement acceptable to both spouses.

The Collaborative approach has many benefits. Issues are resolved sooner and often at a smaller cost. The parties are in charge, rather than judges or lawyers. The parties customize their solution so they can come to more creative resolutions than a court can order. Those solutions can also be more tailored to the parties' situation than court orders. It is a private process, so the details are kept out of the public record.

An important aspect of Collaborative Practice is that the parties commit to working out the issues between them, using professionals as needed. They devote themselves to keep working on a resolution until they reach one. While this process can still be difficult, the success rate in reaching an agreement is very high. As the parties control the process, and determine the final result, they are often happier with the outcome, and less angry with the other party than if they battle out the issues in court or arbitration[112].

The Collaborative Practice process is often thought to be better for the children, because the parties are committed to working together, rather that fighting each other, and they come to an agreement that is tailored for the children, rather than having the court impose a resolution. Where the parties need assistance to determine what solution is best for the children, the Collaborative Practice process has them involve Family Professionals, who are social workers, psychologists or other experts on children and families, to advise on the best solution for the family.

An important difference between Collaborative Practice and court or arbitration is that the parties are encouraged to resolve on the basis of what their 'interests' are, rather than what their 'rights'(or entitlements) are. With this focus, parties often learn that each of them can get what they really want while

---

[112] The above discussion is based on information available from the Collaborative Practice Toronto Website: http://www.collaborativepracticetoronto.com.

John P. Schuman, C.S., Family Lawyer, Mediator and Arbitrator

still allowing the other party to get what he or she really wants. It is not the case that the winner gets what he or she wants and the loser does not, or both parties get a result that they do not want, which can be the result in court or arbitration.

Since Collaborative Practice if focused on the party's interests rather than their legal positions, the negotiations are very different from traditional negotiations – to the point where they may not seem like negotiations at all. Rather than working from positions where one party starts high and the other starts low and then they exchange offers, Collaborative Practice feels more like a brainstorming sessions where everyone throws out possible resolutions to issues and then parties and lawyers discuss the strengths and weaknesses of each possible resolution. If a parenting or financial professional is at the meeting, they weigh in with some professional advice on each option.

Collaborative Practice usually involves several meetings as the parties work through each aspect of the process together. Each meeting will have an "agenda" so that parties have a clear idea of what matters will be addressed at the meeting, and to reduce the possibility of parties becoming overwhelmed, frustrated or tired. At the end of each meeting, the parties agree on their "homework", which usually involves considering or preparing something in advance of the next meeting. The lawyers will also create and circulate "progress notes" which are brief summaries of the meeting that give the parties a reference as to what they accomplished at each meeting and where they should focus their energy going forward.

The Collaborative Practice process does not work for everyone. It will not work where both parties will not commit to working out an agreement. It will also not work where one or both parties are acting in bad faith, being dishonest, or concealing important facts or information. Collaborative Practice requires that the parties commit themselves to reaching an agreement, and using whatever professionals and tools they need to reach an agreement, as opposed to asking a judge or arbitrator to impose a resolution.

Using Collaborative Practice does not mean the parties can avoid producing disclosure or reach an agreement that is contrary to the law.[113] While parties are free to consider creative solutions to their legal issues, they cannot do anything that the law prohibits and any agreement reached must still fulfill the legal requirements of an enforceable separation agreement.

---

[113] *Webb v. Birkett*, 2011 ABCA 13.

Parties are often more satisfied after reaching an agreement through Collaborative Practice than those who have a resolution imposed by a judge, where neither party may get what they want. If the parties are able to commit themselves to the process and are acting in good faith, the Collaborative Practice process is one that separated couples should consider.

When It's "Just Math" – Resolving Child Support Through the Online Service

The *Child Support Guidelines* were designed to avoid conflict between separated parents by making the issue of child support no more than a mathematic calculation for most parents. The simplicity of the child support formula (it is based only on the income of the payer and the number of children) allowed the Ontario Government to implement an Online Child Support Calculation Service to replace court proceedings where the only issue between parents is child support. When the service calculates child support, the result is binding on the parents and enforced by the Family Responsibility Office – just like a Court Order.[114] The online service costs only $80.00 per parent and it avoids issues with financial disclosure. The service operates by allowing the Ontario Ministry of Finance, which does the child support calculation, to access both parents' income tax information from the Canada Revenue Agency. That information allows the online service access to not only the parties' incomes, but also what "Section 7 Expenses" they reported on their tax returns (which are daycare, medical and health expenses.) The calculation service does not calculate other Section 7 Expenses (such as tuition or extracurricular activities) that are not reflected on a party's income tax return.[115]

To access the online child support calculation service, either parent can go to this webpage and complete an application: https://www.ontario.ca/page/set-up-or-update-child-support-online .

The calculation service notifies the other parent asking them to sign in and use the service. The service can only be used if the support payer agrees to use it, or both parents if the service is asked to calculate section 7 expenses.[116] The service uses the parents' income tax information from the CRA to calculate the correct amount of base child support and then reports the

---

[114] *Family Law Act*, R.S.O. 1990, c. F-3, s. 39(14),
[115] O. Reg. 190/15, s. 3(1).
[116] O. Reg. 190/15, s. 5(4).

John P. Schuman, C.S., Family Lawyer, Mediator and Arbitrator

adjusted amount of child support to the Family Responsibility Office, which then enforces the calculated amount of child support.[117] Either parent can apply to have any errors in the calculation corrected through the service, [118] provided that parent asks for the correction within 15 days of being notified of the results of the calculation.[119] However, addressing any issues other than calculation errors requires a trip to court.

The online child support calculation services is only a calculation service. It bases the amount of support on the numbers in parents' tax returns –it does not investigate or 'look behind' the numbers. For the majority of separated parents, who earn most, if not all, their income as salary or government benefits and whose children reside primarily with one parent, setting child support is a simple calculation. It involves looking up the payer's income on the tables and applying a formula to determine contribution to Section 7 expenses. The on-line service will not make any determination of parents' rights and obligations that involves more that just doing math. For that reason, parents cannot use the online child support calculation in any of the following eleven situations:

1. Either parent or the child resides outside of Ontario;
2. The parents have shared custody of a child or split custody of children;
3. A child is over 17.5 years old, or a parent is paying for post-secondary education expenses pursuant to s. 7 of the *Child Support Guidelines*;
4. The support payer earns more than 20 per cent of his or her annual income from self-employment, or reported a self-employment income loss in the most recent taxation year.
5. The support payer earns more than 20 per cent of his or her annual income from a rental property;
6. The support payer earns more than 20 percent of his or her annual income from season employment in certain cases;
7. The support payer's income includes income from a corporation of which the parent is a director, officer or majority shareholder, or from a partnership of which the step payer is a partner;
8. A parent has an annual income of more than $150,000;
9. There is more than one parent who has to pay base child support;
10. Less than six months has passed since the child support order was made;

---

[117] *Family Law Act*, R.S.O. 1990, c. F-3, s. 39(15),.
[118] *Family Law Act*, R.S.O. 1990, s. F-3, s. 39.1(1).
[119] O. Reg. 190/15, s. 25(2).

11. The Child Support Order to be changed was not made by an Ontario Court.[120]

If any of the above applies, child support must be determined by a judge. Parents eligible for the online service can still opt to have child support determined by a judge, but the court system is much more complicated than the online recalculation service.

Should the Children be Involved in the Process?

The long-term impact of divorce on children is not related to the fact of the divorce as much as the degree to which children are exposed to conflict. Children who are exposed to parental conflict after separation adjust more poorly to their new situation and suffer more negative long-term effects[121]. However, it is also important for separating parents to listen to what their children have to say, and even more important for those parents to hear the emotions and meaning behind the children's words[122]. Many judges are now considering that the United Nation Convention on the Rights of the Child[123] requires that children have a voice in court proceedings that affect them. They struggle about how best to get that voice before the court. The requirement is that the court hear the child, but it does not specify whether that is as a witness, through a judicial interview or through an interview by a professional who reports to the court. The key to this balance is to listen to the children's opinion without involving them in the conflict or using them as foot soldiers in the war on the other spouse.

A child's wishes do not determine any matter before a Family Court. No child should think that he or she gets to make the important decisions after his or her parents separate. It is important to note that when a court or arbitrator has to decide custody and access issues, the opinion of the children is only one of at least eight factors that the court must consider[124]. The opinion of young children has little influence on a court or arbitrator. The opinions of

---

[120] O. Reg. 190/15, s. 2, 12, 14(3).
[121] Rachel Birnbaum and Nicholas Bala, "Toward the Differentiation of High-Conflict Families: An Analysis of Social Science Research and Canadian Case Law," *Family Court Review*, 48:4 (July 2010) at page 404.
[122] Joanne Pedro-Carroll, *Putting Children First: Proven Parenting Strategies for Helping Children Thrive Through Divorce* (Avery, 2010).
[123] UN General Assembly, *Convention on the Rights of the Child*, 20 November 1989, United Nations, Treaty Series, vol. 1577, p. 3.
[124] *Children's Law Reform Act*, R.S.O. c.C-12, s.24, as amended.

John P. Schuman, C.S., Family Lawyer, Mediator and Arbitrator

teenagers, who have the physical ability to decide where they are going to live, have much greater influence on a court, but are still not determinative. Judges give no weight to a child's expressed views where the judge believes that the child is only a mouthpiece for one parent or had been brainwashed or manipulated by either parent.[125]

How should the views of the children be presented to a court (or arbitrator)? The traditional view is that children should be shielded from the court process, or any other process that is the battleground for the fight between their parents. Also important is that children should not be forced to take sides, or choose between their parents. Children can feel enormous guilt if they have to make a decision in favour of one parent to the detriment of the other. Consistent with this view, Ontario has the Office of the Children's Lawyer. In Family Law disputes, that office may provide legal representation to a child[126], or appoint a social worker to investigate the circumstances of the child and make recommendations to the court.[127] These mechanisms allow the opinions of children to be heard by the court, without the child participating directly. However, a judge can only request that the Office of the Children's Lawyer become involved in a particular case. It is still up to that agency to decide if it will become involved.[128] The Office of the Children's Lawyer does not become involved in private arbitrations. An alternative is to privately retain a children's mental health professional to report on the child's views[129]. Children can also retain their own lawyers[130].

It is also possible for a judge (or arbitrator) to interview a child in an attempt to determine that child's views and preferences[131]. Until recently, judges avoided interviewing the children. They were afraid of putting children 'in the middle' and risking anxiety and trauma that could befall a child just by walking into a courthouse. However, research showing that children want their opinions taken into account, even if they are not followed, has led many judges to consider interviewing children.

---

[125] *L.(A.F.) v. D.(K.B.)* (2009), 93 O.R. (3d) 409 at para 143-148 (S.C.J.)
[126] *Courts of Justice Act*, R.S.O. 1990, c.C-43, s.89(3.1), as amended.
[127] *Courts of Justice Act*, R.S.O. 1990, c.C-43, s.112(1), as amended.
[128] *Bhajan v. Bhajan,* 2010 ONCA 714 at para 43.
[129] A court can appoint an assessor to report on any aspect of a child's situation, including the child's views and preferences: *Children's Law Reform Act*, R.S.O. 1990, c.C-12, s.30.
[130] *S.G.B. v. S.J.L.*, 2010 ONCA 578.
[131] *Children's Law Reform Act*, R.S.O. 1990, c.C-12, s.64(2).

John P. Schuman, C.S., Family Lawyer, Mediator and Arbitrator

Practical Tip: Getting Your Child's Voice Before the Court

Dragging a child to court to speak to a judge is still a bad idea. Few things anger judges more than a parent deliberately involving a child in any form of litigation. A parent who brings a child to court, without a specific invitation from a judge, makes it clear to the judge that that parent does not make good parenting decisions. Judges will only consider interviewing a child when it is clear that child wants to be heard in the process. If that interview makes it clear to the judge that the child has been manipulated or taught by a parent to tell the judge a certain story, that parent should not expect a favourable outcome in the court case. On the other hand, independently and carefully considered opinions of a child can be quite influential on a judge in a custody-access case.

It is also a bad idea for parties to interview their children personally and record the interview. Judges have seen lots of parents try to manipulate the child into saying things "for the record." Some judges also believe that recording children to use as evidence in court is bad parenting and see it as a way of parents exposing their children to the conflict between them. Judges do not want to encourage parents recording children and it is only in exceptional circumstances that judges will even listen to the recording. It is a criminal act for a parent to record a conversation involving a child when the parent is not present for the conversation.[132] Not only is a judge unlikely to admit such evidence, it may also result in criminal charges against the parent who made the recording.

If a child feels strongly about an issue, than the child should express those feelings to both parents. One or both parents can then express to a judge that it is important to hear from the child and ask the judge to consider one of the methods described above to receive evidence from the children. Asking a judge to hear from a child is more persuasive than telling a judge to listen to a child. Any request should focus on the child's particular needs, why the court should hear from the child, and what the best process (usually the one that is least intrusive for the child) is to hear from the child.

---

[132] *Criminal Code*, R.S.C., 1985, c. C-46, s. 184(1)

After a Court Hears a Child, the Child Must Do What the Court Orders

Once the court has had the opportunity to take a child's views into account, the court will make an order that the court feels is in the child's best interest. That Order may not be consistent with what the child said or what the child wants. The court expects that parents will obey that order even if the child does not agree with it. Adults are also expected to use all reasonable efforts, short of using physical force, to get children to comply with the parenting schedule in an access order. Parents must make children go for access visits, even if the child does not want to go, in the same way that parents have to make children go to school, to the doctor, to the dentist or to spend time with relatives.

Current social science thinking suggests that it could harm a child, or at least a child's relationship with their parents, to force them to decide what relationship they will have with each parent. Doing so can place a child in a conflict of loyalties. This can cause guilt and stress where child has to tell their mom or dad that they want to spend more of their time with one over the other. Regardless of a child's decision, being in this position will usually strain the child's relationship with both parents. A child who is given no say in how much time they spend with each parent will not experience the stress, guilt and emotional harm that comes with that decision. If there is something that seriously concerns a child, both parents should encourage the child to express their feelings to both parents and should address the issue in a balanced and cooperative manner.

There are Always Exceptions to Rules and Different Paths to Take

The above is a general discussion of the processes that spouses go through after they separate. There are exceptions to the above rules. In addition, there are also several other steps that lawyers and parties can take to advance their position and move the case forward. The complexity of the above rules, the exceptions to those rules that have not been fully discussed above, and the other procedures that are available, are reasons why it is important for spouses to have a lawyer after they separate. You should discuss with your lawyer if you have any questions about the above processes. A lawyer can also help you determine whether you should be taking, or avoiding, any other steps as you work towards a final resolution of the matters arising from your separation.

John P. Schuman, C.S., Family Lawyer, Mediator and Arbitrator

Part 2: What You Really Need to Know Before Making Any Decisions after Separation: The Basic Family Law Issues

Separation agreements and Family Court proceedings address four main areas of legal issues. They are:

1. parenting (custody and access),

2. child support,

3. spousal support, and

4. property issues (division of accumulated wealth).

There are other legal issues that can arise between spouses and parents after separation, although they are seen less frequently. They are:

5. restraining orders,

6. determination of paternity,

7. matters related to name changes,

8. addressing the removal of religious barriers to remarriage, and

9. a few other Family Law issues.

In addition, the *Family Law Rules* contemplate that the parties in a Family Court proceeding will address all of the issues between the parties in those proceedings and not just the Family Law issues. Judges do not want the parties litigating in a series of separate court proceedings[133]. It is, therefore, not only possible, but preferable to address issues such as tort (personal injury) claims, contract issues, corporate oppression remedies, further relief claims and other non- Family Law issues between the parties in Family Court proceedings[134]. The same type of issues can also be included in separation agreements. However, just because an issue is dealt with in a separation agreement does not mean that Family Law trumps the law that would otherwise apply. Parties who want to deal with non-Family Law issues in Family Court proceedings or separation agreements should seek the advice of lawyers who practice in the area of law that applies to those issues.

> *Molly has shares in the corporation that owns Desmond's store. Rather than buying those shares, Desmond is issuing new shares to make Molly's shares worthless. In her Family Court application, Molly asks the court for shareholder's remedies under the Ontario Business Corporations Act. Those types of matters would usually be heard in commercial court, not Family Court, but Molly knows that all the matters between two people should be addressed on one court proceeding.*

> *Meanwhile, Desmond has heard that Molly is telling everyone that the fruit at his store has parasites. In the Family Court proceedings, Desmond asks for damages for defamation of character.*

Since the law applies differently to the various situations in which parties find themselves, there can be variations in the outcome of Family Court proceedings. In addition, on many issues, it is possible for separated parties to think outside the box when they are negotiating the terms of a separation agreement. The parties can apply all the laws of Ontario Law, and not just Family Law in their separation agreements to make their agreement work. The possible resolutions in a separation agreement are almost endless, as compared to the decisions that the law allows judges to make. However, there are some general principles that apply.

---

[133] Rule 1(5) of the *Family Law Rules*.
[134] *Children's Aid Society of Durham v. C.(V.)*, 2004 CarswellOnt 3812 (Ont. S.C.J.)

John P. Schuman, C.S., Family Lawyer, Mediator and Arbitrator

Who Gets the Kids? Parenting (Custody/Access) Issues

The overarching principle on parenting issues is that the courts will always make the order that is "in the best interests of the children". The Family Law Legislation mandates that principle[135]. When parties are negotiating a separation agreement, they must be governed by the same principle, because the court will not enforce a parenting agreement that is not in the best interests of the children. Before making any order, even orders to which both parties consent, a judge must make an inquiry to determine whether the order is in the child's best interest.

A court takes into account several specific factors when deciding what parenting order is in a child's best interest. One factor is the "love, affection and emotional ties" between the child and each parent, and also the other members of the child's family and other people involved in the child's care and upbringing[136]. The court is also required to consider a child's relationship with people who are linked to the child either "by blood" (genetically) or an adoption order[137]. That means the court considers the biological parents and extended family even when the "love, affection and emotional ties" are not strong.

Another obvious factor that the court must take into account is the ability of each person applying for custody or access to act as a parent[138]. One of the considerations regarding whether a person can act as a parent is whether that person can not only encourage, but also facilitate, the child's relationship with other people with whom the child has "love, affection and emotional ties." Judges frequently comment that one of the best indications they have as to whether a person is a good parent is whether that parent supports the child having a relationship with the other parent. Judges have taken custody away from parents who have undermined their children's relationship with the other parent[139].

---

[135] *Divorce Act*, R.S.C. 1985, c.3 (2nd Supp.), s.16(8), as amended; *Children's Law Reform Act*, R.S.O. 1990, c.C-12, s.24(1), as amended.
[136] *Children's Law Reform Act*, R.S.O. 1990, c.C-12, s.24(2)(a), as amended.
[137] *Children's Law Reform Act*, R.S.O. 1990, c.C-12, s.24(h), as amended.
[138] *Children's Law Reform Act*, R.S.O. 1990, c.C-12, s.24(g), as amended.
[139] *L. (A.G.) v. D.(K.B.)* (2009), 93 O.R. (3d) 409 (S.C.J.)

John P. Schuman, C.S., Family Lawyer, Mediator and Arbitrator

In assessing what order is in the "best interests of the child," the court also considers many other factors related to parenting. These include the length of time the child has lived in a stable home environment, the ability and willingness of each person applying for custody to provide the child with guidance, an education, the necessaries of life and meet any special needs of the child, the person's plans for the child's care and upbringing, and the permanence and stability of the family unit in which it is proposed the child will live[140].

Courts also consider the child's views and preferences on parenting matters[141]. However, judges do not always give those views and preferences much weight. Courts usually give no weight to the views and preferences of very young children, but frequently place a lot of weight on the views and preferences of teenagers. In between those ages, the court gives some weight, but not great weight, to a child's views and preferences, although the more mature the child, the more weight that a court will give to a child's opinion. However, courts give no weight to the views and preferences of a child where the child's opinion is the product of manipulation, coercion or brainwashing[142].

Who Makes the Decisions? – The Legal Definition of Custody

The terms "custody" and "access" have fallen out of favour in separation agreements, because they are loaded terms. Furthermore, there is a proposal to change the Family Law legislation to replace those terms with terms such as "parenting rights and responsibilities." However, since "custody" and "access" are still the legal terms, it is important to understand with they mean.

The concepts of custody over a child and where that child lives are separate issues. A parent can have custody of a child who lives primarily with the other parent.

"Custody" refers to who gets to make important decisions concerning the child. The term does not refer to where a child lives. The important decisions that must be made regarding a child are the following:

---

[140] *Children's Law Reform Act*, R.S.O. 1990, c.C-12, s.24(c), (d), (e) and (f), as amended.
[141] *Children's Law Reform Act*, R.S.O. 1990, c.C-12, s.24(b), as amended.
[142] *L. (A.G.) v. D. (K.B.)* (2009), 93 O.R. (3d) 409 at 143 (S.C.J.).

John P. Schuman, C.S., Family Lawyer, Mediator and Arbitrator

1. educational decisions (that is where the child will go to school or what special educational placement the child will be in);
2. medical decisions;
3. decisions regarding religious upbringing; and
4. the determination of what extracurricular activities a child will participate in (and when).

There may also be an issue about who can decide where the child is going to live. The general rule is that one parent will not move the child away so as to frustrate the child's time with the other parent unless both parents agree or there is a court order permitting the move.

Another important decision that must be made is where the child will live. In many circumstances, the child spends most of his or her time with one parent (usually, but not necessarily, the parent with custody). However, in many circumstances, the children continue to reside an equal amount with each parent. The schedule by which children reside with their parents is not subject to any specific formula. It is determined based on what is in each "child's best interest", and frequently changes over time as the child's needs, interests and desires change. When the parents have worked out a schedule for the residence of the children, judges usually, but not always, respect that schedule as being in the child's best interest.

Two other important decision-making areas are those pertaining to a child's education or healthcare. Where there is an order for custody, the party who has custody has the right to make the final decisions with regard to major educational decisions (such as which school the child attends, what programs the child is placed in), and decisions regarding the child's healthcare. However there may be an exception in emergencies when it is not possible to reach the custodial parent, in which case the other non-custodial parent may direct the treatment on an emergency basis.

Parents must also make decisions about their children's extra-curricular activities. This can be a thorny issue since it can affect the amount of child support that is paid between the parties. It can lead to difficult situations where one parent schedules activities during the other parent's time. When a parent has custody, that parent is entitled to make decisions regarding a child's extra-curricular activities. However, agreements and orders frequently have a condition that one parent cannot schedule activities during the child's time with the other parent. Another common restriction, even where one parent has custody, is that one parent will not enrol the child in activities that require financial contributions from the other parent without that other parent's

John P. Schuman, C.S., Family Lawyer, Mediator and Arbitrator

consent. Even where a court order or agreement does not specifically prohibit a parent from registering the child for activities in ways that offend the other parent, judges view that behaviour very negatively if the matter ever returns to court.

The final two areas where parents make important decisions about their children involve religious upbringing and the children's names. Usually, if a child has been raised in a particular faith and the parties agreed to that before they separated, there would be an agreement or an order that the child's faith cannot be changed unless the child decides to change it. A similar principle applies to changing a child's name. When an order or agreement is silent with regard to whether a child's name can be changed, the Ontario government will not allow a legal name change without both parents' consent.

Obviously, there may be other issues that arise with regard to the parenting of children. If these issues ever make it before a court, they are always determined according to the "child's best interest".

It is common for court orders or agreements to place restrictions on the rights of one parent to make a decision without the input of the other parent. Court orders and separation agreements can also assign some decision-making powers to one parent and other decision-making powers to the other parent. As long as both parents are competent to make decisions for their children, the court generally respects the parents' arrangements for the dividing of decision-making authority. Where there is high conflict, the court looks for arrangements that minimize the conflict for the child while doing as much as possible to maintain a meaningful relationship between the child and each parent.

> *Desmond and Molly do not agree about anything regarding their kids and they fight over even small issues. The case management judge recommended a long, detailed parenting order. Such an order will set out what Desmond and Molly will do in almost every situation regarding the children. By doing this, Desmond and Molly do not have many decisions left to make, or fight about.*

Access Parents Still Have a Right to Information

It is important to note that if one parent does not have custody or does not have decision-making authority regarding a particular area, it does not mean that that parent is not entitled to information. Both the *Divorce Act* and Ontario's *Children's Law Reform Act* state that, unless a court orders otherwise, both parents are equally entitled to information regarding their children regardless of who has final decision-making authority. The entitlement to access includes both the right to visit with the child, but also be given information about the health, education and welfare of the child. It is not necessary for an Access Parent to get an order specifically giving that parent access to information, because both the *Divorce Act* and the *Children's Law Reform Act* give the access parent that right[143].

Giving up Your Rights – the Concept of De Facto Custody

Even immediately after separation, someone may have to make decisions regarding children. To avoid a situation where there are problems getting a parent to participate in making a decision, the *Children's Law Reform Act* says that the parent who is living with the children has the authority to make all the decisions. If one parent leaves the matrimonial home (or the family home if the parents are not married) and leaves the children in the care of the other parent, the leaving parent forfeits all rights to custody until a separation agreement or court order provides otherwise. In legal terminology, the staying parent has "de facto custody." By leaving the home, the law assumes that the leaving parent is giving consent, or at least acquiescing to the other parent having custody[144].

The provision in the law giving the staying parent temporary custody is one reason why separated parents stay living under the same roof; neither of them wants to give up custody of the children. It is also a reason why, as will be discussed later, that the *Family Law Act* gives both married spouses the right to stay in the matrimonial home after separation until there is a separation agreement or court order that states otherwise.

> *After Desmond and Molly decided that their marriage was over, neither one of them wanted to move out of the matrimonial home. That was because neither of them wanted to give up the right to make decisions regarding the children. Separated parents continuing to live under the same roof can cause a lot of stress for children. If Desmond and Molly cannot keep the hostilities out of the home, the court may have to intervene to create a parenting plan that allows both parents to remain in the children's lives after Desmond and Molly start living apart.*

---

[143] *Divorce Act*, R.S.C. 1985, c. 3 (2nd Supp.), s. 16(5) as amended; *Children's Law Reform Act*, R.S.O. 1990, c. C-12, s. 20(5) as amended
[144] *Children's Law Reform Act*, R.S.O. 1990, c.C-12, s.30(4), as amended

John P. Schuman, C.S., Family Lawyer, Mediator and Arbitrator

Joint Custody and When It Can Be Ordered

Ontario Law permits any person, not just a child's parents, to apply to the courts for custody of, or access to, a child. However, upon the breakdown of relationship, the child's biological or adoptive parents are equally entitled to have custody of a child of their relationship[145]. That said, courts and child professionals believe that it is best to keep the parenting arrangements as similar as possible as to what existed during the marriage. If during the marriage, the child had one primary parent, after separation, the expectation will be that the child will continue to have one primary parent and a secondary parent who will also play an important role in the child's life. If a child had two equal parents during the marriage, the courts and child professionals' hope that the parents will be able to put aside their differences and continue as equal parents after separation.

In some circumstances, it is possible for parents to continue to equally parent children after the end of the parent's relationship. However, in many cases, conflict, poor communication between the parents, or other factors prevents them from doing so. In all cases where parents separate, they must determine how they will continue to parent their children in light of their new circumstances.

The general rule is that where parents have such a high level of conflict that they cannot work together to parent a child, the court will not order joint custody[146]. Joint custody in high conflict circumstances exposes the children to too much unhealthy conflict. However, another authoritative line of court decisions suggest that courts are willing to order joint custody where there is even a slight hope that the parents will be able to get along in the future[147]. Courts may order professionals to intervene to help with, or make parenting decisions, if the parents cannot cooperate to make them. Courts are particularly likely to order joint custody where either of the parents would use sole custody to marginalize the other parent in the children's lives[148].

---

[145] *Children's Law Reform Act*, R.S.O. 1990, c.C-12, s.20(1), as amended.
[146] *Kaplanis v. Kaplanis* (2005), 10 R.F.L. (6th) (C.A.).
[147] *May-Iannazzi v. Iannazi*, 2010 CarswellOnt 5353 at para 2-4 (C.A.)
[148] *Young v. Young* 2010 ONCA 602.

John P. Schuman, C.S., Family Lawyer, Mediator and Arbitrator

Moving With the Kids

Judges frequently say that the hardest cases to hear are those where one parent wants to move away and take the children far away from the other parent. This can be one of the most upsetting things to happen to the parent who is left behind. The law agrees with the principle that it is preferable for the children to have a relationship with both parents[149]. However, sometimes that is just not possible.

Courts expect that court orders and agreements regarding parenting schedules will be obeyed. A parent cannot move to the children to a new residence that makes the existing parenting schedule, or the children's relationship with the other parent, unworkable. A parent who wants to disrupt the children's time with the other parent, must either get the other parent's agreement or a court order.

It is very difficult to predict whether a court will allow a move. Every case is decided on its own set of facts and on what is in the child's best interests rather than the needs and desires of each parent[150]. There are some general principles. However, which principle a judge thinks is most important is up to the judge. Here are the main considerations in deciding whether to allow a parent to move away with a child:

1. The strength of the child's relationship with the moving parent.
2. The strength of the child's relationship with the non-moving parent. A feature of this consideration can be whether the non-moving parent will have the ability to travel to visit with the child.
3. The desirability of allowing the child to have a continued relationship with both parents. (It may not be desirable for a child to have a continued relationship with both parents if doing so exposes the child to conflict between the parents or one of the parents is not a positive influence on the child.)
4. The views and preferences of the child.
5. Any disruption that the move will cause to the child's relationship with other family members, schools or the community to which the child has become accustomed[151].

---

[149] *Divorce Act*, R.S.C. 1985, c. 3 (2nd Supp.), s. 16(10).
[150] *Woodhouse v. Woodhouse* (1996), 29 O.R. (3d) (C.A.).
[151] *Goertz v. Gordon*, [1996] S.C.J. no. 52.

John P. Schuman, C.S., Family Lawyer, Mediator and Arbitrator

6. Whether the move is being undertaken for legitimate reasons, or to deprive the child of a relationship with a parent. Moving a child so that a parent can "go back home to family", go someplace with a better support network[152], follow a new spouse who has relocated or to get a significantly better job are all legitimate reasons to move. It is often considered that a child will be better moving to be with a parent who is happier or in a better job[153], than staying in the same place but having a parent who is miserable.

A parent who is "left behind" but is determined to maintain a relationship with the child does have some tools available. First, judges are often willing to give that parent a much time as can still be managed in light of the move. That can mean that the child spends most or all vacation times with the non-moving parent and the schedule for visits is tailored to the non-moving parents travel schedule. Also, where there is a cost associated with travel for visits, the non-moving parent can have her child support obligations reduced to take into account that cost[154].

What To Do If A Parent Disappears With the Kids

Judges look very poorly on parents who unilaterally deprive children of their relationship with both parents. If a parent poses a danger, then there should be no problem getting a court order that access be suspended or supervised until the danger subsides. A parent who takes the children away from the other parent, without court authorization, can lose custody.

Anyone who bought this book because the other parent has disappeared with the children has made a serious mistake. The first thing to do is to contact the police. The police may not be able to do much initially if there is no court order setting parenting times. But, it is important to get the formal search underway and then go immediately to Court.

Family Court Judges do not have the authority to cancel children's passports,[155] but they do have the authority to order a parent to return the passports to Passport Canada within a specified period of time, failing which they will be deemed stolen and Passport Canada can then cancel the

---

[152] *Oldfield v. Oldfield* (1991), 33 R.F.L. 234 (Ont. Gen. Div.).
[153] *Appleby v. Appleby* (1989), 2 R.F.K. (3d) 307 (Ont. H.C.J.).
[154] *Child Support Guidelines, s.* 10(2)(b).
[155] *Canadian Passport Order*, SI/81-86, s. 10(2), as amended; *Children's Law Reform Act*, R.S.O., c. C-12, s. 28(1)(c)(v), as amended.

John P. Schuman, C.S., Family Lawyer, Mediator and Arbitrator

passport.[156] A Family Court Judge can also order that one or more parents, or other people, cannot take a child outside of Ontario. To give effect to that order, the judge can order that any Ontario police officer (and any Canadian Customs Officer who has been given the powers of a peace officer[157]) to apprehend a child who has been "unlawfully withheld" from a parent and then take that child to whoever the Judge may direct.[158] The police can enter such orders on their data base so the children, and their passports, will be "flagged" to keep the children from leaving the province. Getting the police involved early facilitates the quick entry of the court order into their database. Parents can also contact Passport Canada directly and provide a copy of the Court Order to have the children's passports put on the "System Lookout List."

If a parent has unlawfully removed a child from Canada and taken the child to a country that is a member of the *Convention of 25 October 1980 on the Civil Aspects of International Child Abduction* (the *"Hague Convention"*),[159] then the remaining parent can contact the "Central Authority for Canada", either in Ottawa or for your province, *to* coordinate assistance with the authorities in that country for the return of the child. If the parent has removed the child to a country that is not a member of the *Hague Convention*, then the parent will have to contact Foreign Affairs Canada to see what diplomatic assistance Canada can provide in that country. It is often very helpful to have a lawyer assist with these steps, particularly if that lawyer is familiar with international child abduction cases.

Getting Professional Help Making Parenting Decisions

After separation, parents who are in conflict frequently employ professionals to assist them with parenting issues. Alternatively, a court may order assistance from professionals. In separation and divorce matters, these professionals are most commonly involved as either parenting coordinators or as custody/access assessors. The same professionals can also act as mediators to help parents develop a parenting plan for their children.

---

[156] *Canadian Passport Order,* SI/81-86, s. 11.2, as amended.
[157] *Customs Act,* R.S.C. 1985, c. 1 (2nd Supp), s. 163.5(1), as amended,
[158] *Children's Law Reform Act,* R.S.O., c. C-12, s. 36(2), as amended.
[159] Hague Conference on Private International Law, *Hague Convention on the Civil Aspects of International Child Abduction,* 25 October 1980, Hague XXVIII
[

John P. Schuman, C.S., Family Lawyer, Mediator and Arbitrator

Parenting coordinators help fighting separated parents resolve on day-to-day parenting issues. Parenting coordinators are almost always child-focussed social workers or psychologists. They take a child-centered approach to suggest solutions to disagreements between parents. Parents can agree, or the court might be able to order[160], that a parenting coordinator will have the powers of an arbitrator to make a decision when the parents cannot agree. Since the process involves a child-centred mental health professional, parenting coordination is a popular way to address minor parenting issues between parents who are always in conflict. Although parenting coordinators are privately retained, it is usually cheaper to pay one parenting coordinator than two lawyers to resolve issues such as when and where access exchanges will take place, how to get information from a child's school, or which parent will attend a school function. The downside of parenting coordination is that it can provide easy access to a forum to keep fighting if one or both parents want to continue the conflict. However, if both parents want to find ways to end their conflict, parenting coordinators may be able to teach them how.

A custody/access assessment, which is also called a "Section 30 Assessment"[161], is very different from parenting coordination. Judges often feel that they do not have the proper training to determine what is in a child's best interests, because a judge's training is in the law and not in child welfare[162]. So, judges often like to have a child-focused mental health professional provide advice as to what the custody/access or parenting plan should look like. There are two methods to obtain custody/access assessment. The first is that the parties can agree to have a custody/access assessment. The second method to obtain a custody access assessment is that a judge can order one if he or she is of the opinion that there are clinical issues that are outside the scope of the judge's legal training[163].

Custody/access assessors are social workers, psychologists or psychiatrists who are familiar with how to conduct custody/access assessments and regularly do that type of work. They meet with the lawyers, and then with the parties, usually several times, sometimes together and sometimes apart. The custody/access assessor usually meets with the children as well. Often the

---

[160] *Young v. Young* 2010 ONCA 602.
[161] The order for these assessments are made pursuant to section 30 of the *Children's Law Reform Act*, R.S.O. 1990, c. C-12, as amended.
[162] *Przygocki v. Przygocki* [1993] O.J. No. 1743.
[163] *Levine v. Levine (1993)*, 50 R.F.L. (3d) 414.

John P. Schuman, C.S., Family Lawyer, Mediator and Arbitrator

assessor will speak to other professionals and other people who are important in the children's lives.

At the end of this process, the assessor forms an opinion as to which parent should make which decisions regarding the children and what time the children should spend with each parent. The assessor then communicates his or her opinion to the parties. If the parents do not agree with that opinion, the custody/access assessor's role is limited to being a witness at trial. The Trial Judge can accept or reject the assessor's opinion[164]. However, the opinion of a custody/access assessor is usually very persuasive to a judge.

The Office of the Children's Lawyer can be involved in custody/access disputes before the court. A court can ask the Office of the Children's Lawyer to become involved to assist a child. The Office of the Children's Lawyer still has the discretion as to whether or not it will become involved in custody/access matters. In addition, the Office also decides whether it will appoint a lawyer for the child[165], or appoint a social worker to conduct a "Clinical Investigation,"[166] which is very similar to a custody/access assessment, or whether the agency will provide both. The Office of the Children's Lawyer, which exists only in Ontario, takes the position that it is not necessarily its job to advocate for a child's views and preferences, but rather to advocate for that child's best interest. The child's views and opinion are only one consideration that the lawyer representing them through the Office of the Children's Lawyer will consider. The agency will consider all the circumstances surrounding the child and tell the court what it believes to be in the child's best interests. The position of the Office of the Children's Lawyer is very influential on a judge, because judges often view that Office as being impartial.

There may be many other issues besides custody and access between separating partners or spouses other than the ones discussed above. This is why it is important for you to consult a Family Law lawyer regarding your specific custody and access concerns.

---

[164] *Weaver v. Tate,* [1989] O.J. No. 2201 (H.C.J.).
[165] Pursuant to section 89(3) of the *Courts of Justice Act*, R.S.O. 1990, c. C-43, as amended.
[166] Pursuant to section 112 of the *Courts of Justice Act*, R.S.O. 1990, c. C-43, as amended.

John P. Schuman, C.S., Family Lawyer, Mediator and Arbitrator

Child Support- Who Pays and How Much?

Child support is a relatively simple issue in Ontario. When parents separate, the parent who is not continuing to live with the children must pay child support to the parent with whom the children reside, pursuant to the *Child Support Guidelines*[167]. The law does not allow parents to opt out of the *Child Support Guidelines* unless the provisions they are making benefit the child more than the payment of support under the *Child Support Guidelines*[168].

For most people, the calculation of the child support obligation is very simple. The parent who should pa support provides a copy of her income tax return. Child support is based on the total income (line 150) of the payer's most recent tax return[169]. Child support tables specify exactly what the monthly child support payment is going to be for each income level for the number of children who need support. That number is called "the Table Amount." A parent who does not immediately start paying child support in the amount set out in the table will make a Family Court Judge angry.

"It's Not My Kid" – Child Support and Non-Biological Children

Liability for child support is not based only on biology (or an adoption order). Natural (biological) and adoptive parents are always liable for child support for their children. However, anyone who assumes the role of a parent of a child also becomes liable for child support[170]. Assuming the role of parent means more than being the spouse of a child's parent and occasional babysitter. To be liable for support, a stepparent must take an active role in parenting the child. Some facts that show that include: making major decisions for the child, disciplining the child, referring to the child as "my child", providing financial

---

[167] The *Child Support Guidelines* are regulations that have been enacted by the Government of Canada (Can.Reg. 97-175) and the Government of Ontario (O.Reg. 391/97) and all of the other provinces. The wording of the federal and Ontario *Child Support Guidelines* is almost identical. The difference is that the federal regulation only applies to divorcing spouses. The provincial regulation applies to all separated or separating parents.

[168] *Divorce Act*, R.S.C. 1985, c. 3 (2nd Supp.), s. 15.1 (5)-(8) as amended; *Children's Law Reform Act*, R.S.O. 1990, c. C-12, s. 37(2.2)-(2.6) as amended.

[169] *Child Support Guidelines*, section 16.

[170] *Child Support Guidelines*, section 5.

John P. Schuman, C.S., Family Lawyer, Mediator and Arbitrator

assistance to the child and having a close emotional relationship with the child[171].

It is possible for a child to have three or more parents for the purposes of child support and for two or more parents to pay the full Table Amount of child support to the parent with whom the child resides. Biological or adoptive parents always pay the full table amount. Stepparents may or may not pay the full table amount. However, the more the step parent acted liked a full parent, the closer the child's relationship with the step parent, and the more the child is financially dependent on that step parent, the more likely it is that a judge will order the full Table Amount of child support[172].

Another scenario is when a child's mother makes a claim against a person she alleges is the child's father. If the alleged father has lived with the child, or otherwise treated the child as his own for a period of time, he will likely be liable for child support whether he is the child's biological child or not. However, if the alleged parent is not the biological parent and has never parented the child, then there is no child support obligation. Where there is an issue about a child's parentage, a judge may order DNA testing[173]. As DNA testing is a medical procedure, the child, or the child's substitute decision maker, who is often the person claiming support, still has the right to refuse the testing. Where that occurs, a judge may draw the inference that the alleged father is not the biological father[174].

Before meeting Molly, Desmond had a "one night stand" with Michelle and fathered a daughter. Desmond pays table support to Michelle. At the time of the one night stand, Michelle was in a relationship with Jude. She let Jude believe he was the father for several years. Jude was an active parent to the girl and became close to her. The relationship ended when Michelle told Jude he was not the father. Michelle obtained full table support from Jude. Michelle then lived with Dr. Robert for a couple of years. Dr. Robert was also a good parent and actively involved in the girl's life, but never as much as Jude. He did not hire a lawyer when asked to pay child support. The court ordered Dr. Robert to pay one quarter of the Table Amount of child support for Dr. Robert's income.

---

[171] *Andela v. Jovetic*, 2011CarswellOnt 1452, 2011ONSC892 (S.C.J.).
[172] *Hilliard v. Popal*, 2010 CarswellOnt 10488, 2010 ONCJ 619 (O.C.J.).
[173] *Children's Law Reform Act*, R.S.O. 1990, c. C-12, s. 10(1).
[174] *Children's Law Reform Act*, R.S.O. 1990, c. C-12, s. 10(3), (4).

John P. Schuman, C.S., Family Lawyer, Mediator and Arbitrator

Extraordinary Expenses Are Not Included in Base Child Support

There is a second component of child support. This component is called either "Special or Extraordinary Expenses" or "Section 7 Expenses"[175]. They are two types of expenses that parents pay on top of the amount under the child support tables.

Special Expenses are certain specific expenses that are necessary for the child. A court may order that the child's parents share these expenses in proportion to their incomes. These expenses are not covered by the amounts paid by base support. They include necessary child care expenses, medical and dental insurance premiums, health related expenses that exceed insurance reimbursement by at least $100 annually, expenses related to special education requirements in primary or secondary school and most post-secondary education expenses[176].

Extraordinary expenses are the ones that are out of the ordinary for families of the income level of the separated parents. They are usually the large expenses related to some form of extracurricular activity that the parent requesting the payment could not reasonably cover with her own income and the base child support payments. These expenses are related to special needs or talents of the child such as participating in sports or the arts at an elite level, tutoring or other special education expenses[177]. As with special expenses, parents share these expenses in proportion to their incomes. A parent's contribution to special or extraordinary expenses is paid over and above the child support she pays pursuant to the tables.

Not every expense for a child is special or extraordinary. Some expenses are covered by base child support. Other expenses are simply unaffordable for a family so calling them an extraordinary expense and requiring the parents to share them would be too burdensome. Whether an expense is extraordinary does depend on the size of the parent's incomes and, consequently, the size of the child support payments. However, the following chart gives some examples of what usually will and will not be a special or extraordinary expense.

---

[175] The payment of these expenses is governed by section 7 of the *Child Support Guidelines*.
[176] Section 7(1)(e) of the *Child Support Guidelines*.
[177] *Child Support Guidelines*, section 7(1.1).

John P. Schuman, C.S., Family Lawyer, Mediator and Arbitrator

Examples of What Is and Is Not a Special or Extraordinary Expense	
Child Care Expenses to allow employment	Special Expense
Medical/dental insurance premiums	Special Expense
Tutoring and educational assessments	Special Expense
Post Secondary education Expenses	Special Expense
Transit Pass	Generally not a special or extraordinary expense
Rep Hockey or Riding Lessons	Extraordinary Expense except for very high income parents
Swimming Lessons	Not a special extraordinary expense except for very low income parents
Swim Team (Provincial/National Level)	Extraordinary Expense

Also, it is important for parents to remember that section 7(3) of the *Child Support Guidelines* says that tax credits, tax deductions, benefits and subsidies must be deducted from the cost of a Section 7 expense before dividing it between the parties. The most common example of this is the tax deduction available for childcare costs. The party who gets that deduction must take it off the total cost before dividing the expense.

> *Molly earns $60,000 per year. Desmond earns $40,000 per year. Their two children play "rep hockey", which costs the family $10,000 each year. Since the total family income is $100,000 per year, Molly is responsible for 60 percent of the cost of the "special and extraordinary expenses." Desmond is responsible for 40 percent of those same expenses. If the children live primarily with Molly, Desmond will have to pay $4,000 per year to Molly in addition to his base child support. Unless they agree differently, Desmond will pay "special and extraordinary expense" ($4,000 divided by 12). Every month, Desmond will pay Molly child support totalling $934. Molly will pay the hockey expenses.*

John P. Schuman, C.S., Family Lawyer, Mediator and Arbitrator

An important consideration for parents who are experiencing issues with payment of Section 7 Expenses is that that the Family Responsibility Office will not enforce support orders that do not specify exactly how much support has to be paid and how frequently it has to be paid. Put another way, you cannot simply send your receipts for expenses to the Family Responsibility Office and expect them to collect the percentage set out in the Court Order (or Agreement). If the other parent is refusing to contribute to special or extraordinary expenses, and the order or agreement doesn't specify the exact amount and when it is owed, the process to collect the amount in default is complicated. It involves bringing a motion and having a judge look at all the receipts and consider other factors such as available tax deductions and credits or subsidies, and set an amount owed. In most cases, the cost of bringing that motion will be far more than is owed. Due to the complexity of this process, it may be preferable to specify monthly amount for special and extraordinary expenses in the agreement or order, even if parties cannot do it with exact precision. Even if the monthly amount the parties agree to is off, the difference may not be worth the trip to court.

Back to (paying for) school: child support and post-secondary education

In Ontario, child support does not necessarily end when a child turns 18 years old. It can continue if the child remains dependant on her parents because she is pursuing full-time education[178] or, if she is the child of married, parents, suffers from some infirmity that prevents her from becoming financially independent[179]. However, child support can change a lot after a child turns 18 because the parents, and the court, have greater freedom to deviate from the child support tables.

The cost of post-secondary is a Special Expense under section 7 of the *Child Support Guidelines.*[180]. Parents share those costs, over and above that the child can reasonably contribute (if post-secondary education is affordable for the family)[181]. Parents share those costs in proportion to their incomes. The amount that a child is expected to contribute to her post-secondary education costs goes up with every year of that education as that child can earn more from summer employment or other sources. However, families that can easily

---

[178] *Family Law Act*, R.S.O. 1990, c. F-3, s. 31(1), as amended.
[179] *Divorce Act*, R.S.C. 1985, c.3 (2nd Supp), s. 2(1), as amended.
[180] *Child Support Guidelines,* s. 7(1)(e).
[181] *Lewi v. Lewi* (2006), 80 O.R. (3d) 321.

afford those educational costs may be expected to pay the bulk of them the whole way through, while lower income families may be simply unable to contribute at all. All "children" are expected to take advantage of any scholarships, bursaries, or grants that are available to them.

Child support often works very differently for children who stay at home for their post-secondary education versus those who go away for school. For children who stay at home, base child support often continues under the tables while parents share the required cost of tuition, books and other education related expenses. However, parents can agree to other arrangements to meet the child's financial needs.

A child going away to school creates more opportunities, or issues, to meet that child's financial needs. Part of the cost of going away to school, which the parents will share, includes the cost of housing, food, and similar expenses while away at school. However, those expenses are supposed to be covered by base child support. One option is for the parents to share all of the away from school education costs and to reduce the base child support while the child is away to reflect the fact that the recipient parent only has the cost of keeping a home for the child to come back to. If the child moves back for the summer, then the table child support resumes for those months. If the child does not show any interest in returning home, then the question arises to whether their base child support should continue at all. However, this is just one option. Sometimes, the support payer offers to pay the full costs of all the child's expenses related to school away from home, without contribution from the other parent, in exchange for an end to the base child support payments. There may be other options that work well for the family.

Once a child turns 18, but is still dependant due to her education or health, parents have the freedom to restructure child support to whatever works best for them. The system of having base child support in accordance with the tables, and a sharing of Special and Extraordinary expenses, is no longer mandatory. Still, judges will expect that the child support arrangements will benefit the child as much as that system, even if the arrangements are very different.

John P. Schuman, C.S., Family Lawyer, Mediator and Arbitrator

Child Support When There Are Children Living with Both Parents

When one or more children live full-time with one parent and one or more children live full-time with the other parent, each parent pays child support based on that parent's income, to the other parent based on the number of the children who live with that parent[182]. Where each parent has one or more children living with them full-time, child support is calculated for each parent with respect to the child or children in the custody of the other parent. Each parent pays the table amount of child support to the other parent for the children living primarily with the other parent.

> *Desmond now earns $100,000 per year and lives with one child. Molly earns $80,000 pear year and also lives with one child. Desmond does pay some child support. He pays the table amount of child support for one child for an income of $100,00 ($877) minus the table child support payable for one child on an income of $80,000 ($719). Desmond pays Molly table child support of $158 per month. He does not pay support for one child based on $100,00 nor does he pay based on an income of $20,000 for two children (which would be $308 per month).*
>
> *The parties would still share the special and extraordinary expenses in relation to their incomes. Desmond now makes 55 percent of the total of $180,000 per year. If Molly is still paying the $10,000 per year hockey expense, Desmond will have to give her an additional $5,500 per year, or $458 per month.*

When the children divide their time approximately evenly between their parents (the children do not spend less than 40 percent of their time with one parent), then different rules apply[183]. Ideally, the parents will share all the costs associated with raising the children in proportion to their incomes. However, keeping track of all the costs associated with children can be a huge task. In *Contino v. Leonelli-Contino*, the Supreme Court of Canada said that when calculating child support in shared custody situations, the first step is to calculate what each parent would owe the other under the *Child Support Guidelines* Tables and set those amounts off against each other. This simple approach has the parent with the higher income writing a child support cheque

---

[182] *Child Support Guidelines*, section 8.
[183] *Child Support Guidelines*, section 9.

to the other parent. The Supreme Court said this approach should be followed unless it does not result in a fair sharing of the children's expenses.[184]

By way of example, if there is one child who lives equally with both parents and Mom earns $50,000.00 and Dad earns $40,000.00, Mom will pay to Dad child support for one child based on income of $50,000.00 and Dad will pay Mom child support under the tables for an income of $40,000.00. Previously, parents simply set off the amounts owing each other and, in the above example, Mom would pay Dad the difference in what was owed. However, for the reasons set out below, that may no longer be the best choice. The *Child Support Guidelines* do allow for a number of other ways to calculate support obligations in these circumstances. For a parent who lives in such a situation to determine what his or her child support obligation is, he or she must consult a lawyer.

Child Support in Various Parenting Situations

Parenting Situation	Mom Pays	Dad Pays
1 Child with Mom, 1 with Dad	Table support for 1 child	Table support for 1 child
2 children with Dad, 1 with mom	Table support for 2 children	Table support for 1 child
3 children with Mom, 2 with dad	Table support for 2 children	Table support for 3 children
2 children each spending equal time with Mom and Dad	Mom and Dad share the expenses associated with both children in proportion to their income, or each pays child support for 2 children to the other.	

---

[184] *Contino v. Leonelli-Contino* [2005] S.C.J. No. 65 at para 49.

John P. Schuman, C.S., Family Lawyer, Mediator and Arbitrator

From a "saving money" perspective, it is often not worthwhile for parents to seek shared custody simply in order to reduce child support. The cost of raising a child in two homes is greater than raising a child in one. A parent who seeks shared custody may find that he or she is paying more in child support *and* directly in relation to the costs of raising the children, than they would have paid in child support. Where spousal support is an issue, a decrease in child support payments can increase spousal support. There are many trappings in trying to get shared custody for financial savings. Before pursuing a claim for "shared custody" for financial reasons, speak to a lawyer. In any case, and especially if you asked any judge, parenting decisions should be based on love not money.

Important Tax Considerations for Child Support: Yes - Child Support Impacts Tax

Since 1997, with the implementation of the *Child Support Guidelines* and related changes to tax law, child support is "tax-free" – the child support payer does not get a tax deduction for, and the child support recipient does not have to pay tax on, support that is paid. However, the ways in which parents pay child support in shared or split custodial situations can have large tax implications. Parents in those situations should do some careful planning. Unless the parents have unique objectives, they should not set-off child support payments but each parent should make the full table child support payment to the other parent.

The set off approach can cause some tax problems for parents. Even though:

1. The Supreme Court of Canada, in *Contino v. Leonelli- Contino*, endorsed that parents with shared custody should set-off the amount of child support owed by each of them so that only the higher income parent has to write a cheque;[185]
2. The amount of child support payable under the tables already takes into account the tax deductions/benefits available to parents for having children,[186] and;

---

[185] *Contino v. Leonelli-Contino* [2005] S.C.J. No. 65 at para 49.
[186] *Children Come First: A Report to Parliament Reviewing the Provisions and Operation of the Federal Child Support Guidelines - Volume 1* (Ottawa: Government of Canada, 2002), Appendix 2: available at: http://www.justice.gc.ca/eng/rp-pr/fl-lf/child-enfant/rp/v1/v1a2.html.

3. The CRA's policy on tax credits and benefits for parents in shared custody situations states that parents must rotate the deductions/credits for children such that each parent gets the benefits for the children for six months of the year.[187]

Despite all of the above, the Tax Court of Canada held in *Harder v the Queen*[188] that where parents use the 'set-off' method described above, only the person who actually gets the support cheque gets to claim any of the tax benefits; the payer does not. Section 118(5) of the *Income Tax Act* states that a person who has to pay support for a dependent cannot claim tax deductions or benefits with respect to that dependent. Children are considered dependents under the *Act*. So, notwithstanding the Canada Revenue Agency policy that benefits must be rotated in shared custodial arrangements, the parent who has a larger income cannot claim those benefits. It may seem that in shared or split custody situations, by setting off support each parent is paying support to the other. However, the decision of *Harder v. the Queen* held that the only way for parents to rotate benefits as contemplated by the *Child Support Guidelines* and the Canada Revenue Agency is for them to actually write cheques for the full table amount to each other and have those cheques cross in the mail.

Obviously, any parent involved in a child support case should consult a lawyer and an accountant about the tax implications associated with different child support arrangements. Parents can arrange their support obligations in a way that maximizes the available tax benefits or in a way that has them paying more tax unnecessarily.

Self-Employed? Your Income For Child Support May Be Greater Than Your Income On Your Tax Return

The calculation of child support becomes complicated when one parent is either self-employed, or earns the bulk of his or her income from sources other than a salary. When that occurs, the *Child Support Guidelines* recognise that the income on line 150 of the tax return may not adequately reflect that parent's income[189].

---

[187] Canada Revenue Agency, *Benefits Entitlements in Shared Custody Cases*, available at: http://www.cra-arc.gc.ca/gncy/bdgt/2010/shrdcstd-eng.html#q3
[188] *Harder v. The Queen* 2016 TCC 197.
[189] *Child Support Guidelines*, Section 18 and Schedule III

John P. Schuman, C.S., Family Lawyer, Mediator and Arbitrator

The courts have adopted the view that the purpose of the *Child Support Guidelines* is to provide some uniformity for what parents pay for child support regardless of how they earn their income. Therefore, when a parent earns some or all of his or her income from a source other than a salary (which that parent does not control), the court looks at how much money actually ends up in the parent's hands and then determines the gross salary that parent would have to earn to have the same amount of after-tax money in his or her hands. The court "grosses up" the parent's income from what is indicated on his or her tax returns to the salary that parent would have to earn to have the same amount of money in his or her hands[190]. In the words of Justice Benotto:

> The *Child Support Guidelines* base support on the payer's gross taxable income. One of the objectives of the *Guidelines* is to ensure "consistent treatment" of those who are in "similar circumstances". Thus, the *Guidelines* have provisions to impute income where a parent is exempt from paying tax, lives in a lower taxed jurisdiction, or derives income from sources that are taxed at a lower rate. Where a parent arranges his or her affairs to pay substantially less tax on income, the income must be grossed up before the table is applied. This is the only way to ensure the consistency mandated by the legislation[191].

The effect of adjusting a parent's income as described above can result in quite a substantial increase in a parent's income over what is reported on a parent's tax return. In fact, it can be several times what is reported on a parent's tax return. The calculation of the income of a self-employed parent, or a parent who earns her income from sources other than a salary, can be very complicated. It is necessary for that parent to speak to both a lawyer and to an accountant who has special training in how to calculate income for the purpose of the *Child Support Guidelines*.

---

[190] *Orser v. Grant*, 2000 CaswellOnt 1354 at para 11 (S.C.J.), aff'd by *Holland v. Riel*, 2003 CarsewllOnt 3828 at para 33 (C.A.).
[191] *Riel v. Holland*, 2003 CarsewllOnt 3828 at paras 28 and 36 (C.A.).

John P. Schuman, C.S., Family Lawyer, Mediator and Arbitrator

Quitting Your Job To Avoid Support Does Not Work

Another circumstance in which a parent's child support obligation is not based on line 150 of his tax return is when that parent is intentionally unemployed or underemployed. Specifically, the *Child Support Guidelines* state that a parent cannot simply avoid their child support obligation by quitting his job. When a parent is unemployed, or underemployed as result of that parent's own actions, the court will require that parent to pay child support on the income that that parent would be earning if he were fully employed[192]. A parent who is earning little or no income may pay child support based on a large income, because that parent was somehow responsible for the circumstances resulting in that parent having little or no income.

There are a number of other discreet issues that may arise in child support cases. The only way for a parent to know how these would apply to her particular circumstances is to consult a lawyer.

The Thorny, and Often Misunderstood, Issues around Spousal Support (Alimony)

Spousal support is money paid by one spouse to the other for the support of the spouse (not the children). It is a separate issue from child support. Spousal support is determined in an entirely different manner than child support. It is important to understand that judges have very wide discretion with respect to whether to order spousal support and, if the judge does order spousal support, the amount of spousal support. Judges have ordered spousal support for marriages that have lasted less than two weeks[193] and refused to order spousal support for marriages lasting more than 20 years. Further, unlike child support, spousal support can be ordered to be paid on a weekly, biweekly, monthly, or annual (or theoretically, bi-annually, daily or in any other interval) basis, or as a single lump sum payment. Where there are periodic payments, they can be either for a period of time or indefinitely. Spousal support is a complex issue that requires consideration of many factors and even then, there is still a range of appropriate spousal support depending on the circumstances.

The first factor to consider is whether a person is permitted to make a claim for spousal support. To bring a claim for spousal support, a person must fall into one of four categories:

---

[192] *Child Support Guidelines*, Section 18(1)(a)
[193] *Hindocha v. Patel*, 2009 CarswellOnt 2611.

John P. Schuman, C.S., Family Lawyer, Mediator and Arbitrator

1. The person must be legally married to the person from whom they are claiming support;[194]; or
2. The person must have lived continuously for a period of not less than three years with the person from whom they are claiming spousal support;[195] or
3. The person must be in a relationship of some permanence with the person from whom they are claiming spousal support and the partners must be the natural or adoptive parents of a child[196] or
4. The parties must have entered into a domestic contract requiring spousal support to be paid between them.

If a person does not fall into one of the four categories above, the law does not permit them to claim spousal support. Even if a person does meet one of the criteria described above, that does not necessarily mean that the person is entitled to spousal support. The court must consider several other factors to determine whether a person is entitled to spousal support, and if so, how much support and for how long.

When a court is considering making an order for spousal support, or the parties are negotiating an agreement regarding spousal support, they should take into account the purposes of spousal support. The federal *Divorce Act*[197] and Ontario's *Family Law Act*[198] both set out the same four purposes for spousal support. The purposes of spousal support are:

1. to recognize a spouse's contribution to the relationship and the economic consequences of that relationship with the other spouse, which includes any economic advantages or disadvantages to the spouse arising from the relationship or its breakdown;
2. to apportion between the spouses any financial consequences arising from the care of any child of marriage over and above any of those addressed by child support. The most obvious example of this is where a spouse is unable to work because he/she is caring for the children. Child Support under the *Child Support Guidelines* does not compensate for that inability to work;

---

[194] *Divorce Act*, R.S.C. 1985, c. 3 (2nd Supp.), s. 2(1) and 15.2(1) as amended.
[195] *Family Law Act*, R.S.O. 1990, c. F-3, s. 29-30, as amended.
[196] *Family Law Act*, R.S.O. 1990, c. F-3, s. 29-30, as amended.
[197] See section 15.2(6).
[198] See section 33(8).

John P. Schuman, C.S., Family Lawyer, Mediator and Arbitrator

3. as far as is practicable, to promote the economic self sufficiency of each spouse within a reasonable period of time; and
4. to relieve any financial hardship to the spouses. When the spouses have been married, the court can take into consideration a payment for the equalization of family property and consider whether a party is facing financial hardship.

The law has also set out several factors that the court must consider in determining what amount of support to order. These include, but are not limited to:

a) the length of the period of cohabitation;
b) the financial situation of each spouse;
c) each spouse's ability to earn an income; and
d) the lifestyle to which the spouses became accustomed during the marriage.

The court should consider several other factors and specific details about the family when it decides how much spousal support should be paid and for how long, or if spousal support is even appropriate in the circumstances.[199]

The grounds on which a party can establish entitlement to support, and then on which a court determines what amount of support is appropriate are often condensed into three:

1. Non-compensatory support;
2. Compensatory support;
3. Contractual support.

A spouse can claim support on more than one ground and, in many cases, a spouse's entitlement to support is based on a mix of the grounds.

Non-compensatory support is meant to ensure that a spouse has a sufficient income to support a lifestyle that is close or equal to the one they had during the relationship. It is often summarized as support based on "need and ability to pay." Need and ability to pay are also the main considerations when judges make temporary support spousal support orders – the spousal support orders that are intended to provide for a spouse until the conclusion of a trial

---

[199] *Family Law Act*, R.S.O. 1990, c. F-3, s. 33(9), as amended; *Divorce Act*, R.S.C. 1985, c. 3 (2nd Supp.), s.15.2 (4) as amended.

or final settlement'. However, the purpose of spousal support is not merely to ensure a spouse can meet his or her expenses.

Compensatory support is intended to compensate a spouse for work that he or she performed during the marriage, but for which he or she did not receive compensation. One spouse may be ordered to pay the other spouse for doing house work, caring for the children, maintaining the house, or any number of other tasks for which the spouse would have been compensated, had that spouse not been providing those services to assist the other spouse. One way to look at this is how much the payer spouse would have had to pay to obtain those same services from someone else.

Compensatory support is also intended to compensate a spouse for any financial sacrifices made for the benefit of the other spouse or the family. This often occurs where a spouse has given up a career, or passed on promotions or other advancements in order to take on a larger role at home for the other spouse and any children. This amount can often be quantified by determining how much past and future income the claimant spouse gave up as a result of the marriage or relationship. However, not every spouse (married or not) is entitled to support. In relationships without children, and where neither spouse made any career sacrifices for the other, it is near impossible to establish an entitlement to compensatory support. A very large equalization payment may also give sufficient compensation to spouse such that he or she loses entitlement to spousal support.[200]

Contractual support is rare. It is most often found in marriage contracts and cohabitation agreements where spouses agree, that notwithstanding any other factors, including a consideration of entitlement, one spouse will pay a specific amount of support to the other spouse. Sometimes, spouses do this unintentionally by setting an amount of support and not giving any thought to whether a spouse is or will be entitled to support. While this more commonly happens in marriage contracts and cohabitation agreements, it can also happen when a spouse agrees to pay spousal support in a separation agreement without first looking at the situation in the marriage or relationship and contemplating whether that situation gives rise to any entitlement to support.

---

[200] *Halliwell v Halliwell,* 2017 ONCA 349, para 11-114

In most cases, consideration of entitlement is important and should not be overlooked. No entitlement means no spousal support. A weak basis for entitlement should mean less spousal support, while a strong basis for entitlement should mean more spousal support.

Also, there can be situations where the factors go both ways: some factors suggest one spouse should get spousal support while other factors suggest the other spouse should get support. Generally, one spouse has a larger claim to support than the other so that these factors do not negate each, although that is possible. Usually, the factors that give one spouse entitlement to support are used to reduce the amount of support going to the other spouse.

Spousal Support Is Not Child Support - It Does Not Change with the Payer's Income

While judges consider the parties' incomes when deciding spousal support – particularly for non-compensatory support, it is usually the payers' income during the relationship that matters. While judges have discretion to consider post separation changes in the payer's income, a dependent spouse is not automatically entitled to share in an increase in their former spouse's income.[201] A former spouse cannot have more "need" than he or she had during the marriage just because the support payer's income went up. Therefore, it is only in cases of compensatory support where a post-secondary change in income can affect spousal support. This occurs on the basis that the change in income is linked to the relationship and therefore the parties should share in each other's fortunes because they both contributed to those fortunes. The longer the time between the end of the relationship and the change in income, the harder it will be for a judge to link the two together to change spousal support.[202]

A decrease in the payer's income may affect ability to pay, which may result in change in support. Similarly, a recipient spouse having an increase in income may eliminate need. So, both may change support, although neither happens automatically. In these cases, the parties, and the court, has to look at entitlement again.

---

[201] *M. (A.A.) v. K. (R.P.)*, [2010] O.J. 807.
[202] *Thompson v. Thompson* 2013 ONSC 5500 at para 103.

Trying to be Predictable: the Spousal Support Advisory Guidelines

In the past, the application of the above principles could result in wide variations in the amount of spousal support that was ordered. To simplify that process, and provide some consistency, the Government of Canada commissioned two law professors to develop spousal support guidelines. The final version of the *Spousal Support Advisory Guidelines* came out in July 2008.[203] No government in Canada has made those guidelines into law. However, the Ontario Court of Appeal held that, in most cases, the *Spousal Support Advisory Guidelines* reflect the principles, discussed above, that the law says judges must consider when determining spousal support. The Court of Appeal also held that judges should not depart from the *Spousal Support Advisory Guidelines* unless he or she can provide a reason for doing so.[204]

The *Spousal Support Advisory Guidelines* are very important for the parties to consider. They do not contain tables as do the *Child Support Guidelines*. Instead, they consist of complex calculations that incorporate a number of variables. The calculations result in a range of spousal support values that reflect the principles discussed above. They result in a "low", "mid" and "high" value for spousal support. The *Spousal Support Advisory Guidelines* only presumptively apply when the support payer's income is between $20,000 and $350,000. Where a spouse's income is below $20,000.00, spousal support will only be payable in exceptional circumstances.[205] There are many decisions where the courts have ordered support below the range when the payer's income is below $30,000.00[206]. The *Spousal Support Advisory Guidelines* are not to be applied automatically when the payers' annual income is greater than $350,000.00. However, in many decisions, courts have used the *Spousal Support Advisory Guidelines* calculations to set the amount of spousal support paid by people earning more than $350,000.00.[207]

---

[203] Carol Rogerson and Rollie Thompson, *Spousal Support Advisory Guidelines* (Ottawa: Government of Canada, July 2008).
[204] *Fisher v. Fisher (2008)*, 88 O.R. (3d) 241 at paras 98 and 103.
[205] *M.(W.M.) v. M.(H.S.)*, 2007 CarswellBC 2667 (S.C.).
[206] *Kajorinne v. Kajorinne*, [2008] O.J. No. 2789, 2008 CarswellOnt 4229 (S.C.J.); *Maitland v. Maitland*, [2005] O.J. No. 2252 (S.C.J.).
[207] *Denofrio v. Denofrio*, [2009] O.J. No. 3295, 2009 CarswellOnt 4601 (S.C.J.), *Elgner v. Elgner* (2009), 85 R.F.L. (6th) 51.

John P. Schuman, C.S., Family Lawyer, Mediator and Arbitrator

People often look at the results of *Spousal Support Advisory Guideline* calculations and assume that if those calculations show an amount of support being paid, then support should be paid. That is a serious mistake. Before the calculations are even applied, the person claiming support must show that she is entitled to support pursuant to the legal principles discussed above. For example, the principle of self-sufficiency may mean that the spouse claiming support is not entitled to support where there has been a shorter, childless marriage or where the recipient already has significant income through employment or investments, or where a large property award will generate income.[208] If the spouse claiming support is not entitled to support, then it does not matter what result comes from the *Spousal Support Advisory Guideline* calculation. Neither the parties nor the court should even look at the calculations until a spouse has established entitlement to support.

The text of the *Spousal Support Advisory Guidelines*, which explains how the calculations are to be completed, is almost 200 pages in length (although, the formulas themselves are not that long.) Most Family Lawyers have computer software that completes the calculation. However, the *Spousal Support Advisory Guidelines*, and the subsequent "User Guides" that the authors of the *Guidelines* have published, describe a number of considerations that are not included in the formulas, and explain special situations where the *Guidelines* may not be appropriate to use, and where the amount of spousal support should be above or below the calculated ranges. The judge or arbitrator (or the parties and/or their lawyers in settlement discussions) must consider the factors described above, as well as whether the case is a "special situation," to determine whether spousal support should awarded at all and then look at whether support should be at the low end of the range or the high end of the range or in the middle. The guidelines also allow payments to be "restructured." That means there can be a lump sum payment, then a lower monthly payment or high payments for a period followed by low payments.[209]

Spousal support remains a very complicated issue. It is affected by the determination of other issues in the case (properly, the determination of spousal support is done after the other financial issues are determined). In addition, sometimes it is appropriate the paying spouse to make a lump sum payment of support rather than periodic payments of support. In deciding

---

[208] Carol Rogerson and Rollie Thompson, *Spousal Support Advisory Guidelines* (Ottawa: Government of Canada, July 2008), 131.

[209] Carol Rogerson and Rollie Thompson, *Spousal Support Advisory Guidelines* (Ottawa: Government of Canada, July 2008), 102.

John P. Schuman, C.S., Family Lawyer, Mediator and Arbitrator

whether payment should be made on a periodic or a lump sum basis, a court considers the same factors described above to determine what the appropriate order for spousal support should be. These can be complex determinations. It is also important to remember that periodic spousal support payments are tax deductible for the support payer and the support recipient pays tax on them. That is not true for lump sum support payments. The parties should consult with a lawyer (and possibly and accountant) to determine how the principles apply to their situations.

Ignoring Support Orders Can Really Hurt: Support Enforcement

When a judge makes a child or spousal support order, or a party files a separation agreement regarding support with a court,[210] that order is automatically enforced by the Family Responsibility Office.[211] The Family Responsibility Office (FRO) is a provincial government agency that collects support from the support payer and pays support to the support recipients. Unless the parties agree to withdraw from the FRO, all support payments must go through that agency. Judges are not allowed to order the parties to withdraw from the FRO, but they can make an order that the parties cannot withdraw.[212]

It can take the FRO up to four months to start collecting support. That process can move a little faster if the person receiving support is diligent in sending back the forms that the FRO sends to them (those forms are called the FRO Filing Package). Just because the FRO it not yet collecting does not mean that the support payer does not have to pay. The FRO will collect all the support that is owed pursuant to the Order, including support that was due before the FRO started collecting. It is important for the support payer to keep proof of having made support payments for the period before the FRO starts collecting. If the payer does not keep that proof, the FRO may collect that support again.

---

[210] Pursuant to section 35 of the *Family Law Act*, R.S.O, 1990, c. F-3
[211] *Family Responsibility and Support Arrears Enforcement Act, 1996*, S.O. 1996, c. 31, s. 9(1) and 10(1), (4).
[212] *Family Responsibility and Support Arrears Enforcement Act, 1996*, S.O. 1996, c. 31, s.9(1)(2).

John P. Schuman, C.S., Family Lawyer, Mediator and Arbitrator

In most cases, support just comes off the payer's paycheque as a payroll deduction, or the support payer gives the FRO post-dated cheques. However, one of the reasons for the existence of the FRO is to collect from people who do not voluntarily pay their support. For that reason, the FRO has a number of powers to collect support from people who do not pay as ordered. Some examples of those powers are that the FRO can:

1. garnish bank accounts,[213]
2. garnish tax refunds, Canada Pension Plan payments or other amounts owed to the support payer by the Government of Canada,[214]
3. register the debt against title to land owned by the support payer,[215]
4. register a lien against the support payer's personal property (cars, etc.),[216]
5. seize the support payer's lottery or gaming winnings or the support payer's assets,[217]
6. suspend the payer's passport, driver's licence or other licences[218], or
7. ask that the court order that the payer be put in jail for up to 180 days.[219]

---

[213] *Family Responsibility and Support Arrears Enforcement Act, 1996*, S.O. 1996, c. 31, s. 45.
[214] *Family Orders and Agreements Enforcement Assistance Act*, R.S.C. 1985, c. 4 (2nd Supp), s. 24, as amended.
[215] *Family Responsibility and Support Arrears Enforcement Act, 1996*, S.O. 1996, c. 31, s. 42.
[216] *Family Responsibility and Support Arrears Enforcement Act, 1996*, S.O. 1996, c. 31, s. 42.
[217] *Family Responsibility and Support Arrears Enforcement Act, 1996*, S.O. 1996, c. 31, s. 44, 46(2).
[218] *Family Orders and Agreements Enforcement Assistance Act*, R.S.C. 1985, c. 4 (2nd Supp), s. 67, as amended; *Family Responsibility and Support Arrears Enforcement Act, 1996*, S.O. 1996, c. 31, s. 37(1).
[219] *Family Responsibility and Support Arrears Enforcement Act, 1996*, S.O. 1996, c. 31, s. 41(10)(h)(i).

John P. Schuman, C.S., Family Lawyer, Mediator and Arbitrator

Unless the above enforcement measures result in the FRO receiving money to forward as support, they do not reduce the amount of support owing.[220] For example, if a support payer is put in jail for failing to pay support, she will still owe all the support when she is released. The amount of support may even have increased by the amount of support payable during the term of imprisonment.

When a support payer receives a notice that his licence will be suspended, he is entitled to ask for a court hearing to stop the suspension[221]. Before a support payer is imprisoned, there has to be a court hearing[222]. However, at the hearing the judge cannot reduce the amount of support owed. The judge can only make an order as to how that support will be paid[223]. If the support payer wants the amount of support reduced, she must start a Motion to Change that support[224]. A judge cannot stop the FRO from suspending the payer's licence unless the payer starts a Motion to Change Support.[225]

If both the support payer and support recipient agree, they can withdraw from the services of the Family Responsibility Office. Both parties must sign a Notice of Withdrawal and file it with the FRO.[226] When the parties file that form, the FRO will take no steps to collect or enforce support. The payer will make the support payments directly to the support recipient. However, either the support payer or recipient can unilaterally opt to have the FRO enforce support again. The FRO charges a small fee to reinstate its services after a support order has been withdrawn from the agency for enforcement.

---

[220] *Family Responsibility and Support Arrears Enforcement Act, 1996*, S.O. 1996, c. 31, s. 35(3), 42(11).
[221] *Family Responsibility and Support Arrears Enforcement Act, 1996*, S.O. 1996, c. 31, s. 35(1).
[222] *Family Responsibility and Support Arrears Enforcement Act, 1996*, S.O. 1996, c. 31, s. 41(1).
[223] *Family Responsibility and Support Arrears Enforcement Act, 1996*, S.O. 1996, c. 31, s. 35(1), 41(10)(a).
[224] Part 3 of this book explains Motions to Change.
[225] *Family Responsibility and Support Arrears Enforcement Act, 1996*, S.O. 1996, c. 31, s. 35(1),(4).
[226] The Notice of Withdrawal Form is available at: http://www.theFRO.ca.

John P. Schuman, C.S., Family Lawyer, Mediator and Arbitrator

Property Matters (How the Family's Assets and Debts Are Divided)

During a marriage, or a relationship of some permanence, the parties usually acquire assets (and debts). At the end of the relationship, the parties usually have to divide up the wealth they accumulated during the relationship. It makes a difference whether the parties last lived together in Ontario or elsewhere. From a legal standpoint, it also makes a huge difference whether the parties were married or were living together in a common law relationship.

When couples live in Ontario, and separate from each other in Ontario, Ontario's *Family Law Act* governs the division of their assets and debts. However, if the last place the parties lived together was someplace other than Ontario, their assets and debts are divided according to the law of that other place.[227] If, for example, the last place a couple lived together was North Carolina, then their assets and liabilities will be divided according to the law of North Carolina. The spouses can still proceed before the Ontario Courts if one of them resides in Ontario at the time of the Court Application,[228] however the Ontario Courts will apply the law of the last place the spouses lived together.

Common Law Couples Do Not Share in Each Other's Property under the Family Law Act.

At the end of a marriage in Ontario, spouses equalize their Net Family Properties, which means that they share in the increase in the spouses' net worth during the marriage. However, unmarried, or common law partners, are not entitled to an "equalization." Unmarried partners have no rights under the *Family Law Act* to share in her partner's net worth[229]. Regardless of how long two people live together, if they do not marry, they do not have any rights to their partner's property that are any greater than people who are not in a romantic relationship at all. By choosing not to be married, a couple is choosing not to share their property under the *Family Law Act*.[230]

---

[227] *Family Law Act*, R.S.O, 1990, c. F-3, s. 15 as amended.
[228] *Divorce Act*, R.S.C. 1985 c. 3 (2nd Supp), s. 3(1) and 4(1), and Rule 5(1)(a) of the *Family Law Rules*.
[229] *Family Law Act*, R.S.O. 1990, c.F-3, s.1(1) and 5, as amended. The definition of "spouse" for the purpose of the Parts of the *Family Law Act* addressing property and matrimonial homes only includes two people who are married or have entered into a marriage that is voidable or void in good faith.
[230] *Nova Scotia (Attorney General) v. Walsh*, [2002] 4 S.C.R. 325.

John P. Schuman, C.S., Family Lawyer, Mediator and Arbitrator

Married Couples Share Some of the Value of Some Property

The most significant property issue between married spouses is the equalization of their Net Family Properties. The *Family Law Act* does not give married spouses (who separate in Ontario) an interest in the assets owned by the other spouse. Put another way, being married does not mean that the spouses own each other's property. Except in rare circumstances, married spouses are also not responsible for each other's debt.

Broadly speaking, married spouses are entitled to share in the increase in the growth of the spouse's net worth during the marriage. This is done by adding up the value of each spouse's assets as of the date of separation, subtracting the value of the debts as of the date of separation, and also subtracting the value of the assets that the spouse brought into the marriage, less the value of the debt that the spouse brought into the marriage. The resulting number for each spouse is called that spouse's Net Family Property.[231] Net Family Property roughly approximates the increase in each spouse's net worth during the marriage. The equalization process requires the spouse with the higher Net Family Property to make a payment to the spouse with the lower Net Family Property. The amount of the payment is the amount that makes their Net Family Properties equal.[232]

Essentially, the spouse with the higher growth in his or her net worth during the marriage must make a payment to the other spouse that is half of the amount that the first spouse's net worth has grown more than the net worth of the second spouse. At the end of this process, the growth in the net worth of both spouses during the marriage is equal.

There are some important exceptions to the general rule regarding equalization. The exceptions are as follows:

1. At separation, the full value of the matrimonial home[233] must be included in the net family property of the spouse or spouses who own it.[234] If a spouse brings a house into the marriage and that house is the matrimonial home on the date of separation, the spouse who owned it is not entitled to a credit for the value of the house at the time of

---

[231] *Family Law Act*, R.S.O. 1990, c. F-3, s. 4(1) as amended.
[232] *Family Law Act*, R.S.O. 1990, c. F-3, s. 5(1) as amended.
[233] See the next section on "matrimonial homes" for what properties are "matrimonial homes."
[234] *Family Law Act*, R.S.O. 1990, c. F-3, s. 4(1) and 4(2), as amended

marriage. This is an important consideration that is the subject of many marriage contracts. Any other house (or any other property) that a spouse owned at the date of marriage is deducted from a party's net worth when calculating net family property. Further, if the spouse brings a house into the marriage, and the parties occupy that house as a matrimonial home, but before the parties separate, they move into a new matrimonial home, the spouse who brought the original house into the marriage still gets a credit for the value of that house.

2. Anything that a spouse acquires during the marriage either by way of a gift or inheritance from a third party (not the other spouse), is not included in a party's net family property unless that gift or inheritance is transferred into a joint asset and the value of the gift and inheritance cannot be traced within that joint asset[235].

3. Payments for damages for personal injury or other claims in tort paid to one spouse are not included in that spouse's net family property unless, as with gifts and inheritance, those payments are then transferred into a joint asset and cannot be traced in the joint asset[236].

4. Income that is created by a gift or inheritance is also excluded if the donor has expressly stated that the income is not to form part of the spouse's net family property. Note, however, that income from a gift or inheritance is included in the calculation of a spouse's child support obligation[237].

5. Proceeds of a life insurance policy that are payable on the death of a spouse are not included in the spouse's net family property. However, any cash surrender value of a life insurance policy is included in a spouse's net family property[238].

6. As noted above, matrimonial homes owned on the date of separation can never be excluded from a spouse's net family property regardless of how or when the matrimonial home was obtained.

7. In a marriage contract, the parties can specifically state that specific assets will be excluded from a spouse's net family property[239]. If the marriage contract is valid, then the property will not be included in the spouse's net family property (in marriage contracts, spouses can also exclude all of their property from the equalization process and if the

---

[235] *Family Law Act*, R.S.O. 1990, c. F-3, s. 4(2), as amended
[236] *Family Law Act*, R.S.O. 1990, c. F-3, s. 4(2), as amended
[237] *Family Law Act*, R.S.O. 1990, c. F-3, s. 4(2), as amended
[238] *Family Law Act*, R.S.O. 1990, c. F-3, s. 4(2), as amended
[239] *Family Law Act*, R.S.O. 1990, c. F-3, s. 4(2) and 52(1)(a), as amended

John P. Schuman, C.S., Family Lawyer, Mediator and Arbitrator

marriage contract is not set aside, then there will be no equalization of net family properties).

When Desmond and Molly were married, Desmond owned his store, worth $20,000 and a house worth $100,000. Molly did not own anything, but during the marriage she inherited $100,000 from her great aunt. She kept the money in a separate bank account. On the date of separation, the store was worth $40,000 and the house was worth #200,000. The inheritance also grew to $200,000.

Desmond's Net Family Property includes the $20,000 increase in the value of the store. It also includes the entire value of the house ($200,000) since it was the matrimonial home on the date of separation. Molly has no net family property, since she inherited all of her assets. Desmond must pay Molly $110,000.

A court might not equalize the net family properties of the spouses in certain situations. The spouses would still divide their Net Family Properties, but not so that each spouse receives an equal share. The spouses' Net Family Properties might not be equalized in the following situations[240]:

1. where one party has improvidently depleted his or her net family property, regardless of whether the spouse did so for the purpose of defeating the other spouse's equalization claim;
2. where a spouse failed to disclose debts or other liabilities existing at the date of marriage;
3. where a large portion of a spouse's net family property is made up of gifts made by the other spouse;
4. when the parties have been married for less than five years and the equalization payment that would otherwise be required is disproportionately large considering the short duration of the marriage;
5. when one spouse has incurred a disproportionately larger amount of debts or other liabilities to support the family during the marriage; and
6. other circumstances where the court thinks it is fair to make an order that does something other than equalizing the net family properties of the parties.

---

[240] All of these circumstances are found at *Family Law Act*, R.S.O. 1990, c. F-3, s. 5(6), as amended.

If a spouse's net worth declines during the marriage, such that the spouse's net family property would be less than zero, the *Family Law Act* deems that that spouse's net family property is zero[241]. It is not possible to have a negative net family property. This makes it impossible for one spouse to receive a payment that is more than half of the other spouse's net family property as an equalization payment. Where one spouse's Net Family Property is less than zero (but deemed to be zero), a court can still order an unequal division in the circumstances described above.

Can I Be Liable for My Spouse's Debts?

As a general rule, spouses are not responsible for each other's debts. The equalization process requires one spouse to make a payment to the other spouse to equalize the net family properties. It does not require that one spouse become responsible for the other's debts. There are a few exceptions:

1. Where parties have joint debts, meaning they have both signed the loan documents saying that they are responsible for the debt, the creditor can come after either spouse for the full amount of the debt. The creditor does not have to come after each spouse for only half of the debt. It does not matter who uses the money from the loan. This rule applies generally to all joint debts, not just to the debts of married spouses.
2. Where two people are married or are living together in a common law relationship, one spouse has authority to render himself or herself and his or her spouse jointly liable to a lender for necessities of life. However, a third party cannot rely on this provision if one of the spouses has specifically told the lender that the spouses will not be jointly liable for the debt[242].
3. Where the spouses jointly own a property together, and taxes are owed by one of the spouses, the Canada Revenue Agency can seize the entire property for payment of the outstanding taxes.

---

[241] *Family Law Act*, R.S.O. 1990, c. F-3, s. 4(5), as amended.
[242] *Family Law Act*, R.S.O. 1990, c. F-3, s. 45(1).

John P. Schuman, C.S., Family Lawyer, Mediator and Arbitrator

The Problems Surrounding Pensions in Divorces

Pensions have historically been an area of great stress in family law cases. In one of his decisions, Justice Quinn wrote "I confess that there is one word which, given the choice, I would prefer not to hear in a matrimonial proceeding: 'pension'."[243] Married spouses share in the value of each other's pensions that accrued during the marriage[244]. Prior to January 1, 2012, that sometimes caused a problem because a spouse might have to share in the value of a pension, even though that spouse could not access the money in the pension for many years. The changes that came into effect on January 1, 2012 may have made things easier. But, the changes are too new to comment on how the courts will implement them.

How the value of a pension, or the pension itself, is divided on separation depends on what kind of pension it is. There are three main types of pensions:

1. the Canada Pension Plan;

2. defined contribution (or "DC") pension plans; and

3. defined benefit (or "DB") pension plans.

There are many other investment/retirement planning devices that can be similar to pensions. These include profit sharing plans, Restricted Stock Units (RSU), deferred payment plans, life insurance programs and many others. These are not technically pensions. The value in them is divided based on the difference in their value between the date of marriage and date of separation. How that is done depends on how each particular device is set up. This guide will discuss only actual pensions.

Canada Pension Plan

Canada Pension Plan pensions are easy to deal with. Spouses must share the pension credits they accumulated during the marriage. The number of pension credits that a person has determines how much he or she will get from the Canada Pension Plan on retirement. After the spouses have a separation agreement or a divorce, either of them has from the date of separation to file the necessary forms with the Canada Pension Plan to cause the pension credits

---

[243] *Iurincic v. Iurincic,* [1998] O.J. No. 2197 (Gen. Div.)
[244] *Family Law Act,* R.S.O. 1990, c. F-3, s. 4(1).

earned by both spouses during the marriage to be divided equally between them.

Defined Contribution Pensions

Defined contribution pensions are increasing in number. They are plans in which the employer agrees to contribute a specific amount each year to an investment account in the employee's name (the plan may also require the employee to contribute). Sometimes the terms of the plan require that the contributions be "locked in" until retirement. However, it is up to the employee to decide how to invest the funds. The employer does not guarantee that any amount will be available when the employee retires. The account is essentially an RRSP. On retirement, the employee has saved a certain amount of money to spend. That amount is the total amount in the account less any taxes owing. Determining the value of defined contribution plans is relatively easy: it is the value of whatever is in the account less the taxes that will be owed when that money is withdrawn.

Defined contribution programs are included in a spouse's net family property. The increase in the value of the pension during the marriage is not directly shared, but included in the calculation of the equalization payment as described above in the section "Married Couples Share Some of the Value of Some Property."

There are two ways to share the value in defined contribution plans between the spouses. The first is to include the value of the pension funds, less the tax payable on those funds in the pension members' net family property. If the pension is the only asset in his net family property, then the other spouse will receive half of the after-tax value of the pension.

The second way to share in the value of defined contribution pensions is to a "rollover." A rollover is a transfer of an asset that also transfers the tax associated with that asset pursuant to the provisions of the *Income Tax Act*[245]. One spouse transfers a portion of the defined contribution plan to the other without taking off anything for tax. Then both spouses file the required documents with the Canada Revenue Agency. When each spouse withdraws his or her share of the defined contribution pension, he or she pays tax on it at the time of that withdrawal.

---

[245] *Income Tax Act*, R.S.C. 1085, c. (5th Supp.) s. 74.5(3)(b), as amended.

John P. Schuman, C.S., Family Lawyer, Mediator and Arbitrator

Molly has a defined contribution plan from working for an orchestra. On the date of separation, she has $100,000 in the pension account. She earned all of it during the marriage. As Molly and Desmond's other assets have equal value, she will have to share her pension with Desmond.

Molly wants to make a payment to Desmond representing half of the value in her pension. She believes that she will pay tax at the rate of 25% when she starts withdrawing from the pension after she retires. Since that is a few years away, and she will not be paying the tax soon, she believes she should reduce the value of her pension by 20%, making it worth $80,000. She wants to pay Desmond $40,000 now.

Desmond wants to do a rollover. He wants Molly to transfer $50,000 from her pension into his RRSPs. He will pay tax when taking that money out.

Defined Benefit Pensions

Defined benefit pensions are pensions in which the pension plan guarantees a certain income for the employee when he or she retires. That amount is based on how long the employee worked for the company. As a result, part of those payments may be related to the employee's service before or after the marriage. That can make the value of the pension hard to determine. The value of the pension for family law purposes was the value, on the date of separation, of the pension payments the spouse would receive after separation. That value was also related to when the spouse retired and how long he was expected to live. Before January 1, 2012, the value of the pension that a separated spouse had to include in his net family property was often a contested issue between the separated spouses. There were often contradictory reports prepared by actuaries. Since pensions were not divisible, the spouse with the pension sometimes had to make an equalization payment with money he was not going to receive until retirement.

Since January 1, 2012, all pension plans in Ontario have the potential to be divisible before retirement. This means that after separation, the portion of the pension that a spouse acquired during the marriage can be divided by the pension plan as long as the spouse with the pension has not already retired. Under the new rules, the pension is still included in a spouse's net family property. However, the value of the pension is calculated by the pension administrator, not an actuary, according to a set formula.[246] To satisfy an equalization payment, or other form of property settlement, the spouse with the pension can transfer up to fifty percent of his pension to the other spouse rather than making a cash payment.[247] To make the calculation simpler, separating spouses can agree to divide the pension equally at source and then exclude it from any equalization calculations. While this is simpler, it may ignore some of tax advantages and disadvantages possible from paying more or less of an equalization payment by way of a pension transfer. It is best to look at all the options, and their ramifications, before deciding what to do with a pension after separation.

For the pension to be divided at source, there must be a court order, arbitration award or separation agreement setting out how it will be divided[248] and the pension must be sufficiently financially solvent to permit the division. There are options for doing that division. The first option is have a lump sum, representing up to half the value of the pension, transferred out of the pension to the other spouse. The pension funds must be transferred into either another pension or an RRSP.[249] The second option is to have the pension divided so that both separated spouses become entitled to a share of the pension[250]. The pension becomes two pensions with the same pension plan. Each separated spouse receives payments from the pension plan on retirement. However, the payments to the spouse who originally had the pension are reduced by the amount transferred to his former spouse.[251] Either of these options for dividing a pension may not be available if the circumstances of the pension plan do not permit it.

In deciding property issues between spouses, a court does not have to order that a pension be divided. A judge can order that the spouse with the pension keep the pension and make a cash payment to the other spouse as an equalization payment. The calculation of that equalization payment will use the value of the pension as calculated by the pension administrator. In deciding

---

[246] *Pension Benefits Act,* R.S.O. 1990, c. P-8, s. 67.2(5), as amended.
[247] *Pension Benefits Act,* R.S.O. 1990, c. P-8, s. 67.3(6), 67.4(5), as amended.
[248] *Pension Benefits Act,* R.S.O. 1990, c. P-8, s. 67.3(1), 67.4(1), as amended.
[249] *Pension Benefits Act,* R.S.O. 1990, c. P-8, s. 67.3(2), as amended. This section also authorized the transfer of the pension into other retirement savings arrangements that may become permitted by law.
[250] *Pension Benefits Act,* R.S.O. 1990, c. P-8, s. 67.4(2), as amended.
[251] *Pension Benefits Act,* R.S.O. 1990, c. P-8, s. 67.4(4), as amended.

John P. Schuman, C.S., Family Lawyer, Mediator and Arbitrator

whether the pension should be divided, or whether there should be a cash payment, the judge must consider the following factors:

1. The nature of the assets available to each spouse at the time of the hearing.
2. The proportion of a spouse's net family property that is made up of the value of the pension.
3. The liquidity of the lump sum pension payment in the hands of the spouse who would be receiving it.
4. Any contingent tax liabilities related to the lump sum that would be transferred.
5. The resources available to each spouse to meet his or her needs in retirement[252].

> *Molly also has a defined benefit pension from her musicians' union. She earned two-thirds of that pension during the marriage. All of their other assets have been divided equally. Molly knows that she will never be able to make a cash payment to Desmond representing half of the value of the pension that she earned during the marriage. Desmond would like to have a pension, and so wants a portion transferred to him.*
>
> *The pension will pay Molly $3000 per month after tax. Molly has to share two thirds of her pension, which represents $2000 per month. She and Desmond agree to divide the pension so that Molly receives $2000 per month and Desmond will receive $1000 per month. They sign a separation agreement that says that, then Desmond applies to the pension administrator to do the division.*

Pensions and Spousal Support

Pensions also affect spousal support. Pensions are a right to receive income after retirement. If a spouse has to pay half the value of his or her pension to the other spouse, then the other spouse has already received half of the pension income. The Supreme Court of Canada held that it is unfair for spousal support to be based on pension income when the pension has already been equalized as the recipient spouse has already received a payment representing the value of the post retirement pension income[253]. There are some exceptions

---

[252] *Family Law Act*, R.S.O. 1990. c. F-3, s. 10.1(4).
[253] *Boston v. Boston*, [2001] 2 S.C.R. 413 at para 75.

John P. Schuman, C.S., Family Lawyer, Mediator and Arbitrator

to this rule. However, they are complicated and based on particular circumstances so these issues should be discussed with a Family Law lawyer.

Child Support is the right of the child, and so pension income is always income for child support purposes, regardless of whether the pension has already been divided, actually or notionally, through the equalization process.

Stock Options Are Great –Except in Divorce Proceedings

Some executives of banks and other large corporations receive part of their compensation through stock options or other profit sharing plans. These represent a great way to be compensated because the employee can receive money from the company usually at a lower tax rate. If the stock goes up in value before the employee exercises the stock option, the benefits are even greater. However, stock options create some particularly difficult problems in divorce proceedings.

The simplest explanation for stock options is that they are a method by which a company pays an employee by allowing that employee to purchase stocks in the company at a certain price. If the market price is greater than the price set in the stock option, the employee can sell the stock and keep the profit. When the employee sells the stock, she reports a capital gain, rather than a salary, on her tax return. Capital gains are taxed at a lower rate than salary. The company may put a restriction on when the employee is entitled to keep the stock options (or when the stock option "vests"), even if stop working for the company and when the employee can exercise the stock option to purchase the stock, and then sell it.

Stock options can be considered both property and income for support in divorce proceedings. They are property that a spouse must include in his net family property on the date of separation[254]. In most cases, the employee will not exercise the stock options on the date of separation. That makes determining the appropriate value for the stock options a particularly difficult task, as the value will depend on when the employee earned the options (as opposed to when the company gave them to him)[255], when the employee can exercise the options, when the employee does exercise the options, the risk associated with the volatility of the stock price, the risk that the employee may never be able to exercise the options and the taxes associated with the

---

[254] *Ross v. Ross* (2006), 83 O.R. (3d) 1, 34 R.F.L. (6th)229 at para 22 (C.A.).
[255] *Ross v. Ross* (2006), 83 O.R. (3d) 1, 34 R.F.L. (6th)229 at para 22 (C.A.).

options[256]. Stock options existing on the date of separation will be equalized as property, even though the employee may not be able to exercise them until later. This can create a problem when the employee does not have the funds to make an equalization payment until he exercises the options. If the terms of the options prevent the employee from exercising them for a while, that can cause hardship.

To the extent that an employee receives stock options as a form of compensation, they are income that must be taken into account when calculating support[257]. However, the stock options that existed at the time of separation, and were included in the equalization calculations, may not show up on the employee's tax return until several years until the employee exercise them. At that time, the other spouse may want them included in income for calculating support, even though she has already received half the value. In some cases, including the same stock options in both property and support calculations can result in the other spouse receiving payments in relation to the options that total more than the entire value of the options. That is not fair. Careful attention is required to keep that from happening.

Where one or both separating spouses have stock options, both spouse need skilled family law lawyers to assist with the complicated issues associated with stock options or other profit sharing plans.

There's No Place Like a Matrimonial Home (or Homes)

Matrimonial homes are special assets. They are properties in which spouses live together as husband and wife. Only legally married spouses can have matrimonial homes (the matrimonial home provisions of the *Family Law Act* do not apply to common law couples[258]). It is possible for the parties to have several matrimonial homes (for example, a principal home, a cottage, and a vacation property can simultaneously be matrimonial homes) unless the parties have jointly (both of them signed the document) registered a designation on title that one specific property is a matrimonial home[259].

---

[256] *Ross v. Ross* (2006), 83 O.R. (3d) 1, 34 R.F.L. (6th)229 at para 65 (C.A.).
[257] *Ewing v. Ewing*, 2009 ABCA 227, 67 R.F.L. (6th) 280 at para 33.
[258] *Family Law Act*, R.S.O. 1990, c. F-3, s. 1(1) and 18(1), as amended.
[259] *Family Law Act*, R.S.O. 1990, c. F-3, s. 20(4), as amended

The basic legal principle that makes matrimonial home special is that Ontario's *Family Law Act* gives both of the spouses the equal right to be in possession of the matrimonial home after separation[260]. "Being in possession" essentially means living in the home. The purpose of this provision is to keep one of the spouse's from throwing the other spouse out onto the street after separation. Not only are spouses not allowed to throw out the other spouse, but they are not allowed to sell, mortgage, or otherwise encumber title to a matrimonial home without the others spouse's permission[261]. This is why both married spouses must sign real estate documents when a matrimonial home is being sold or mortgaged.

Married spouses cannot opt out of these provisions related to matrimonial homes in the *Family Law Act*. However, they can have a domestic contract that opts out of the provisions in the *Family Law Act* that requires that an ownership interest in a matrimonial home be included in a spouse's net family property (that provision in the *Family Law Act* means that the parties must share the value of any matrimonial homes unless they have a Marriage Contract).

The court can make orders that affect spouses' rights with regard to matrimonial homes. First, a court can make an order that only one spouse may be in possession, or live in, a matrimonial home. Secondly, a court may permit a spouse to sell, mortgage, or otherwise encumber a matrimonial home[262]. It is important to note that the *Family Law Act* only governs the rights of spouses in relation to each other regarding a matrimonial home. The *Family Law Act* does not prevent third parties from exercising rights they may have over a matrimonial home. By way of example, the fact that a property is a matrimonial home does not prevent a bank from foreclosing on it if the mortgage goes into default.

A spouse cannot throw the other spouse out of a matrimonial home, change the locks, sell the matrimonial home, or re-mortgage a matrimonial home without the other spouse's consent. Obviously, there are times when it is good, if not essential, for one spouse to take one of the above actions. If the spouses do not agree, the court may order that any of the above events take

---

[260] *Family Law Act*, R.S.O. 1990, c. F-3, s. 19(1).
[261] *Family Law Act*, R.S.O. 1990, c. F-3, s. 21(1), as amended.
[262] *Family Law Act*, R.S.O. 1990, c. F-3, s. 23(b), as amended

John P. Schuman, C.S., Family Lawyer, Mediator and Arbitrator

place. When deciding whether one spouse lose his or her rights regarding a matrimonial home, the court considers the following criteria:[263]

1. the best interest of any children affected (which involves a consideration of the possible disruptive effects on a child of being moved to other accommodations and the child's views and preferences where they can be reasonably ascertained);[264]
2. any existing orders for the equalization of the spouses net family properties and any existing orders with regard to support;
3. the financial position of both spouses;
4. any written agreement between the parties;
5. the availability of other suitable and affordable accommodation; and
6. any violence committed by a spouse against the other spouse or the children.

Where a court has made an order giving one spouse possession of a matrimonial home or to do any of the things described above, it is an offence, for which a spouse can be arrested, to contravene that order. The offence is punishable, on a first conviction, of a fine of not more than $5,000, or imprisonment for a term of not more than three months, or both. In the event of a second or subsequent offence, the maximum penalty is a fine of not more than $10,000, imprisonment for a term of not more than two years, or both[265].

If a spouse mortgages, encumbers, or sells a matrimonial home without the other spouse's permission, the court can set aside that transaction[266].

Separated spouses commonly make a serious mistake by assuming that after a period of separation they can deal with the matrimonial home without the other spouse's consent. That is not the case. Even if parties have been separated for 20 years, but they remain married, neither spouse can deal with a matrimonial home. They cannot even renew a mortgage without the other spouse's consent. Even when a separated spouse has lived together with a new partner for more than three years, which makes the new partner a spouse for the purposes of support, the person to whom the first spouse is still legally married is still a spouse for the purposes of matrimonial homes.

---

[263] *Family Law Act*, R.S.O. 1990, c. F-3, s. 24(3), as amended
[264] *Family Law Act*, R.S.O. 1990, c. F-3, s. 24(4), as amended
[265] *Family Law Act*, R.S.O. 1990, c. F-3, s. 24(5), as amended
[266] *Family Law Act*, R.S.O. 1990, c. F-3, s. 23(d), as amended

> *Desmond and Molly's divorce proceedings have dragged on. Molly bought a new home. Desmond's new partner, Eleanor, moved into the house that Desmond lived in when he separated from Molly. They have lived together for 3 years, making Eleanor Desmond's spouse for the purpose of spousal support.*
>
> *When it was time, Desmond renewed the mortgage with the same bank. A month later, then bank called him to demand that the mortgage be paid back immediately. Molly had called the bank calming the new mortgage was not valid. She is still married to Desmond, and so the house is still a matrimonial home. She had not signed the spousal consent for the renewed mortgage. Even though Eleanor is now Desmond's spouse for spousal support, Molly still has to consent to transactions involving the matrimonial home until Desmond and Molly are divorced, or there is a court order allowing the transaction. Desmond has no say regarding Molly's new house.*

After spouses separate, any properties that they buy cannot, by definition, be a matrimonial home since the spouses do not live in them together. This is even true when one spouse sold a matrimonial home, with the others spouse's consent, and purchased a new home with the proceeds.

When two people are divorced, they are no longer spouses and so they can no longer have matrimonial homes. On divorce, any property that was a matrimonial home ceases to be a matrimonial home and the divorced spouses lose any rights they may have had to that property as a matrimonial home under the *Family Law Act*.

Forcing Your Ex-Partner Out: Partition and Sale of Property

Often, married spouses and common-law partners purchase property (which may include real property such as a home, or investments, or any other type of possession) as joint tenants. "Joint Tenancy" is a legal term meaning that both parties own the property entirely. When they register title as joint tenants, the spouses (or common-law partners) have equal ownership to the property and equal rights to it. Holding a piece of property as joint tenants is good estate-planning, because on the death of one joint tenant, the title to the property passes to the other joint tenant without going through a last will and testament, or requiring the payment of estate taxes on the transfer of ownership. Where there is a dispute over the property, joint tenants are presumed to own equal shares in the property, although that can be refuted by evidence such as an agreement between the owners.

John P. Schuman, C.S., Family Lawyer, Mediator and Arbitrator

If the jointly held property is a matrimonial home and the owners are married, then the provisions described above with regard to matrimonial homes apply to prevent the married owners from dealing with the property. Further, married spouses are subject to the terms of the *Family Law Act* that allow a court to determine their respective ownership interests in jointly-held property[267]. A court can decide that one married spouse owns more than 50 percent of a jointly held property and the other spouse owns less than 50 percent of that same property.

If the property is not a matrimonial home, or the owners either have never been married or are divorced, then any owner can force the property to be sold. This is done by way of a court application pursuant to the *Partition and Sale Act*. At the same time, the court can make a determination of what each owner's interest is in the jointly held property and distribute the proceeds of sale accordingly. Where this application is not brought in Family Court, the process for doing this is a very streamlined and a relatively quick one.

What to Do If Everything So Far Does Not Help: Other Remedies

The Ontario Superior Court of Justice may grant some other common remedies with regard to property in Family Law cases. These remedies grant one party an ownership interest in a property that is legally owned by another party. Such remedies are available to both married and unmarried partners. In cases involving common-law relationships, they are frequently employed to correct an injustice where all of the wealth accumulated during the relationship was accumulated in the name of one of the common-law spouses to the detriment of the other spouse.

These remedies are remedies that are based in equity and not in law. The difference between "equity" and "law" is not usually important for a non-lawyer to understand except that a person who is making a claim in equity must "come to the court with clean hands". What this means is that if a person has behaved badly towards either the court or the other party, that person may be barred from obtaining any of the remedies described below.

---

[267] *Family Law Act*, R.S.O. 1990, c. F-3. s. 10, as amended.

John P. Schuman, C.S., Family Lawyer, Mediator and Arbitrator

There is a wide range of remedies available in equity. Many of them could have application in Family Law cases if the circumstances are right. However, a review of all of equitable remedies is beyond this discussion. Parties often seek a few equitable remedies in family proceedings. These remedies are discussed below.

The first group of remedies are those that are collectively called "trust remedies". The basic idea behind this principle is that a person who holds legal title to a property is not the actual owner but is holding that property for somebody else. The person who has legal title is holding the property in trust for a "beneficial owner", who is the real owner of the property. It is not uncommon, for variety of reasons, for one person to hold property in trust for another person on purpose. In some cases, both parties agree to this, as giving a gift to another person in this way that has certain advantages (most of them tax-related). However, in Family Law proceedings, one of the most common equitable remedies sought is a declaration from the court that says that one person is not the real owner of property, but is actually holding that property in trust for a second person (the beneficial owner). That second person is the real owner. The court can make that declaration over the objections of both the legal owner and the person who is purported to be the beneficial owner.

Claims in equity, especially the ones in family proceedings, are very technical, complex, and fact-driven, which means that in making or responding to these claims, it is very important for a party to have a lawyer who can explain how equity applies to his situation.

One common situation in which a party may want to make a claim in equity is where one spouse put property into the name of another person for the purposes of defeating her spouse's entitlement to an equalization payment. The court will be concerned about what transpired in circumstances where the spouse put an asset of significant value into the name of another person, but continues to control that asset and to collect any income or other benefits related to that asset. The court will be suspicious that the spouse did not intend to transfer ownership of the asset but rather to retain ownership while making it appear that the asset should not form part of the spouse's net family property. In such circumstances, the court can impose a Resulting Trust. In doing that, the court will declare that the spouse is the actual owner of the property, despite title being registered in the name of another person and will order that the asset be included in the spouse's net family property.

A court can also make a declaration that property belongs to the person who is making the claim in equity. The court can make a declaration that, despite what is registered on title, the second spouse holds part of the ownership of the asset in trust for the first spouse. These claims are very popular among common-law spouses, who are denied any equalization payment under the *Family Law Act*. Since the law does not allow unmarried spouses with long term relationships to share in their increases in net worth during the relationship, spouses may bring a claim in equity saying that the claimant spouse actually has an interest in the property owned by the other spouse. The spouse making this claim does so to share in the others spouse's increase in net worth during the relationship.

In *Kerr v. Baranow*,[268] the Supreme Court of Canada recognized that in intimate or familial relationships, "spouses", whether married or not, could acquire an equitable interest in each other's property without proving that they made a direct contribution to it. Where spouses can show that there was a certain degree of financial integration of the spouses and the parties had consciously arranged their affairs such that one spouse would primarily look after the family and the other would primarily support the family. The Supreme Court of Canada called this situation a "Joint Family Venture" because, as the names applies, the parties joined together financially to advance the financial wellbeing of the family as a whole rather than their individual fortunes. Usually a Joint Family Venture will involve one spouse suffering an economic disadvantage because they didn't earn an income and accumulate assets in their name. If a party can prove they were in a Joint Family Venture with their spouse, they are usually entitled to a monetary payment from the other spouse to compensate for the inequity. In rare cases where money isn't sufficient (such as where a spouse contributed to a business or other asset that continues to grow in value), a court may declare that the spouse actually has a legal interest in the other spouse's property.

The fact of a long-term relationship does not, in itself, entitle one common-law spouse to share in the property of the other common-law spouse. One situation that does create that interest in property is where the spouses specifically discuss that they intended to share the ownership of a specific piece of property, no matter whose name title is registered. The other circumstance is where the spouse who does not have a titled interest contributes something of value, either money, or his own labour, toward a piece of property without receiving anything in return, and in such a way that the contribution creates

---

[268] *Kerr v. Baranow*, 2011 SCC 10.

value for the titled owner. Further, the non-titled spouse must suffer some form of detriment as a result of having made the contribution. By way of example, just cleaning a house may not give a non-titled spouse an interest in that property if that spouse did not have to pay any rent to live in the property. However, if that spouse contributed work that was more valuable than the rent that the spouse would otherwise have paid then that spouse might gain an interest in the property.

Another limitation on the ability of a party to acquire an interest in property through a claim in equity is that a claim in law, which would involve a payment of money, must be inadequate. For example, equalization claims for married spouses can erase any claims to share in the increase in value in a spouse's property during the marriage (the equity claim may be necessary to address post-separation changes in value. Further, the factors that would lead a court to find the existence of a "Joint Family Venture" are very similar to the factors a court would consider in making a spousal support order. So, the Joint Family Venture claim may only be appropriate where a spousal support order does not address the situation fairly. Where neither of those claims are sufficient, a court would prefer to have the titled spouse pay the non-titled spouse an amount equivalent to the value of the work that the non-titled spouse performed, rather than give an interest in the property. However, if the property is somehow special such that the only appropriate result is that the non-titled spouse be given an interest in it, and money would be inadequate compensation, then the court may declare that the titled spouse holds all or part of the property in trust for the non-titled spouse.

The above discussion refers to claims in equity being made for property. "Property" does not just mean "real property" or land. It can also mean chattels, which are things like cars, furniture, pieces of art, bank accounts, or just about anything else a person can own that is not land. It is possible to make a trust claim in relation to anything a person can own (you cannot, by way of example, claim to hold an interest in someone else's heart, because Canadian Law says that human organs cannot be bought and sold).

Obviously, these types of claims are very complicated. They result from complex fact situations and require the application of complex principles. The above is only a very short and oversimplified overview of these principles, to give a brief introduction into the type of claims that can be made in Family Law proceedings. Parties need lawyers both to make and defend the claims described above, because the concepts are more complicated when they are applied in real life.

John P. Schuman, C.S., Family Lawyer, Mediator and Arbitrator

Stopping Your Spouse From Giving Everything to Someone Else: Preservation Orders

In the Family Law context, "Preservation Orders" are orders that restrain a party from dealing with his or her assets or debts. These orders are also known as "Freezing Orders", as they are the orders that freeze bank accounts and other assets. Judges make Preservation Orders when they are concerned that one spouse is divesting herself of her assets, or is running up debts, to prevent the other spouse from collecting on any amount that the court may find is owed to the other party. Preservation Orders can be made to freeze a party's assets to preserve them either to make an equalization payment[269], or to pay support[270].

If a party is worried that he or she may have difficulty collecting on support, such that some form of order may be needed to freeze the other party's assets, that party should commence a court proceeding in the Ontario Superior Court of Justice. The Ontario Court of Justice has much more limited powers with regard to freezing or seizing assets[271]. The Ontario Superior Court of Justice has quite broad powers in that regard and can even order that an asset be transferred to the other party either in fulfilment of a support obligation or as security for payment of future support payments[272]. For example, when a support payer owns half of a house with the recipient, but has not been paying support, the court can transfer the payer's half interest in the house to the recipient as security for the support payments.

How to Get Paid Pursuant to a Non-Support Order

Sometimes former spouses do not pay the equalization payments, other property payments, or costs awards made against them. The *Family Law Rules* give spouses who are entitled to these payments much greater powers to enforce them than are enjoyed by other judgment creditors. Family law orders for payment of money can be enforced through judgment-debtor examinations, writs of seizure and sale, garnishment, and the appointment of a receiver[273], which are all enforcement steps that are available to anyone who has a judgment. However, people who are owed a payment pursuant to a family court order can also demand a financial statement, or request disclosure from

---

[269] *Family Law Act*, R.S.O, 1990, c. F-3, s. 12.
[270] *Family Law Act*, R.S.O, 1990, c. F-3, s. 34(1).
[271] *Family Law Act*, R.S.O, 1990, c. F-3, s. 34(2).
[272] *Family Law Act*, R.S.O, 1990, c. F-3, s. 34(1)(c).
[273] *Family Law Rules*, Rule 26(3)

an income source[274]. If the person who owes the money does not provide the financial information as required, he or she can be imprisoned continuously or intermittently for not more than 40 days[275]. If an income source for the person who owes the money fails to provide the required information, the judge can order that the income source post a bond or a quantity of money[276]. These remedies are much more severe than those available to people who are owed money under a civil judgment.

As noted above, there are additional enforcement steps that are available when the order is an order for spousal or child support.

Bankruptcy Can Change Everything or Nothing

People who are going to separation or divorce are not immune from financial problems, nor are they exempt from the *Bankruptcy and Insolvency Act* ("BIA")[277]. To the contrary, going through a separation or divorce forces people to pay attention to, and come to terms with, their financial circumstances. Many people who have not paid attention to the family's financial situation for a long time suddenly think about bankruptcy when they confront financial realities. Additionally, the period after separation is a very difficult time when many people are driven by emotion rather than reason. They may behave badly, or without sufficient consideration to what they are doing, which may result in court orders or arbitration awards that cause financial hardship. Finally, family courts have seen a lot of cases in which a spouse has intentionally bankrupted herself in an attempt to prevent her spouse from receiving money.

One separated spouse, or both, going bankrupt can have a profound effect on both spouses, their options for resolving the matters between them, and any litigation between them. It is important for separated spouses to have some understanding of what their bankruptcy, or their spouse's bankruptcy, will have on post-separation financial issues so that they can make appropriate decisions.

---

[274] *Family Law Rules*, Rule 26(3)
[275] *Family Law Rules*, Rule 27(6)
[276] *Family Law Rules*, Rule 27(10)
[277] *Bankruptcy and Insolvency Act*, R.S.C. 1985, c. B-3, as amended.

A person "goes bankrupt" by retaining a trustee in bankruptcy and making an assignment in bankruptcy or committing any a series of acts designed to defeat creditors[278]. Some people try to avoid bankruptcy by making a proposal to their creditors, but if a majority of the creditors (majority by value of the debt owed) do not accept the proposal, the person becomes bankrupt[279]. Alternatively, sometimes creditors will put a person into bankruptcy[280]. When a person goes bankrupt, the following three important things happen:

1. All the bankrupt's property (land and personal property), with the exception of the basic things that the bankrupt needs to live, established retirement savings, life insurance policies and pension plans, is turned over to the bankruptcy trustee[281]. The trustee can then use that property to satisfy the claims made by the creditors.
2. All of the bankrupt's income, except that which is needed to pay for basic necessities, becomes the property of the trustee[282]. The trustee uses that income to pay creditors.
3. All court proceedings, related to financial matters, brought by or against the bankrupt are stopped[283]. For family court matters, the proceedings can be restarted again relatively easily.[284] However, the trustee replaces the bankrupt as the party in the proceedings for financial matters. The trustee directs the financial litigation, not to the bankrupt.

It is a common misconception that bankruptcy erases all debts. That is not true and it is especially not true with regard to child and spousal support[285]. Creditors who have security in place for the entire debt owed by the bankrupt are not affected much by a bankruptcy[286]. Secured creditors are creditors who have security such as mortgages or liens against property. They can call the

---

[278] *Bankruptcy and Insolvency Act*, R.S.C. 1985, c. B-3, s. 42(1) as amended.
[279] *Bankruptcy and Insolvency Act*, R.S.C. 1985, c. B-3, s. 62 and 66.28, 71 as amended.
[280] *Bankruptcy and Insolvency Act*, R.S.C. 1985, c. B-3, s. 43(1) as amended.
[281] *Bankruptcy and Insolvency Act*, R.S.C. 1985, c. B-3, s. 67(1) as amended.
[282] *Bankruptcy and Insolvency Act*, R.S.C. 1985, c. B-3, s. 68(1) as amended.
[283] *Bankruptcy and Insolvency Act*, R.S.C. 1985, c. B-3, s. 69.3(1) as amended.
[284] *Bankruptcy and Insolvency Act*, R.S.C. 1985, c. B-3, s. 69.4 as amended.
Support cases easily meet the test for lifting of the automatic stay of proceedings under the BIA. Suspending support proceedings prejudices the children and dependent spouse of the bankrupt.
[285] *Bankruptcy and Insolvency Act*, R.S.C. 1985, c. B-3, s. 178(1)(c) as amended.
[286] *Bankruptcy and Insolvency Act*, R.S.C. 1985, c. B-3, s. 88 as amended.

mortgage or exercise the lien in the event of the bankruptcy to recover their entire debt. It is unsecured creditors who are most affected by a bankruptcy.

The trustee divides up the bankrupt's unencumbered assets and surplus income to satisfy as much of the debt owed to unsecured creditors as possible. People do not go bankrupt if they have the means to pay off their debts. This means that some unsecured creditor do not get paid, or at least do not get paid in full. The BIA sets out priorities for which creditors get paid before others. Fortunately, child and spousal support are quite high up on the list of priorities (support ranks fourth in the list of priorities). Unfortunately, payments in relation to family law property orders or settlements rank very low. A bankrupt's spouse and children will get paid their support before most other creditors receive anything. If there is money to be shared, it is likely they will get some. However, despite the priority given to support in a bankruptcy, the Family Responsibility Office does not aggressively enforce support until a step payer is discharged from bankruptcy.

Child and spousal support debt is also different from other types of debt in that it is not erased by a bankruptcy. Any support arrears that the bankrupt owes at the time of bankruptcy will still be owed after the bankruptcy unless they are paid down during the bankruptcy[287]. Further, support arrears continue to accumulate during the bankruptcy. If the bankrupt does not make the full support payments during the bankruptcy, the support arrears will continue to increase and will still be owed after the bankruptcy. The support recipient may have to wait to receive support, knowing that the bankrupt will still owe the support after the bankruptcy. The only way that the bankrupt can reduce the amount of support owed is to bring a Motion to Change support[288]. The bankruptcy may be a change in the bankrupt's financial circumstances that is sufficient to justify a change in support.

Costs awards that are clearly related to support issues are considered to be part of the support order or award. They also survive bankruptcy.[289]

---

[287] *Bankruptcy and Insolvency Act*, R.S.C. 1985, c. B-3, s. 178(1)(c) as amended.
[288] See Part 3 of this guide.
[289] *Champagne v. Chapagne*, 2010 ONSC 4469 at para 33, *Bankruptcy and Insolvency Act*, R.S.C. 1985, c. B-3, s. 178(1)(c) as amended.

John P. Schuman, C.S., Family Lawyer, Mediator and Arbitrator

Equalization payments are not exempt from the bankruptcy. Also, they do not get any priority, which means the trustee will pay an equalization payment after all secured creditors and all creditors with priority receive full payment[290]. Sometimes a court order or arbitration award will give the non-bankrupt spouse an interest in the bankrupt's property, or some form of security against it. However, unless that court award or arbitration award is clear that it is giving some form of interest in property to a spouse, and it does that before the bankruptcy, the non-bankrupt spouse will not have any way to get paid before other unsecured creditors[291].

Costs orders and awards for anything other than support, such as those related to property issues, parenting issues or restraining orders, do not get any priority over other creditors. Claims for payment of those costs are among the last to be paid in a bankruptcy.

The bankruptcy of one separated spouse can have unfair consequences for the non-bankrupt spouse. The bankruptcy can have the effect of depriving the non-bankrupt spouse of all of the wealth accumulated during the marriage. Sometimes, the bankrupt spouse organizes his affairs so that a bankruptcy will prevent the other spouse from being paid. The Supreme Court of Canada recognized that this situation could be terribly unfair. However, that court also recognized that the BIA permits such behaviour and the courts do not have the ability to interfere with the operation of the BIA[292]. Courts can consider the effect of the bankruptcy on both spouses when deciding the issue of spousal support[293]. If a bankruptcy prevents a spouse from receiving the equalization payment to which she otherwise would have been entitled, the non-bankrupt spouse will have a greater need for support. That greater need for support can be used to justify a higher periodic spousal support payment. That higher obligation to pay support will survive the bankruptcy.

---

[290] *Schreyer v. Schreyer*, 2011 SCC 35 at para 29.
[291] *Thibodeau v. Thibodeau*, 2011 ONCA 110, 104 O.R. (3d) 161 at paras 30 and 43.
[292] *Schreyer v. Schreyer*, 2011 SCC 35 at para 40.
[293] *Schreyer v. Schreyer*, 2011 SCC 35 at para 37.

John P. Schuman, C.S., Family Lawyer, Mediator and Arbitrator

> *Molly is going to owe Desmond a significant equalization payment. The judge said that Desmond should not get any spousal support as a result. Rather than paying the equalization payment, Molly went bankrupt. All the money that Molly had, except for her pensions, was divided between Desmond, her credit cards, her unsecured line of credit and even her family law lawyer. Desmond received about twenty percent of his equalization payment owed to him.*
>
> *Molly also owed child support to Desmond – both table and payments toward special and extraordinary expenses. Molly did not make those payments after she went bankrupt. However, the Family Responsibility Office started collecting all the missed payments after Molly was discharged from her bankruptcy.*

Bankruptcy can profoundly impact on the financial results for spouses after separation. Bankruptcy law is much more complicated than just the simple principles described above. There are several very difficult steps that the bankrupt spouse or the non-bankrupt spouse can use to lessen the impact of the bankruptcy on them. If the bankruptcy of one of the spouses looks like a possibility, then both spouses should immediately consult with lawyers who are familiar with family law, insolvency law, and how the two interact.

Protecting the Safety of You and the Kids: Restraining Orders

Both the *Family Law Act*[294] and the *Children's Law Reform Act*[295] allow courts to make an order preventing two people from "harassing, molesting or annoying each other. However, in Family Law, the court can only make orders of this type apply to limited groups of people. Restraining/Non-Harassment Orders can be made with respect to the following groups of people:

---

[294] *Family Law Act*, R.S.O. 1990, C. F-3, s. 46(1).
[295] *Children's Law Reform Act*, R.S.O. 1990, c. C-12, s. 35(1).

1. parents of children;
2. married or common law spouses;
3. one person as against another, so long as they lived together for any length of time – possibly as short as one night;[296]
4. any person whose behaviour provides reasonable grounds for concern for the safety of a parent or a child in the parent's lawful custody.[297]

The above categories cover every type of romantic or familial relationship except "dating relationships", (where the parties have not spent nights together) or stalkers, (where the parties have never had a relationship at all). A person in those two situations cannot get a Restraining Order under the *Family Law Act* or *Children's Law Reform Act*. If that person requires protection from another person, she should consult with a criminal lawyer to have an order made under the *Criminal Code*.

The courts have held that the wording in both the *Family Law Act* and the *Children's Law Reform Act* is broad enough to allow a court to make an order that stops people, who do not fall into one of the above categories, from harassing a spouse or parent on behalf of the other spouse or parent, who falls within the categories above[298]. A spouse cannot have his or her friends or employees harass the other spouse to try to get around the provisions of the legislation.

One of the purposes of a Restraining Order, when made at the beginning of a court case, or during a court case, is to permit both litigants an opportunity to conduct their litigation in as reasonable an atmosphere as may be possible[299]. The courts can make permanent Restraining Orders at the end of a court case, although the police tend to keep a record of such orders for 5 years. To make a permanent Restraining Order, the court must be convinced that one or both parties are determined to make the other's life as miserable as possible for as long as possible, such that a police-enforceable order is necessary.

---

[296] The applicable section pertains to "spouses" and "former spouses", but is in Part III of the *Family Law Act*, which defines "spouses" not only as married spouses, but as also including people who have lived together for not less than three years or who are the natural or adoptive parents of a child.
[297] *Children's Law Reform Act*, R.S.O. 1990, c. C-12, s. 35(1).
[298] *Callon v. Callon*, [1999] O.J. No. 3108 (Div. Ct.) at para 1.
[299] *Callon v. Callon*, [1999] O.J. No. 3108 (Div. Ct.) at para 1.

John P. Schuman, C.S., Family Lawyer, Mediator and Arbitrator

When a court makes a Restraining Order, the order is entered into the nationwide police database. This means that the order will come up when a police officer searches a person in a car or station computer. A person who violates a Restraining Order may be charged with Criminal Harassment, pursuant to the *Criminal Code of Canada*. The *Criminal Code* mandates harsher sentences for people who have breached a Family Court Restraining Order[300].

There is wide variation between judges with respect to the circumstances in which they will grant Restraining Orders. Some judges will grant the orders when a spouse feels uncomfortable around the other spouse. Other judges will not grant the order unless there is reliable evidence that there is a danger to the safety of a spouse, parent or child. However, Family Court Judges will generally not make Restraining Orders where there is already another court order preventing spouses from having contact. It is typically not necessary to get a Family Court Restraining Order where one spouse has conditions of bail, probation, or parole, that prohibit contact with the other spouse.

You Can't Put it Off Forever – There are Limits on How Long You Can Ask For Things

After parties have separated, they have a limited time in which they can make family law claims against their former spouses. People need to move on with their lives without fearing that they will be sued for things that happened a long time ago. To promote this, the law sets out different time limits for making different claims. In law, these time limits are called "limitation periods." Once a limitation period expires for a particular type of claim, anyone's claim and their right to make it, disappears completely. If one former spouse gives the other anything in relation to a claim after a limitation period has expired, the first spouse is giving a gift. For a spouse to preserve his or her rights to a claim, he or she has to start a court proceeding before the limitation period expires. In special circumstances, a separated spouse may be able to extend a limitation agreement by way of an agreement with his or her spouse. However no spouse should do that without speaking to a lawyer first.

Here is a list of limitation periods that commonly apply to Ontario Family Law Cases:

---

[300] *Criminal Code of Canada*, R.S.C. 1985, c. C-46, s. 264.

John P. Schuman, C.S., Family Lawyer, Mediator and Arbitrator

ISSUE	LIMITATION PERIOD
Equalization of Net Family Property (Usual Family Law Property Claims)	**6 Years** from date of separation **2 Years** from date of a divorce order **6 Months** from the date of death of a spouse[301]
Claims in Equity for Real Property (Claims that the legal title to land does not reflect the true owner)	**10 Years** from date claim arose (may be before date of separation)[302]
Claims in Equity for Other Property (Claims that the legal title to a bank account or other asset, other than land) does not reflect the true owner)	**2 Years** from date claim arose (may be before date of separation)[303]
Application to Divide Canada Pension Plan Credits	**4 Years (48 months)** from the date of separation (unless former spouse gives written consent later)[304]
Support/Retroactive Support and Requests for Income Disclosure	**No fixed period** but refusal to pursue a claim or seek disclosure can nullify a support claim, but intentionally hiding income can extend the right to ask for support.

---

[301] *Family Law Act*, R.S.O. 1900, c. F.-3, s. 7(3).
[302] *McConnell v. Huxtable*, 2014 ONCA 86 at para 39.
[303] *McConnell v. Huxtable*, 2014 ONCA 86 at para 50, 53.
[304] For more see: http://www.servicecanada.gc.ca/eng/services/pensions/cpp/credit-split.shtml

Custody and Access	**When child turns 18 years old**[305] unless the parents were married and the child remains legally unable to make own decisions.[306] However, the *Health Care Consent Act*, allows children to make health care decisions for themselves as soon as they understand the treatment and risks.[307]
Related Non-Family Claims	Claims for personal injury, defamation, battery, malicious prosecution and other claims that are not family law claims but may be made in family law claims, have **various limitation periods**.

In many cases, it is clear the day on which spouses separate, and so there is little issue over what their limitation periods are. However, some spouses do not agree on when they separated. In some cases, spouses are 'on again, off again' and will disagree on when they finally separated. Some spouses 'held out hope' longer than the other, and disagree on when they concluded that there relationship was over. Some spouses will try to argue that parties separated later to extend a limitation period. If there is a dispute over the date of separation, it is best to assume that the limitation period expires based on the earliest separation date. If a party doesn't, and a judge later finds that the earlier date of separation was the correct one, that party may find that they can no longer pursue their claims.

The law is not settled as to when the ability of a parent to claim retroactive child support from the other parent expires. In *D.B.S. v. S.R.G.*[308], the Supreme Court of Canada held that the right of a parent to claim retroactive child support from the other ends when the child no longer qualifies for support (usually 18).[309]

---

[305] *Children's Law Reform Act*, R.S.O., 1990, c. C-12, s. 18(2).
[306] *Divorce Act*, S.C. 1986 c. 3 (2nd Supp) s. 2(1).
[307] *Health Care Consent Act 1996*, S.O. 1996, c. 2, Sched. A., s. 4(1).
[308] *D.B.S., v S.R.G.,* 2006 SCC
[309] *D.B.S., v S.R.G.,* 2006 SCC 37 at paras 88-101

John P. Schuman, C.S., Family Lawyer, Mediator and Arbitrator

Some judges in Ontario have applied the '*DBS* rule' broadly and have decided that, absent blameworthy conduct, no claim for child support can be made after the child stops being eligible for support.[310] However, a number of judges have applied the *DBS* rule very narrowly, and have decided that it only applies in the very limited circumstances that occurred in *DBS*.[311] Judges have found that parents can make claims for retroactive child support after the children are no longer eligible in the following situations:[312]

1. Where the parent is not seeking to start child support, but seeking to change an existing child support order through a Motion to Change; or

2. Where there is blameworthy conduct on the part of the payer that contributed to the failure of the recipient to make the claim within the required time. Blameworthy conduct includes where the payer hides their true income, intimidates the recipient from claiming support, or claims to be paying the required amount of support when they know they are not.

Where children are no longer eligible for support, but a party may be entitled to claim retroactive child support, it is important to speak to a lawyer immediately.

Death May Not Change Anything in Family Law

The rights and obligations that a spouse or parent had during life can continue after death. Orders for child and spousal support continue to be binding on a spouse or parent's estate after death, regardless of whether the deceased person was married[313] or living common-law or neither but the parent of a child.[314] The death may result in a change in circumstances that would justify a change in support, which is covered in the next Part of this book.

---

[310] *Durso v Macherin,* 2013 ONSC 6522; *Krivanek v Krivanek,* 2008 CanLII 44732 (ON SC)
[311] *B.(P.M.) v A.(A.R.C.),* 2015 ONCJ 720; *Meyer v Content,* 2014 ONSC 6001; *George v Gayed,* 2014 ONSC 530; *Catena v. Catena,* 2015 ONSC 3186
[312] *B.(P.M.) v A.(A.R.C.),* 2015 ONCJ 720 at para 91
[313] *Katz v Katz,* 2014 ONCA 606 at para 71, 72
[314] *Family Law Act,* R.S.O. 1990, c. F-3, s. 394 (4).

John P. Schuman, C.S., Family Lawyer, Mediator and Arbitrator

However, if a parent or spouse dies before there are support proceedings in court, or signing a separation agreement that binds his or her estate, the deceased's partner or spouse cannot bring a support claim. Fortunately, the *Succession Law Reform Act*, allows most people who could have claimed child or spousal support to seek money from the estate as a "dependent."[315] These "dependents' relief claims" are very different from support claims because neither the *Child Support Guidelines* nor the *Spousal Support Guidelines* nor the other family law support considerations apply in these cases. In stead, the court considers the needs of the dependents and what moral obligations the deceases had to those dependents.[316] Those considerations can result in a different amount than an order for child or spousal support. In addition, a judge making an order in favour of dependents has a many options for the payment of the "support" from the estate. The judge can choose periodic or lump sum payments, or a transfer of property, or other options to meet the needs of the dependent.[317]

A married spouse who has separated before the death of a spouse can seek an equalization payment in the usual way and the spouses' Net Family Properties will be equalized as of the date of separation.[318] However, if the deceased spouse did not commence a court proceeding seeking the equalization before dying, his or her estate cannot start proceedings to claim an equalization payment after death.[319] When a spouse dies while the marriage continues, the surviving spouse can chose to receive whatever is left for them in the Will (or under the *Succession Law Reform Act* if there is no will) or make an equalization claim.[320] The surviving spouse must make this choice within 6 months of the death of his or her spouse, unless a court makes an order extending the period to make that choice.[321] Obviously, the existence, or non-existence of a Will can have a big impact on a surviving spouse and children.

---

[315] *Succession Law Reform* Act, RSO 1990, c.S-26, s. 57.
[316] *Cummings v Cummings*, 2004 CanLII 9339 (ON CA) at para 50.
[317] *Succession Law Reform* Act, RSO 1990, c.S-26, s. 63(2).
[318] *Panangaden v Panangaden Estate*, 1991 CarswellOnt 538 at paras 6-8
[319] *Family Law Act,* R.S.O. 1990, c. F-3, s. 5(2).
[320] *Family Law Act,* R.S.O. 1990, c. F-3, s. 6(1).
[321][321] *Family Law Act,* R.S.O. 1990, c. F-3, s. 6(10), 6(16).

John P. Schuman, C.S., Family Lawyer, Mediator and Arbitrator

A Special Note about Last Wills and Testaments – Why Everyone Needs One

After a couple separates, each partner should make it a priority to create a new last will and testament (commonly called "a will"). While a Divorce Order or a legal annulment automatically voids all the parts of a will that involve the former spouse, a separation does not[322]. (A divorce can cause problems for the whole will if the former spouse is the executor or otherwise has a big part in it.) A separated spouse with a will, who left most, or all, of her estate to her former partner may obviously want to change those provisions after separating. However, it is not just separated spouses who already have wills that should make new wills. When a separated spouse dies without a will, their spouse, even though separated, still has a claim to all of the deceased's property where there are no children[323], and a preferential share of the deceased's estate where there are children[324]. Without a will, some or all of the deceased's estate may automatically go to his or her former husband or wife, rather than to the deceased's loved ones.

Another consideration for parents who have custody of their children, or unmarried parents, is that it is possible for them to appoint a guardian for the children for the first 90 days after their death[325]. This allows the custodial parent to direct with whom the children will live until there is time for a court to make an order for custody of the children.

Anyone who holds property as joint tenants with his or her former partner should also contact a lawyer to sever the joint tenancy. If the partner dies while the property is still registered as a joint tenancy, the deceased's interest in that property will automatically transfer to the other joint tenant. At the end of a relationship, a person may no longer want to give that interest in property to a former partner but may want to transfer it to his or her other heirs pursuant to a will. That can only be accomplished by severing the joint tenancy.

---

[322] *Succession Law Reform Act,* R.S.O. 1990, c. S-26, s. 17(2). Note. Section 1 of the Act defines spouses as to people who are married to each other. It does not treat separated spouses any differently from spouses who are still together.
[323] *Succession Law Reform Act,* R.S.O. 1990, c. S-26, s. 44.
[324] *Succession Law Reform Act,* R.S.O. 1990, c. S-26, s. 45.
[325] *Children's Law Reform Act,* R.S.O. 1990, c. C-12, s. 61(1), (2) and (7).

John P. Schuman, C.S., Family Lawyer, Mediator and Arbitrator

Sometimes Family Law Is Not About Family Law

Family Law often touches on many other areas of law. Tax law, employment law, education law, health law, personal injury law, and many other areas of law can become relevant in Family Court cases. Parties can make many other claims or raise other issues that are outside of this discussion. This is another reason why it is important to consult a lawyer when separating. The discussion above has only focused on the most common Family Law issues to give a basic understanding of the general matters that appear when a couple separates.

John P. Schuman, C.S., Family Lawyer, Mediator and Arbitrator

John P. Schuman, C.S., Family Lawyer, Mediator and Arbitrator

Part 3: Going Back.... Changing an Order or Agreement

It is often said that, in Family Law, nothing is forever. The idea behind that statement is that even after former spouses have resolved the matters between them on a final basis, they can still seek a change to the deal because circumstances have changed. The *Divorce Act*, the *Family Law Act* and the *Children's Law Reform Act* all have specific provisions to change the arrangements that former spouses have reached either through the court process, or by way of agreement. In addition, the *Family Law Rules* create a streamlined process by which former spouses can change a final support order or agreement[326].

The idea behind all the provisions that allow changes to final arrangements is to recognize that families grow and evolve, and their circumstances change. What may have been fair and worked well at one time may become unfair or unworkable as things change in the lives of the family members. However, courts also recognize that there needs to be some finality to the arrangements between former spouses. It is not healthy for a family to be engaged in never ending litigation because the family members are always trying to change the arrangements, perhaps only because they are not happy

---

[326] *Family Law Rules*, Rule 15. However, it is important to note that only the Ontario Court of Justice or the Family Court of the Superior Court of Justice can change agreements using this procedure. [*Family Law Act*, R.S.O. 1990, c. F-3, s. 35(1)(2) as amended]. The Superior Court of Justice can only change orders, not agreements. These provisions mean that a person wanting to change an agreement should speak to a lawyer particularly if the change involves property or if the parties have been involved with more than one court.

John P. Schuman, C.S., Family Lawyer, Mediator and Arbitrator

with them. Both the Family Law legislation and the courts have placed limits on what can be changed, and in what circumstances.

There is a general rule that pertains to all requests to change an order or agreement. A former spouse should not be entitled to ask for a change just because he or she did not like the existing final order or agreement. If a former spouse thinks that a court order or an arbitration award is incorrect, he or she should appeal the decision. Since the basic idea behind allowing changes to final arrangements is the recognition that families change and evolve, the party seeking a change must show that there has been a "material change in circumstances."

The term "material change in circumstances" is an important one to understand. Not any change in the circumstances of family members will give rise to a right to seek a change to a final order or agreement. The word "material" is legal jargon meaning "significant". So, the change in circumstances must not be a small one, but must be big enough to make a change to the final order or agreement an absolute necessity.

There are a number of court decisions that provide guidance as to what constitutes a "material change", and in the case of child support, the legislation specifies what sort of changes should result in a change to a court order or agreement. In most cases, the change must be so significant or meaningful so as to show a clear impact on the family members.

Often in separation agreements, separated spouses specify what change in their circumstances will justify a change in the terms of the agreement. Those terms in a separation agreement are designed to provide clear guidance to the former spouses regarding when they can ask to change the terms. (In separation agreements, spouses can also create other provisions about when the terms of the agreements can be changed that are different than the "material change in circumstances" requirement. A common one is a provision that says certain terms in the agreement can be reviewed after a specific period of time.)

The first obstacle faced by any former spouse seeking to change an order or agreement is that he or she must show that any change is appropriate, either because the order or agreement specifically allows for changes to be made, or because the circumstances in the family have changed so significantly so as to necessitate a change. Even still, there are some final arrangements that can almost never be changed.

John P. Schuman, C.S., Family Lawyer, Mediator and Arbitrator

What Can Be Changed and What Cannot

Some terms of final orders or agreements are susceptible to change. Other terms are almost impossible to change. A person who wants to change an order or agreement should first determine whether the change he or she wants is something that can be changed. Child support is easily and often changed. Ongoing spousal support and parenting provisions can be changed in the right circumstances. Property settlements, such as equalization payments and the division of assets, are almost impossible to change, unless one of the parties has essentially committed fraud in the process leading up to the determination of the final property terms. Just about any court order can be changed where it was based on fraud or contains a mistake.

Changing Child Support Is Expected and Often Easy

No parent should expect that the child support provisions of an order or agreement will remain the same forever. On the contrary, the *Child Support Guidelines* contemplate that the amount of child support paid will be adjusted on an annual basis to reflect even small changes in the payer's income (or in the case of shared or split parenting, or in relation to special and extraordinary expenses, both parents' income)[327]. Child support can also be changed whenever there is any change (including small changes), in the amount of special or extraordinary expenses[328].

The *Child Support Guidelines* require that parents continue to exchange complete information about their income for as long as there is a child support obligation[329]. For most parents, those who earn most or all of their income through employment, the calculation of their income and the corresponding child support obligation is not complicated. Those parents should be able to agree on the correct amount of child support and adjust the payments accordingly.

Most parents do not want to incur the cost of having to start court proceedings every year to adjust the amount of child support, especially where the change is not large. In order to encourage parents to adjust child support every year, the Government of Ontario has implemented an online service that most parents can use to adjust child support being paid pursuant to a Court

---

[327] *Child Support Guidelines*, section 14.
[328] *Child Support Guidelines*, section 7(2).
[329] *Child Support Guidelines*, sections 24(1) and 25.

John P. Schuman, C.S., Family Lawyer, Mediator and Arbitrator

Order[330], including some section 7 expenses, without having to go to court. Parents who pay a fixed amount of child support pursuant to a separation agreement can also use the service provided that they have not already filed the agreement with the court for enforcement.[331]

The online service is as effective in changing child support as going to court. However, the online service only costs $80.00 per parent and avoids any potential issues with financial disclosure. To use the service, parents allow the Ontario Ministry of Finance, which performs the child support calculation, to collect their income tax information from the Canada Revenue Agency. That information allows the online service to determine not only the parties' incomes but also what they spent on Section 7 expenses that parents report on their tax returns (which are daycare, medical and health expenses.) The calculation service does not recalculate any other Section 7 expenses (such as tuition or extracurricular activities.)[332]

To use the online child support calculation service, a parent goes to the following site and completes an application:

https://www.ontario.ca/page/set-up-or-update-child-support-online.

The calculation service then notifies the other parent that an application has been started and asks them gives them 25 days to sign into the service. The service can only be used to set or adjust child support if the support payer agrees to use it, or if both parents agree to use it to recalculate eligible section 7 expenses.[333] If the other parent doesn't respond, the application is rejected.[334] If both parents participate, then the service then uses the parents' income tax information from the CRA to calculate the correct child support and then reports the adjusted amount of child support to the Family Responsibility Office, which then enforces the adjusted amount.[335] Either parent can apply to have any errors in the calculation corrected through the service, [336] provided that parent asks for the correction within 15 days of

---

[330] *Family Law Act*, R.S.O. 1990, c. F-3, s. 39.1(2).
[331] *Family Law Act*, R.S.O. 1990, c. F-3, s. 39(3)3 as amended.
[332] O. Reg. 190/15, s. 3(1) and 13(1).
[333] O. Reg. 190/15, s. 5(4) and 15(5).
[334] O. Reg. 190/15, s. 5(2)
[335] *Family Law Act*, R.S.O. 1990, c. F-3, s. 39(15), s. 39.1(9).
[336] *Family Law Act*, R.S.O. 1990, s. F-3, s. 39.1(11).

receiving notice of the recalculation.[337] However, fixing problems other than calculation errors requires a trip to court.

The online child support calculation service is only a calculation service. It does not determine legal rights or obligations. It simply calculates an amount based on a strict application of the *Child Support Guidelines* table formula using amounts in two individual's tax returns. For that reason, where a strict application of the table amount based solely on tax returns may not be appropriate parents cannot use the online child support calculation in any of the following situations:

1. Either parent or the child resides outside of Ontario;
2. The parents have shared custody of a child or split custody of children;
3. A child is over 17.5 years old, or a parent is paying for post-secondary education expenses pursuant to s. 7 of the *Child Support Guidelines*;
4. The support payer earns more than 20 per cent of his or her annual income from self-employment, or reported a self-employment income loss in the most recent taxation year.
5. The support payer earns more than 20 per cent of his or her annual income from a rental property;
6. The support payer earns more than 20 percent of his or her annual income from season employment in certain cases;
7. The support payer's income includes income from a corporation of which the parent is a director, officer or majority shareholder, or from a partnership of which the step payer is a partner;
8. A parent has an annual income of more than $150,000;
9. There is more than one parent who is responsible for paying base child support;
10. Less than six months has passed since the child support order was made;
11. The Child Support Order to be changed was not made by an Ontario Court.[338]

In any of the above situations, child support must be determined by a judge. Of course even parents who are eligible for the service can always opt to have child support determined by a judge, although the court system is much more complicated, and expensive, than the online recalculation service.

---

[337] O. Reg. 190/15, s. 25(2).
[338] O. Reg. 190/15, s. 2, 12, 14(3).

John P. Schuman, C.S., Family Lawyer, Mediator and Arbitrator

If parents are ineligible for the online child support recalculation service, but agree to the change in support, there is a simplified procedure they can use to have the amount of child support verified and changed by a judge. [339]. It requires the filing of documents, but no court attendance. There is no reason why child support should not be changed on an annual basis.

When parents do not exchange information about their incomes every year, one parent may find she has to pay child support retroactively[340]. When child support is finally adjusted, the child support payer may have to make up any increases in child support that should have been made in the past. The simple failure of the child support payer to provide income information every year, even if the support recipient did not ask for it, can create an obligation to pay retroactive support. Generally, if the child support recipient did not ask for income information, and the child support payer was not deliberately hiding increases in income, the obligation to make up for what ought to have been paid in the past is limited to three years of child support[341]. However, a support payer who has behaved badly, and deliberately hid increases in her income cannot take advantage of the three-year limit. A child support payer that has deliberately hidden an increase in his income may have to make up what he should have paid from the date of the increase in income. On the other side, where the parent receiving the child support receives accurate information about the other parent's income, child support will generally only be adjusted from the date that the recipient parent asked for child support to be changed[342].

Molly and Desmond have one child living with each of them. Originally, Desmond's income was higher than Molly's so he has been paying her spousal support. However, some of Molly's investments paid off and created a substantial income for her. She does not tell Desmond. To the contrary, she tells Desmond that times have been rough to discourage him from asking to exchange income information to adjust support.

Desmond finds out about Molly's true income five years later. In the circumstances, the court may adjust support back five years, which would require Molly to make a huge payment to Desmond.

---

[339] *Family Law Rules,* Rule 15(18)
[340] *D.B.S. v. S.R.G.,* [2006] S.C.G. No. 37 at para 124 (S.C.C.).
[341] *D.B.S. v. S.R.G.,* [2006] S.C.G. No. 37 at para 123 (S.C.C.).
[342] *D.B.S. v. S.R.G.,* [2006] S.C.G. No. 37 at para 125 (S.C.C.).

John P. Schuman, C.S., Family Lawyer, Mediator and Arbitrator

Unlike initial child support applications, which parents can only bring before the court while the children are still are still children of the marriage, a parent can bring a motion to change child support, including to reduce or increase support retroactively, even after child support is not longer payable.[343]

Annual Changes to Child Support for Self-Employed People Can Be Difficult and Expensive if the Parties Do Not Cooperate

Parents who are self-employed will know from the first time that child support is calculated that the calculation of a self-employed person's income can be quite an onerous process. The calculation of a self-employed parent's income for child support purposes almost always involves complex calculations that have to be performed by an accountant. Where the support payer is self-employed, parents cannot use the online child support recalculation service, but have to go to court.[344] Changing child support in those circumstances requires extensive disclosure of both the payer parent's and the business' finances. Unfortunately, changes to a Child Support Order or agreement, whether to increase or decrease support, involves repeating that same process. Further, the annual requirement to provide financial information includes an obligation to provide the same detailed information about personal and business finances, and to have that parent's income calculated by an accountant, who is qualified to do income calculations for child support purposes.

It is possible that the annual calculation of a self-employed parent's income can lead to perpetual litigation for as long as there is a child support obligation. Often parents in such a situation will try to come to an agreement as a way to streamline the process. That streamlining can be by way of an agreed upon formula that makes the income calculation simpler, an agreement to fix child support for a period of years, or another process agreed upon between the parents. Even though Family Court Judges generally support finding alternative methods to simplify the annual calculation of child support, because it reduces the litigation within the family, the law only permits such arrangements in special circumstances[345]. The special arrangements to simplify the calculation of child support have to be very carefully created to ensure the terms comply with the law. This requires the participation of experienced Family Law lawyers.

---

[343] *Colucci v. Collucci,* 2017 ONCA 892.
[344] O. Reg. 190/15, s. 2, 12,.
[345] *Divorce Act,* S.C. 1986 c. 3 (2nd Supp) s. 15.1(7), *Family Law Act,* R.S.O. 1990, c. F-3, s. 33(12), as amended.

John P. Schuman, C.S., Family Lawyer, Mediator and Arbitrator

Child Support Can Change for Reasons Other than Income

Circumstances other than changes in income can result in a change to a Child Support Order. When a healthy child is over 18 years old, and is no longer in school full-time, child support for that child should end[346]. Child support should also end when the child no longer resides with the parent who is receiving child support. A child's marriage similarly ends the obligation to pay support for that child. In any of these circumstances, the parents should agree to terminate child support for the child. Judges do not like it when a parent, who is getting support, refuses to end child support when that parent is no longer entitled to receive it. A parent who is wrongfully continuing to receive child support should expect to pay all of the legal fees incurred by the parent who has to go to court to terminate the Child Support Order.

A child starting or finishing daycare, or starting or finishing an activity that qualifies as a Special and/or Extraordinary Expense, changes the amount of child support payable to the extent that it changes the additional amount that is payable pursuant to Section 7 of the *Child Support Guidelines*.

As noted in Part 2 of this guide on child support, where a child resides and when affects how much child support is paid. If a child who is living full-time with one parent switches to live full-time with the other parent, the parent who had been receiving child support becomes the child support payer. Child support will also be changed where a child that was living equally with both parents starts living primarily with one parent, or where a child who is living primarily with one parent starts sharing his or her time equally between his or her parents. However, in those cases the amount of the change is depends more on the specific facts of the case. It does not matter why the child's residential schedule changed. The *Child Support Guidelines* give absolutely no consideration to the reasons that a child is living with a particular parent. The mere fact that a child is living with one parent creates a child support obligation for the other parent. If a parent is manipulating a child to live with him or her for the purpose of obtaining child support, it may be appropriate to ask the court to change the order or agreements that deals with custody and access.

---

[346] *Divorce Act*, S.C. 1986 c. 3 (2nd Supp) s. 2(1), 15.1(1), *Family Law Act*, R.S.O. 1990, c. F-3, s. 31(1), as amended.

John P. Schuman, C.S., Family Lawyer, Mediator and Arbitrator

When Parenting Plans Break Down: Changing Custody and Access

Another agreement or order that can always be changed by a court is an agreement or order that addresses parenting (custody, access, and other terms regarding how children will be parented). Ontario Courts are not bound to follow the parents' agreements regarding the parenting of their children[347]. Whenever a court is asked to look at parenting issues, whether under the federal *Divorce Act*, or under Ontario's *Children's Law Reform Act*, the paramount consideration is what court order would be in the best interests of the children[348]. Where the circumstances for the children have changed so much that the existing agreement or court order is no longer in their best interests, the court always has jurisdiction to make a new order[349].

Some examples of situations that would change what order or agreement is in a child's best interests include the following:

1. one parent abusing a child;
2. a child having serious difficulties getting along with a parent;
3. a child starting school if the existing residential schedule impedes the child's attendance at the school, or vice versa;
4. a child wanting to participate in activities that makes the existing residential schedule impossible;
5. a parent moving far enough away to make the existing residential schedule impossible, if the parent is moving for purposes of employment or some other legitimate reason;
6. a change in a parent's work schedule that makes the existing residential schedule impossible;
7. the existing residential schedule being too stressful or too disruptive to the child's life; and
8. other circumstances that are significant enough to require a change to the parenting arrangements because the existing arrangements are contrary to the child's best interest.

---

[347] *Family Law Act*, R.S.O 1990, c. F-3, s. 56(1).
[348] *Divorce Act*, R.S.C. 1985, c. 3 (2nd Supp), s. 16(8); *Children's Law Reform Act*, R.S.O. 1990, c. C-12, s. 24.
[349] *Divorce Act*, R.S.C. 1985, c. 3 (2nd Supp), s. 17(5); *Children's Law Reform Act*, R.S.O. 1990, c. C-12, s. 29.

John P. Schuman, C.S., Family Lawyer, Mediator and Arbitrator

Since court cases over custody and access almost always have an impact on the children, the wording of both the *Divorce Act* and the *Children's Law Reform Act* require that court cases to change an existing parenting arrangement be avoided unless they are absolutely necessary[350]. Parents should consider using the services of a parenting coordinator to see if they can find a way to make the existing arrangements work before heading off to court or using other methods to change the parenting arrangements. Since parenting coordination is a form of mediation (it can also involve arbitration if the contract with the parenting coordinator permits), the process is more likely to end in a result that the parents like, is less destructive for the children, and is much less expensive than going to court. Sometimes judges order that parents must use a parenting coordinator before returning to court[351]. The failure of parenting coordination may indicate to a judge, or an arbitrator, that there is no hope that the current arrangements will work for the children, and a change to the parenting arrangement is necessary[352].

"I Need More" or "I'm Out of Money": Changing Spousal Support

Spousal support is another area where an agreement or order can be changed because of a material change in circumstances. Whether the original arrangements for spousal support can be changed depends a lot on what the original arrangements were. Whether spousal support can be changed at all depends on what the original order or agreement says on the matter:

1. If a court has dismissed an application for spousal support, it is very difficult for a party whose request was dismissed to obtain spousal support;
2. If the parties have signed a release of spousal support in a separation agreement, marriage contract or cohabitation agreement, then it will also be very difficult to obtain spousal support;
3. Similarly, if a court order, separation agreement, marriage contract or cohabitation agreement provides for a lump sum payment of spousal support, then it will be very difficult for a party to go back and ask for more support. The term setting out the lump sum payment will almost always include either a dismissal of further spousal support (if it is in a

---

[350] *Divorce Act*, R.S.C. 1985, c. 3 (2nd Supp), s. 17(5); *Children's Law Reform Act*, R.S.O. 1990, c. C-12, s. 29.
[351] *Young v. Young*, 2010 ONCA 602.
[352] *May-Iannazzi v. Iannazi*, 2010 CarswellOnt 5353 at paragraph 2-4 (C.A.).

court order), or a release of further spousal support (if it is in the domestic contract); and

4. Where there are periodic (usually monthly) payments of spousal support, it is usually possible to seek a change to those payments if there has been a "material change in circumstances". If the agreement was incorporated into a court order, before allowing any change to the support, a court must consider whether there has been a change in the conditions, means, needs or other circumstances of either former spouse since the making of the spousal support order[353]. Court orders or agreements often set out when there can be a change to spousal support and in what circumstances. In the event that the provisions for spousal support state that spousal support cannot be reviewed until a certain date, then it will only be in very exceptional circumstances that support will be or can be changed before that date. Essentially, there would have to be a change in circumstances that was beyond what the parties (or the judge where there was one) would have anticipated at the time that they made the original provisions. The restrictions on what circumstances will give rise to a change in spousal support can be very restrictive. If an order or agreement for periodic spousal support payments does set out when or under what circumstances spousal support can be changed, then periodic payments can only be changed because there has been a material change in circumstances for either of the parties[354].

Spousal support provisions that provide for an annual change in support, either in accordance with the Consumer Price Index, or by a specified percentage, are not subject to the above limitations, because those changes are supposed to be automatic. However, a deviation from the automatic change in periodic support payments will be a change that would be subject to the above limitations.

Further, as noted in the section on spousal support in Part 2, a change in a payer's income does not automatically result in change in spousal support.[355] Either the change in on spouse's income, or a change in a spouse's need, must be linked to the relationship.[356] The exception to this may be

---

[353] *L.M.P. v. L.S.* [2011] SCC 64 at para 29.
[354] *Divorce Act*, R.S.C. 1985, c. 3 (2nd supp), s. 17(4.1), as amended; *Family Law Act*, R.S.O. 1990, c. F-3, s. 37(2), as amended.
[355] *Hariram v. Hariram* 2001 CaswellOnt (Div. Ct.)
[356] *Thompson v. Thompson* 2013 ONSC 5500 at para 103.

John P. Schuman, C.S., Family Lawyer, Mediator and Arbitrator

where a payer spouse has an unforeseen loss in income and cannot afford to continue to pay. To share in a former spouse's increase in income, the spouse claiming support must show that he or she, directly or indirectly, did something that allowed the payer spouse to get that increase in income. That can be easy shortly after the relationship, especially where the parties' finances and goals were intertwined. But, as the spouses establish independence from each other, it becomes increasing difficult to justify a change in compensatory support based on a change in a spouse's fortunes.

Changing Dismissals of Spousal Support and Lump Sum Spousal Support Orders

Where there has been a court order or an arbitration award dismissing spousal support, or requiring a lump sum payment, and then no further support, it will only be possible to change that dismissal and get an order for spousal support where:

1. the requesting spouse shows a new need for support has arisen since the dismissal of support and that, despite the elapse of time, the need is still related to the marriage or its breakdown[357];
2. there were serious problems surrounding the creation of the original support provisions. In the case of an agreement, that can include a failure by one or both spouses to make sufficient financial disclosure to allow the other spouse to understand that spouse's financial circumstances[358]. Where there was a court order, one party must have misled the judge to an extent that constitutes fraud, or the judge must have made a mistake, or a party who should have been present in court did not have the opportunity to be present[359]; or
3. the order is made on consent of both parties and the same circumstances exist that would allow a court to disregard an agreement requiring that no support be paid[360].

Obtaining Support Contrary to the Terms of an Agreement

Lawyers try very hard to write spousal support releases that give the court as little room as possible to change an agreement and award spousal support in the face of a release. Judges and arbitrators are required to consider the

---

[357] *Tierney-Hynes v Hynes*, 2005 CarswellOnt. 2632 at para 76 (C.A.)
[358] *Family Law Act*, R.S.O. 1990, sc. F-3, s. 56(4)
[359] *Family Law Rules*, Rule 25(19).
[360] *Miglin v. Miglin* (2003), 1. S.C.R. 303 at paragraph 60.

John P. Schuman, C.S., Family Lawyer, Mediator and Arbitrator

objectives for spousal support, as discussed in Part 2 of this guide, before making or changing an order or award for spousal support. Any properly worded domestic contract that releases spousal support will include paragraphs that state that no spousal support is consistent with the objectives for spousal support as set out in the *Divorce Act* and the *Family Law Act*, both at the time the agreement was signed, and no matter what may happen to the spouses after signing the agreement.

The *Family Law Act* provides that a court may set aside the spousal support provisions in a separation agreement - even a spousal support release. If a judge sets aside the terms relating to support, he or she can make a support order that is different from the support provisions in the separation agreement. A judge can set aside the support provisions of a marriage contract or cohabitation agreement and order support where:

1. the provision for support or the waiver of the right to support results in unconscionable circumstances at the time the matter is before the court (not just at the time the parties signed the agreement). Note that "unconscionable" means "shocking to the court's conscious" and can be a hard test to meet, because judges believe that it is important for parties to reach settlements, so their settlements should be respected;
2. the provision for support is in favour of, or the waiver of support is by, a dependent who qualifies for an allowance for support out of public money (social assistance, employment insurance, etc.); or
3. there is default in the payment of support under the contract or agreement at the time the party starts the court proceeding for support[361].

The latter two circumstances are quite clear. It is easy to determine that a party is receiving public money or the support payer is not making the required payments. However, it may not be as clear whether a situation is unconscionable, such that the court should create new support provisions despite the terms of the agreement.

In the important case of *Miglin* v. *Miglin*[362], the Supreme Court of Canada set out the circumstances in which the terms of an agreement for spousal support, which has not been incorporated into a court order[363],

---

[361] *Family Law Act*, R.S.O. 1990, c. F-3, s. 33(4) as amended.
[362] *Miglin v. Miglin* (2003), 1. S.C.R. 303.
[363] *L.M.P. v. L.S.* [2011] SCC 64 at para 29.

John P. Schuman, C.S., Family Lawyer, Mediator and Arbitrator

(including a provision requiring that no spousal support be paid) can be set aside. In determining whether the original agreement should be set aside, the court has to engage in a two-step analysis. First, it must look at the circumstances of the original agreement. Secondly, the court must look at the substance of the agreement. A change in circumstances, by itself, does not allow a former spouse to get around a spousal support release and obtain support.

In looking at the circumstances that existed at the time of the agreement, the court should be alive to the conditions of the parties, including whether there were any circumstances of oppression, pressure, or other vulnerabilities, and the conditions under which the negotiations were held[364], such as their duration and whether the parties had professional assistance. If the court does not feel those circumstances were satisfactory, it can order support even though the agreement does not allow further support.

The *Family Law Act* also specifically provides that domestic contracts, including agreements in relation to spousal support, can be set aside if one or both parties did not provide complete and accurate disclosure about his or her financial circumstances at the time of the agreement. Domestic contracts can also be set aside where one or both parties did not understand the agreement, which usually means that one or both parties did not have competent Independent Legal Advice before signing the contract. Domestic agreements can also be set aside where one party was acting under duress, or where there was any other circumstance that the law of contract says would result in an invalid or unenforceable agreement[365].

If the court comes to the conclusion that the agreement should not be discounted as a result of the circumstances under which it was negotiated, then it must look at the substance of the agreement. This step involves looking at the extent to which the agreement takes into account the factors and objectives of spousal support (as described in Part 2 of this guide). Those factors and objectives are seen to result in an equitable sharing of the economic consequences of marriage and its breakdown. If the agreement shows a significant departure from the general objectives of spousal support, the court can change the agreement, even ordering support where there is a release[366]. However, it is important to remember that one of the factors the court must

---

[364] *Miglin v. Miglin* (2003), 1. S.C.R. 303 at paragraph 81.
[365] *Family Law Act*, R.S.O. 1990, c. F-3, s. 56(4).
[366] *Miglin v. Miglin* (2003), 1. S.C.R. 303 at paragraph 85.

John P. Schuman, C.S., Family Lawyer, Mediator and Arbitrator

consider in any spousal support case is the emphasis in the statutes on parties settling their own affairs and having finality.

The second stage of the Miglin analysis is directed toward the present circumstances of the parties. It requires an assessment of whether the new circumstances of the parties were contemplated at the time they signed the agreement. The court must decide whether the agreement should be discounted because of changes in the circumstances of the parties since the agreement was signed. Then the court must considered whether, in light of these new circumstances, the agreement still reflects the parties' intentions and also still reflects the factors and objectives of spousal support[367].

> *Desmond and Molly negotiated a separation agreement in which Desmond pays support to Molly. After separation, Molly's investments did very well, but she did not reveal this to Desmond. The parties did not take this into account when negotiating spousal support terms in the agreement. Five years later, Desmond learns of Molly's increase in income. He can ask to have the spousal support terms of the agreement set aside.*
>
> *Desmond found out about Molly's income when she ran out of money and wanted more support. As Desmond did provide accurate disclosure, it will be difficult for Molly to increase her support.*

The onus of proving that the order, award or agreement should be set aside rests on the shoulders of the party who is asking that it be set aside. Setting aside a separation agreement, arbitration award, or court order generally requires compelling evidence and the burden of proof can be a heavy one. However, an agreement that simply states, "Neither party shall pay spousal support" is clearly insufficient. The agreement must make it clear that no circumstances exist that a court, applying Miglin, could use to change the agreement. Further, the agreement must set out what types of circumstances could exist in the future that would still not justify changing the agreement.

Agreeing to Review Spousal Support

After long-term marriages or cohabitations, it is common for spousal support arrangements to continue for an indefinite period of time. Support may last until the recipient's death. However, in medium and short-term relationships, it

---

[367] *Carrier c. Carrier,* 2007 CarswellNB 155 at para 13 (N.B. C.A.).

is common to see an agreement or court order for support for a specific period of time, after which the parties will review support. Where an agreement or order says that support will be reviewed after a specific date, once that date has passed, neither party has to show that such a review of spousal support is appropriate. Instead, the parties focus on what, if any, support should continue. Before that review date arrives, a party who wants to obtain a change in support will have to prove that the order or agreement should be set aside. The burden that the party must meet to have the order or the agreement set aside is very similar to the requirements that a party must meet to set aside an order dismissing support or an agreement releasing support.

Changing On-Going Support Where There is No Set Review Date

Where an order, arbitration award, or agreement provides for ongoing periodic spousal support payments, but does not provide for a review of spousal support on a specific date, and does restrict when or how spousal support may be reviewed, then a party may be able to get a change in spousal support if there has been a material change in either party's circumstances[368] that can be linked to the relationship.[369] Where the support terms are only contained in an agreement, then the court will use apply the test in Miglin, described above, to determine whether the court should make an order that is different from the terms of the agreement.

Desmond married Eleanor. Eleanor makes a good income, which has significantly improved Desmond's lifestyle. Molly feels Desmond's new circumstances should change spousal support. However, their separation agreement specifically says that the remarriage of either party will not result in a change in support.

To change the support in the separation agreement, Molly must show either that there was a problem in the negotiation of the agreement (such as insufficient disclosure, lack of legal advice or duress) or that the agreement has resulted in a situation that is inconsistent with the objectives of spousal support. In the circumstances, it will be difficult for Molly to succeed.

---

[368] *Divorce Act*, R.S.C. 1985, c. 3 (2nd supp), s. 17(4.1), as amended; *Family Law Act*, R.S.O. 1990, c. F-3, s. 37(2), as amended.
[369] *Thompson v. Thompson*, ONSC 5500 at para 103.

John P. Schuman, C.S., Family Lawyer, Mediator and Arbitrator

If support terms are contained in a court order, then the court will not change them unless one, or both parties has experienced a material change in circumstances. To be a "material change", the change must be one that if known at the time of the order, would likely have resulted in different terms and the change in circumstances must be fairly permanent[370]. It will only be large changes in circumstances that will meet that threshold. It is not possible, as it when asking for a change to an agreement, to argue that there were problems with the circumstances surrounding the making of the order. The judge who is considering the change to support will assume that the judge who made the original order knew and correctly applied the law when making that support order[371]. A judge should not consider what the new spousal support order should be, including giving any consideration to the *Spousal Support Advisory Guidelines*, until that judge is convinced that there is a material and permanent change that the parties and the original judge did not contemplate[372].

Court orders or agreements, even if they do not set a specific review date, may set circumstances in which support may be reviewed. Where such terms exist, judges will follow them when considering whether to change support in an agreement or an order[373]. Examples of such provisions include terms that a change in either party's annual income by more than a set amount can result in a change, or the re-marriage of one of the spouses does not justify a change in support. It is possible to seek a change of support that is not permitted by such restrictions. However, the party seeking such a change faces the difficult task of convincing the court or arbitrator to set aside the terms of the agreement related to those restrictions. To set aside those terms the court, or arbitrator, will consider the same factors, described above, to that change an agreement or order that has a spousal support release.

A change in a spouse's income alone is not enough to justify a change in spousal support. The change in the income must be linked to the relationship that gave rise to spousal support. A judge might also order a change in support if some form of unconscionable circumstances would result if there were no change. However, in determining whether a result is a conscionable, a judge has to consider that one of the objectives of spousal

---

[370] *L.M.P. v. L.S.* [2011] SCC 64 at paras 29 and 35.
[371] *L.M.P. v. L.S.* [2011] SCC 64 at para 29.
[372] *L.M.P. v. L.S.* [2011] SCC 64 at paras 45, 46 and 50.
[373] *L.M.P. v. L.S.* [2011] SCC 64 at para 40.

John P. Schuman, C.S., Family Lawyer, Mediator and Arbitrator

support, and any change to spousal support, is the economic self-sufficiency of the parties. [374]

On such reviews, it is possible for spousal support to go up, or down, or be terminated all together. It is also possible to place restrictions on when or how spousal support will be reviewed in the future. These unrestricted Spousal Support Orders are open to being changed. Other types of orders may be impossible to change.

> *Desmond and Eleanor win the lottery. Molly makes another request for a change in spousal support. She says she did not get a fair deal with the judge made the divorce order, after she challenged the separation agreement. Molly is surprised when the judge tells her that it does not matter if she thinks the order was fair as the judge who made it properly applied the law. All that matters is whether there has been a "material change in circumstances."*
>
> *One of the parties winning a lottery might be a material change in circumstances allowing a change in spousal support. However, the divorce order sets out specific events that will constitute a material change in circumstances. One of the parties winning the lottery is not one of those circumstances, so Molly will have a hard time convincing the judge to order a change to spousal support.*

The Uphill Battle: Changing Property and Lump Sum Damages Payments

Court orders, arbitration awards, or agreements that address the division of property or resolve other issues that are not ongoing in nature are almost always final. Judges and arbitrators do not like to go back and change a final resolution of these issues. Changes in either party's circumstances should not affect these matters, because the resolution was based on historic facts. The *Family Law Act*, which is the legal authority for making equalization payments, provides that the amount of an equalization payment is not to be changed because of a change in either party's circumstances after the payment has been

---

[374] *Divorce Act*, R.S.C. 1985, c. 3 (2nd Supp), s. 15.2(6)(d) and 17(7.)

made[375]. The only permitted change is with regard to the terms by which that payment is made[376].

Changes to the final order setting the amount of an equalization payment can only be made if there was fraud or a mistake, or if one of the parties did not have the opportunity to be in court[377]. Agreements resolving these issues can only be changed if the parties did not exchange full financial disclosure of their assets and liabilities, one or both parties do not understand the terms[378], or where there were problems in the circumstances surrounding the negotiation of the agreement. Examples of those problems can include where one or both parties did not have adequate legal (or accounting) advice, or there was oppression, duress or the calculations were made in haste[379]. Agreements settling property claims on these issues may also be changed only where the agreement was not in writing, not signed or not witnessed[380]. However, a judge would likely be very reluctant to go back and look at these issues again as they do not represent ongoing matters, but instead are based on historic facts that do not need to be re-litigated. Judges are aware of the impact of litigation on families. They do not want to see fights over matters that have already been determined.

Ensuring Continued Safety: Changing and Continuing Restraining /Non-Harassment Orders

Restraining/Non-Harassment Orders must meet strict procedural guidelines. When making a Restraining Order, the judge must set a specific date when it expires[381]. When the Restraining Order expires, all of the terms to control the other party's behaviour will be gone and it is often not necessary to seek changes to the terms. Often Restraining Orders are initially made without notice to the person being restrained out of concern that the person would do something before the order came into effect. However, where a judge makes an order without notice to one of the parties, the motion must be brought back to court within 14 days[382]. At that time, the party restrained by the order can

---

[375] *Family Law Act*, R.S.O. 1990, c. F-3, s. 9(3).
[376] *Ibid.*
[377] *Family Law Rules*, Rule 25(19).
[378] *Family Law Act*, R.S.O. 1990, c. F-3, s. 56(4).
[379] *Miglin v. Miglin* (2003), 1. S.C.R. 303 at paragraph 81.
[380] *Family Law Act*, R.S.O. 1990, c. F-3, s. 55(1)
[381] *Family Law Rules,* Form 25G and 25H
[382] *Family Law Rules*, Rule 14(14).

John P. Schuman, C.S., Family Lawyer, Mediator and Arbitrator

argue that the order should not have been made, or that the terms should be different.

While the order continues to be enforced, it may be necessary to make some changes to it. For example, if the protected party changes his or her address, there should be no problems changing the restraining order to protect the party by keeping the other spouse away from where he or she is, rather than where he or she is not. Changes to Restraining Orders must be made on notice to the other party. If the party bound by the order does not know where the protected party lives, then bringing a motion to change the Restraining Order will reveal that information. Also, if the protected spouse goes to court to ask for such a change, then the other spouse may try to use the opportunity to convince the court that the order is no longer necessary.

The Risk of Asking for a Change to an Order or Agreement

Any person who goes to court or mediation or arbitration to change a part of an order or agreement that he or she does not like or thinks should be changed, because of a change in circumstances, should be aware of the risk in doing so. If one party asks for a change to an order or agreement, the other party may use the opportunity to ask for changes as well. The procedures available to change a court order or an agreement allow both parties to ask for changes and also allow one party to ask for changes after the other party has asked for changes[383].

I Need a Change! What Do I Do? How to Change a Final Court Order

Changing a final court order involves going to court to ask for the change. Where a court order is in place, no one should assume that an agreement with another party, especially an oral agreement, releases them of the obligations imposed by a court order. Court orders continue to bind the people named in them until either the court order is changed or a term of the court order expressly states that the order has expired. There have been many occasions when a person has thought that he or she is safe, because there was an oral agreement to stop support, only to have the support recipient go to court to enforce the order and collect all of the "arrears" despite the agreement. If the terms of a court order need to be changed, then the court order must be

---

[383] *Family Law Rules,* Rule 15(9).

changed and the parties must go to court to do that. If the parties agree to the change, getting the new order may not involve a court appearance.

There is a simplified procedure for changing a final court order. This is based on the premise that most of the issues between the parties will have been resolved in the original court proceedings and a framework may have been set up that helps the parties workout the issues between them in the future. An example of this would be child support. The original court proceedings would have determined which party pays child support and which party receives it (this would have been determined by the terms of the parenting order). Where a support payer's income was difficult to calculate, then the original court proceedings may have resulted in a determination of how that parties' income should be calculated. In those situations, changes in child support are only a matter of getting the disclosure, plugging in the numbers, and doing the calculations. Often in variation proceedings, no facts are in dispute; only questions of law and procedure. This allows for a simplified procedure that avoids putting the parties to the burden of the same type of court process that they experienced their first time at court. Obviously, there may still be times when the issues are more complex and a more complicated court process is required. This will be discussed below.

In Ontario, changing a final Family Court order involves filing a Motion to Change. The court forms involve a lot of "check boxes" and "fill in the blanks", which reflects the fact that often the issues involved in changing the original order are not complex[384]. Further, the usual simplicity of the matters involved has led to a procedure where the issues are decided on a motion rather than at a trial[385]. Motions to Change often have only two steps/court appearances. They are:

1. a case conference before a judge or an appearance before a Dispute Resolution Officer;
2. the motion. At the hearing of the motion, the judge relies on the Motion to Change Forms filed by both parties and does not hear oral evidence as a judge would at a trial.

---

[384] *Family Law Rules*, Forms 15, 15A and 15B.
[385] *Family Law Rules*, Rule 15(26)

Sometimes matters are so simple that they do not require any court appearances. Where the parties agree to the change in the order, the Motion to Change Forms allow the parties to set out the new order that they have agreed to and give the judge an explanation as to why the new order is appropriate. Where the order relates to support, the Motion to Change Forms include simplified financial statements that allow the judge to quickly understand why the order to which the parties have agreed is appropriate.

However, when the change relates to child support, then the new court order must be in accordance with the *Child Support Guidelines*. If it is not, then the parties must explain to the judge how the new order benefits the children as much, or more than, the order that the judge would make if the judge strictly applied the *Child Support Guidelines*. In doing this, the parties must include in their court materials very specific information to address specific issues in the *Child Support Guidelines*[386]. Judges will only make orders that are not in accordance with the *Child Support Guidelines* in exceptional circumstances[387]. If the parties are agreeing to such an order, they must set out carefully, and in detail, why the court order they are seeking is as good or better for the children than an order made pursuant to the *Child Support Guidelines*[388].

Making a Change That Is Complex or Based on Contested Facts

While some changes to final orders may be simple and straight forward, obviously others will be difficult and complex. The simplified procedure for changing an order is not appropriate where the issues are complex. Where factual issues are in dispute (the parties cannot agree on the facts on which the order should be based), then a trial is required. Judges cannot determine credibility by reading affidavits. They must hear witnesses testify to determine which party has the facts right[389]. In those situations, the judge at the Case Conference, or one of the other early appearances, will make an order that the matter proceed to trial following the same steps as the original proceedings[390] (which are described in Part 1). In those circumstances, the Motion to Change Forms become the parties' Application, Answer, and Reply.

---

[386] *Family Law Rules*, Rule 15(21).
[387] *Family Law Act*, R.S.O. 1990, c. F-3, s. 37(2.3), as amended.
[388] *Ibid.*
[389] *Ierullo v. Ierullo* 2006 CarswellOnt 5887 at paragraphs 17-18 (C.A.).
[390] *Family Law Rules*, Rule 15(26).

If the parties resolved the original court proceedings by reaching a settlement, the terms of that settlement may have included terms that require the parties to take alternate steps to change the final court order. The alternate steps may be specific negotiation steps, mediation or arbitration. Those terms can only be put in a final court order if both parties agree. If the settlement contained such terms then the parties must follow them when they want to change that final court order. Often, those terms require the parties to follow procedures very much like the procedure involved in changing an agreement.

How Do I Change Our Agreement?

The steps involved in changing a separation agreement depend on a number of factors, which include whether:

1. the parties agree to the change;
2. either party has filed the separation agreement with a court for enforcement; or
3. the separation agreement sets out the process that the parties must follow to change that separation agreement.

If both parties agree, they can always change the terms of their separation agreement. The new agreement is usually called an "amending agreement," because it amends some (and rarely all) of the terms of the original agreement. Amending agreements are a form of separation agreement and therefore a "domestic contract" pursuant to the *Family Law Act*. This means that the requirements for a valid separation agreement, described in Part 1 of this guide, must still be followed. The agreement must be in writing, both parties must sign the agreement and those signatures must be witnessed[391]. In addition, for the agreement to be enforced, the parties must exchange full disclosure in relation to the issues in the amending agreement, they both must understand the agreement, which usually means they both must have Independent Legal Advice, and the new agreement must not otherwise violate the law of contract[392]. The agreement must also be negotiated in "unimpeachable circumstances" to prevent a court from setting aside the agreement pursuant to the Miglin decision, as described earlier in this chapter.

---

[391] *Family Law Act*, R.S.O. 1990, c. F-3, s. 55(1).
[392] *Family Law Act*, R.S.O. 1990, c. F-3, s. 56(4). For a full discussion of what is needed to have a valid and enforceable separation agreement or amending agreement please see Part 1.

John P. Schuman, C.S., Family Lawyer, Mediator and Arbitrator

Prior to their divorce order setting out spousal support, Desmond and Molly came to a new agreement about spousal support. Since Molly had filed the old agreement with the court to have it enforced, Desmond and Molly knew that they had to file the new agreement. Desmond completed and swore an affidavit for filing the new agreement with the court (Form 26B). He filed that document with the court to advise the court of the change.

Desmond and Molly know that if they had wanted to change child support, the process would have been more complicated. They would have to file a Consent Motion to Change Child Support (Form 15D). That for requires the parties to go into detail about their financial situations and assure the court that the Child Support Order that Desmond and Molly are seeking is right for the children.

If one of the parties has filed the original separation agreement with the court for enforcement, then changing the terms of the agreement requires the involvement of the court. If the parties agree to the change in the agreement, all that should be necessary is for one of the parties to file the amending agreement with the same court to have the court enforce the support provisions of the amending agreement rather than those in the original separation agreement[393] (of course, the court will still enforce the support provisions of the original separation agreement that were not changed by the amending agreement). However, in some circumstances, a judge may want to hear more from the parties before the court enforces the amending agreement. This is particularly the case where the amending agreement deals with child support and is not in accordance with the *Child Support Guidelines*. If it is not clear from the agreement that it benefits the children as much or more than an agreement pursuant to the *Child Support Guidelines*, then a judge may want to receive an explanation from the parties before enforcing the agreement[394].

Obviously, where the parties obtained a court order in accordance with their settlement rather than just filing a separation agreement with a court, and they want to change the terms, then they must follow the procedure for changing the final court order described above.

---

[393] *Family Law Act*, R.S.O. 1990, c. F-3, s. 35(2).
[394] *Family Law Act*, R.S.O. 1990, c. F-3, s. 37(2.3)-(2.6).

John P. Schuman, C.S., Family Lawyer, Mediator and Arbitrator

Where there is a separation agreement that has not been converted to a court order and one or both parties want to change it, then the steps they will have to take will depend on what arrangements they have previously put into place.

It is common for separation agreements to contain a Dispute Resolution Clause. That clause sets out what steps the parties must take if either they disagree about the interpretation of the separation agreement, or they want a change to the separation agreement, or both. Where there is a Dispute Resolution Clause, both parties are bound by it.

It is common for a Dispute Resolution Clause to require the parties to exchange relevant disclosure, and then meet to try to reach a new agreement. If the parties are unable to agree on the change, then it is also common for such clauses to require the parties to participate in mediation, sometimes with a specified mediator, and try to resolve the dispute. If the separation agreement was the result of a Collaborative Law or Collaborative Practice process, then the agreement may require the parties to use a collaborative process again. If the agreement sets out these types of procedures, then the parties *must* follow them before either party can go to court[395]. In addition, sometimes separation agreements require that the parties resolve the issues in dispute by way of an arbitration rather than court. If the separation agreement contains such a clause, the parties cannot go to court and expect to appeal or otherwise seek a review of the arbitration award[396].

If the separation agreement permits the parties to go to court, but the separation agreement itself has never been made into a court order, then the parties have a couple of procedural options to consider. If the court that has jurisdiction based on municipality of where the children or the parties reside is the Family Court of the Superior Court of Justice, then the party who wants to change can opt to proceed by way of the simplified Motion To Change procedure by filing the separation agreement with the court to have it enforced as a court order and then bringing a motion to change the agreement. If the parties, or children, do not live in a municipality with a Family Court of the Superior Court of Justice, and the desired change relates to either parenting or

---

[395] The exception to this is where the Dispute Resolution Clause should not be enforced because of the factors described in *Miglin* as described above.
[396] *Arbitration Act, 1991,* S.O. 1991, c. 17, s. 6, 45 and 46, as amended.

John P. Schuman, C.S., Family Lawyer, Mediator and Arbitrator

support, then a party can file the agreement with the Ontario Court of Justice and then bring the Motion to Change before that court[397].

Another option, where the separation agreement has not been made into a court order, is to start a court application (which might be a divorce application) and ask the court to make an order on the issue that is different from the terms of the separation agreement. Generally, judges like to uphold the terms of separation agreements to encourage parties to settle their issues out of court. However, with regard to parenting issues, the court will only make the order that is in the best interests of the child, regardless of what an agreement says. However, the fact that the parties previously agreed that the terms of the separation agreement were in the best interest of the children is strong evidence that the appropriate order is one in accordance with the terms of the separation agreement.

Except in the circumstances described above, judges will make an order for child support that is in accordance with the *Child Support Guidelines*, unless the court is satisfied that the terms of the agreement benefit the children more than a strict application of the *Child Support Guidelines*. With regard to other issues, generally the court will not make an order that is different from the agreement, unless the court is persuaded that the agreement should be set aside.

As discussed above, the court might be persuaded the agreement should be set aside if there has not been proper financial disclosure, one or both parties do not understand the agreement, or the agreement otherwise has problems pursuant to the Law of Contract. The burden of proof falls on the person who wants an order that is different from the agreement to prove that one of these situations applies.

Going Back Again and Again (and Again…. And Again…)

If a court order or separation agreement is changed once, that does not mean that the agreement cannot be changed again. The same considerations, as described above, apply to determine whether the court order or the agreement amending the separation agreement should be changed further. Again, there will have to be a material change in circumstances for one or both parties before the court will consider making another change. Generally, parties can go back to court to change court orders as many times as they like unless the

---

[397] *Family Law Act*, R.S.O. 1990, c. F-3, s. 35(1), (2)(b), as amended.

court finds that the party requesting the change is acting in a vexatious manner or is not abiding by the court order anyway.[398]

"My Ex Won't Follow the Rules!" - Going Back Because the Other Party Is Not Following the Order, Arbitration Award or Agreement

Another reason why parties go back to court is because one of them is not following the terms of a court order. If the order is a support order, unless the parties have agreed not to use the Family Responsibility Office, then the Family Responsibility Office has exclusive jurisdiction to enforce the Support Order. The party who is owed support cannot take steps on his or her own to enforce the order.[399] The Family Responsibility Office has a variety of powers that are designed to deal with a party who is defaulting on a support order. Those powers include damaging the support payer's credit rating, suspending the payer's passport, driver's licence or other licence, or even asking the court to impose a term of imprisonment.[400]

Where a support payer is not making the payments required by an agreement, this opens the door for the recipient to ask a judge to change the terms of support. The mere fact that support payments are in default gives the court jurisdiction to change the agreement[401]. The support recipient may want new support provisions that make it easier to collect support. Perhaps spousal support should be reduced where the spousal support recipient is in default of child support.[402] Another possibility is to ask the court to make a court order transferring or encumbering certain assets to pay support, or to use them as security for the support owed, or that will be owed in the future.[403]

---

[398] *Family Law Rules*, Rule 14(21)-(23), Rule 15(27).
[399] *Family Responsibility and Support Arrears Enforcement Act*, S.O. 1996, c. 31, s. 6(7).
[400] *Family Responsibility and Support Arrears Enforcement Act*, S.O. 1996, c. 31, Part V, Part VI.
[401] *Family Law Act*, R.S.O. 1990, c. F-3, s. 33(4)(a), as amended.
[402] It would be difficult to obtain an order reducing child support because the child support recipient is not paying spousal support because child support takes priority over spousal support: *Family Law Act*, R.S.O, 1990, c. F-3, s. 38.1, as amended.
[403] *Family Law Act*, R.S.O. 1990, c. F-3, s. 34(1)(c)(k), as amended.

If a party wants to enforce an order for the payment of money other than support, the Family Court provides a variety of procedural options to attempt to collect the money. These can include garnishing the payer's bank account or income source[404], asking the Sheriff to seize the payer's assets[405], or requiring the payer to file a financial statement and submit to cross-examination about his or her financial affairs[406]. All of these options are done through the court, although they do not require a contested court hearing between the payer and the payee. Contempt proceedings are not available to enforce an order for the payment of money[407].

Contempt proceedings are available to assist in the enforcement of court orders other than orders for the payment of money[408]. For example, contempt is available as a remedy where a party is breaching a parenting order. Contempt proceedings are very serious because the court can impose fines or terms of imprisonment as penalties for breaching a court order[409]. Since very serious penalties are available, contempt proceedings are considered quasi-criminal in nature. The person bringing the contempt motion must state with specificity when and how the other party breached the court order, and then must prove that the other party breached the order beyond a reasonable doubt[410]. The party who is alleged to have breached the court order has all of the safeguards in place that are available in criminal proceedings[411], including such rights as the protection from self-incrimination. Due to the heavy burden of proof and the stringent procedural safeguards in place, a party should only bring a contempt motion when he or she is absolutely certain it is possible to prove a deliberate breach of a court order.

Most judges sitting on Family Law matters do not like to make findings of contempt, or impose the resulting penalties. Therefore, it can be very difficult to succeed on contempt motions. Many judges prefer to consider the breach of a court order to be a material change in circumstances that justifies making a change to the original court order. For example, where a parent is

---

[404] *Family Law Rules*, Rule 29.
[405] *Family Law Rules*, Rule 28.
[406] *Family Law Rules*, Rule 27.
[407] *Family Law Rules*, Rule 31(1).
[408] *Family Law Rules*, Rule 31(1).
[409] *Family Law Rules*, Rule 31(5).
[410] *R. v. Glasner* (1994) 119 D.L.R. (4th) 113 (Ont. C.A.).; *Iron Ore Co. of Canada v. U.S.W., Local 4795* (1979)20 Nfld. & P.E.I.R. 27.
[411] *Fisher v. Fisher*, 2003 CarswellOnt 1170 (S.C.J.).

John P. Schuman, C.S., Family Lawyer, Mediator and Arbitrator

breaching a parenting order in such a way as to undermine a child's relationship with the other parent, judges have preferred to find that there has been a material change in circumstances that justify limiting the parent's rights or parenting time with respect to the children[412]. Judges often find that a party's refusal to follow a parenting order justifies changing that order. Judges may also be willing to find that breaches of other types of orders constitute a material change in circumstances that should result in a change to the order to preserve the intent of the original order. Any person who is being disadvantaged by another person's refusal to obey a court order should speak to a lawyer to figure out the best way to put the problem before the court to have it fixed.

If the parties resolved their matters through arbitration, then they have an arbitration award, rather than a court order. The Family Responsibility Office does not enforce arbitration awards, and only a judge can throw a party into jail for contempt. However, if the Family Law arbitration is conducted in accordance with the *Family Law Act*, the arbitration award can automatically be converted into a court order[413]. Once the appeal period for the arbitration award has expired, a Superior Court Judge cannot refuse to make an order on the same terms as the arbitration award (provided the arbitration was conducted in accordance with the *Family Law Act*)[414]. Once the arbitration award has been converted to a court order, it can be enforced as a court order; the FRO will enforce support; a party can obtain garnishments or writs of seizure and sale or bring a motion for contempt.

Judges Do Not Like Changing Temporary Orders Before Trial

As court proceedings (or arbitrations) unfold, there are often a number of temporary orders. These temporary orders can relate to support, parenting, ongoing disclosure, or other issues. The purpose of these orders is to get the parties through to either a trial or a settlement. These orders are not intended to be a determination of the dispute on its merits, or final opinion as to what the best order is in the circumstances. It is very difficult to change temporary orders[415]. Since the purpose of temporary orders is just to put temporary

---

[412] *L. (A.G.) v. D. (K.B.)* 2009 CarswellOnt 188; *McCoid v. McCoid*, [1996] B.C.J. No. 553 (B.C.S.C.); *Lim v. Mullin*, [1996] O.J. No. 2206 (Ont. C.J.).
[413] *Family Law Act*, R.S.O. 1990, c. F-3, s. 59.8.
[414] *Family Law Act*, R.S.O. 1990, c. F-3, s. 59.8(4).
[415] *Biddle v. Biddle*, [2005] O.J. No. 737 (Ont. S.C.J.)

John P. Schuman, C.S., Family Lawyer, Mediator and Arbitrator

provisions in place to make due until the parties get to trial, the correct way to address a temporary order is to move forward to have the trial[416]. Having the trial gives the judge the opportunity to see all the witnesses, hear all the facts and give careful consideration to the appropriate order. It is only in the most serious of circumstances, where a person's welfare is at stake, that a court will change a temporary order rather than just moving the parties onto trial to allow a full exploration of the issues.

---

[416] *Boissy v. Boissy*, 2008 CarswellOnt 4253 (Ont. S.C.J.); *Grant v. Turgeon,* [2000] O.J. No. 970 (Sup. Ct.) at para 15.

Part 4: Last Things First: Planning Your New Life Together With Cohabitation Agreements & Marriage Contracts ("Pre-nups")

Cohabitation agreements are agreements that people usually sign before they live together (in a conjugal relationship)[417], and marriage contracts are agreements that people usually sign before they get married[418]. So why is this guide talking about those agreements after divorce and separation? There are two reasons for this:

1. Marriage contracts do not have to be signed before a couple get married, and cohabitation agreements do not have to be signed before a couple start living together. Couples can organize their affairs with a marriage contract or cohabitation agreement at any time[419], and cohabitation agreements even automatically become marriage contracts if the couple gets married[420]. Sometimes parties choose to sign a marriage contract or a cohabitation agreement instead of separating.
2. Couples may sign cohabitation agreements and marriage contracts to set out what will happen if they separate, or if one of them dies. In so doing, they opt out of the laws that usually apply with regard to spousal support, property division, and many other (but not all) issues that arise on separation. As will be discussed below, it is very important that couples understand what they are doing when they sign a marriage contract or cohabitation agreement. To understand how the agreement

---

[417] *Family Law Act*, R.S.O. 1990, c. F-3, s. 1(1) and 53(1), as amended.
[418] *Family Law Act*, R.S.O. 1990, c. F-3, s. 52(1), as amended.
[419] *Family Law Act*, R.S.O. 1990, c. F-3, s. 52(1) and 53(1), as amended.
[420] *Family Law Act*, R.S.O. 1990, c. F-3, s. 53 (2), as amended.

changes their rights and obligations under the law, they must first understand what their rights and obligations are without a contract[421]. Part 2 of this guide covers what happens without a marriage contract or cohabitation agreement.

What a Marriage Contract or Cohabitation Agreement Can Do

Originally, the law in Ontario did not permit cohabitation agreements and marriage contracts. That changed in 1978, when the Ontario Government specifically allowed these types of agreements[422], and set out what people could and could not include in them.

Marriage contracts and cohabitation agreements can set out how the spouses will organize their affairs while they are or living together, when they separate, or both. There are limits on what matters can be included in a marriage contract or cohabitation agreement. However, the *Family Law Act* specifically allows the parties to make a contract regarding the following issues:

1. **ownership in or division of property**[423] – this includes excluding certain assets or liabilities from equalization, or opting out of the equalization process altogether. It can also limit each partner's right to make other types of claims against each other's property. The agreement can require that property, other than a matrimonial home, be sold on separation or at another time. Where property is not sold, the agreement can set out how and when that property will be valued if the value is to be shared. It can also set out who will own what during the marriage.

2. **spousal support**[424] – the parties can set out exactly what support will be paid between them when they separate or, specify that no support will be paid[425]. The parties can also set out how they will address their finances and pay for their needs during the relationship.

---

[421] *LeVan v. LeVan*, 2008 ONCA 388 at para 52.
[422] With the passing of the *Family Law Reform Act*.
[423] *Family Law Act*, R.S.O. 1990, c. F-3, s. 52(1)(a) and 53(1)(a), as amended
[424] *Family Law Act*, R.S.O. 1990, c. F-3, s. 52(1)(b) and 53(1)(b), as amended
[425] Courts are very reluctant to give much weight to contracts that deny any support after a long-term marriage that has created a situation of economic dependency or when one party has made significant sacrifices to care for the couple's children. In those circumstances the court will look very hard to find reasons to

3. **child support**[426] – but only if the agreement is reasonable having regard to the *Child Support Guidelines*[427]. Further, if the matter of child support makes it before a court, the court must order child support in accordance with the *Child Support Guidelines*[428]. The court can only follow the terms of the marriage contract or cohabitation agreement if those terms benefit the child to an extent that ordering child support in accordance with the *Child Support Guidelines* would be inequitable in light of the provisions of the agreement[429]. Where the support payer is receiving "public money" (social assistance, employment insurance, Canada Pension Benefits, etc.), this exception does not apply[430]. Drafting an agreement for child support other than in accordance with the *Child Support Guidelines* is a risky and tricky process that requires competent Family Lawyers.

4. **the right to direct the education and moral training of their children**, but not the right to custody of or access to their children[431]. However, when determining a matter respecting the education, moral training or custody of or access to a child, a judge may disregard any provision of a domestic contract addressing those issues where he or she feels doing so is in the best interests of the child[432].

5. **any other matter in the settlement of their affairs**[433], with the exception of the matters that the law states specifically cannot be addressed in a marriage contract or cohabitation agreement. For example, a marriage contract or cohabitation agreement might include, for example, provisions such as a requirement that the parties abide by terms of a shareholder's agreement for a business, that a spouse will resign from a family business on separation, or that the parties will designate a certain property as a matrimonial home or many other terms, with the exception of those that are specifically outlawed.

---

set aside the contract pursuant to the considerations set out later in this part of the Guide.

[426] *Family Law Act*, R.S.O. 1990, c. F-3, s. 52(1)(b) and 53(1)(b), as amended.
[427] *Family Law Act*, R.S.O. 1990, c. F-3, s. 59(1.1) as amended.
[428] *Family Law Act*, R.S.O. 1990, c. F-3, s. 33(11) as amended.
[429] *Family Law Act*, R.S.O. 1990, c. F-3, s. 33(12), as amended
[430] Where the support payer is receiving public money, the court must order support that is at least as much as would be required by the *Child Support Guidelines*: *Family Law Act*, R.S.O. 1990, c. F-3, s. 33(14)(b), as amended.
[431] *Family Law Act*, R.S.O. 1990, c. F-3, s. 52(1)(c) and 53(1)(c), as amended.
[432] *Family Law Act*, R.S.O 1990, c. F-3, s. 56(1).
[433] *Family Law Act*, R.S.O. 1990, c. F-3, s. 52(1) (c) and 53(1)(c), as amended.

John P. Schuman, C.S., Family Lawyer, Mediator and Arbitrator

What a Marriage Contract or Cohabitation Agreement Cannot Do

Ontario's *Family Law Act* specifically prohibits four types of terms from being included in marriage contracts and cohabitation agreements. In addition, the *Income Tax Act* does not consider support arrangements in marriage contracts or separation agreements. As a result, marriage contracts and cohabitation agreements cannot:

1. **set parenting terms** (address custody or access). The *Family Law Act* specifically states that marriage contracts and cohabitation agreements cannot contain terms in relation to custody of, or access to, children[434]. Judges always have the right to make the custody or access order that they feel is in the "best interests of a child", regardless of an agreement between the parties[435]. As noted above, while the *Family Law Act* specifically allows marriage contracts and cohabitation agreements to address the education and moral training of children, the *Family Law Act* also says that judges can override the contract if doing so is in the "best interests of the child";

2. **restrict either married spouse's right to be in possession of matrimonial homes.** On separation, married spouses have an equal right to stay in the Matrimonial Homes[436]. As noted in Part 2, there can be more than one matrimonial home. A marriage contract cannot contain terms requiring one spouse to leave a Matrimonial Home[437]. It also cannot authorize one spouse to sell, mortgage or otherwise encumber or otherwise dispose of a Matrimonial Home before the spouses are divorced, unless they sign a separation agreement addressing the Matrimonial Home, or a court permits it by way of an order[438]. Only married spouses can have Matrimonial Homes[439], so this restriction does not apply to cohabitation agreements unless the parties marry with the agreement still in effect;

3. **contain provisions for child support that benefit the child less than the Child Support Guidelines.** As discussed above, if the

---

[434] *Family Law Act*, R.S.O. 1990, c. F-3, s. 52(1)(c) and 53(1)(c), as amended.
[435] *Divorce Act*, R.S.C. 1985, c. 3 (2nd Supp), s. 16(8); *Children's Law Reform Act*, R.S.O. 1990, c. C-12, s. 24.
[436] *Family Law Act*, R.S.O. 1990, c. F-3, s. 19(1).
[437] *Family Law Act*, R.S.O. 1990, c. F-3, s. 52(2).
[438] *Family Law Act*, R.S.O. 1990, c. F-3, s. 19(2), 21(1), and 52(2).
[439] *Family Law Act*, R.S.O. 1990, c. F-3, s. 1(1) and 18(1), as amended.

matter of child support goes before a court, the court will make an order in accordance with the *Child Support Guidelines* unless it feels the terms of the agreement are reasonable in light of the *Guidelines*;

4. **require the parties to resolve any issue arising from the breakdown of the relationship by way of arbitration.** The *Family Law Act* does not allow parties to agree to resolve a Family Law dispute by way of arbitration until after the dispute has arisen[440]. Parties can agree in a separation agreement to resolve future disputes by way of arbitration[441], but they cannot do so in a marriage contract or cohabitation agreement;

5. **result in spousal support payments that are deductible to the support payer and taxable for the support recipient while the parties are still living at the same residence.** For support payments to be recognized under the *Income Tax Act*, one separated spouse must make the payments to the other separated spouse pursuant to a written agreement (or a court order)[442]. People who are living together cannot agree that one will pay support to the other to shift the tax burden to the person who pays tax at the lower rate.

Feeling that he was "stung" once, Desmond wants a cohabitation agreement before he allows Eleanor to move in with him. He wants an agreement that says Eleanor will not discipline or otherwise parent Desmond and Molly's children. However, Desmond's lawyer explains that the cohabitation agreement cannot do that.

Desmond also wants an agreement that says Eleanor will move out of "his" house if they separate, even if they are married. He does not want her hanging around after separation like Molly did. Desmond's lawyer tells him that such a clause would be invalid if Desmond and Eleanor do get married. A marriage contract cannot require a married spouse to leave a matrimonial home.

Finally, Desmond lost the deduction for the value of his house on the date of marriage in his divorce from Molly because they were living in that house when they separated. Desmond wants to make sure he gets credit for bringing the house into the marriage this time. To Desmond's relief, his lawyer tells him that a cohabitation agreement/marriage contract can do that.

---

[440] *Family Law Act*, R.S.O. 1990, c. F-3, s. 59.4, as amended.
[441] *Family Law Act*, R.S.O. 1990, c. F-3, s. 59.7(1)1., as amended.
[442] *Income Tax Act*, R.S.C. 1985, c. 1 (5th Supp) s. 60, as amended.

Marriage contracts and cohabitation agreements are forward-looking documents. They address how the parties want to organize their affairs in the future. It is possible that, in the future, the Ontario Government will add more restrictions on what parties can include in marriage contracts or cohabitation agreements. It is also possible that those new restrictions will be applied to existing marriage contracts and cohabitation agreements, which could invalidate some of the terms in those contracts and agreements. It is not possible to protect a contract from the legislature passing a law making that contract invalid. People signing marriage contracts and cohabitation agreements have to be aware of, and accept, this risk.

People signing a marriage contract or cohabitation agreement must also understand that even if their contract contains only terms that are allowed, those terms might still not be enforced if they do not follow the rules governing the creation of those contracts.

Avoiding Making A Bad Deal That Will Not Hold Up

Many rules apply to the creation of marriage contracts and cohabitation agreements. The failure to follow those rules may result in a court refusing to enforce the contract or agreement.

The basic rules for a valid marriage contract or cohabitation agreement are that the agreement must be in writing, must be signed by the parties, and those signatures must be witnessed[443].

The *Family Law Act* also sets out specific grounds on which a marriage contract or cohabitation agreement can be set aside. Those provisions effectively create additional rules for making an enforceable marriage contract or cohabitation agreement. Some of the additional rules are:

1. the parties must understand the agreement. The courts have said that effectively this means that each party must have had competent Independent Legal Advice from a lawyer who explained the legal significance of the terms of the agreement. "Independent" means that one party must not have interfered with the other party's relationship

---

[443] Witnesses may be called upon later if there is a dispute as to whether the signature on the contract belongs to the person it says or whether someone fraudulently signed on for that person.

John P. Schuman, C.S., Family Lawyer, Mediator and Arbitrator

with his or her lawyer. It is also important for each party to freely select and pay for his or her own lawyer.
2. there must be full, complete, and accurate financial disclosure of all of both parties' assets, liabilities and income sources, and that includes values for each line item.[444]
3. the marriage contract or cohabitation agreement must not offend the general Law of Contract in a way that supports setting it aside. Some applications of the Law of Contract to set aside an agreement or contract are as follows:
    (a) duress: A wrongful act or threat by one party deprives the other of the opportunity to freely make decisions about the contract;
    (b) undue influence: One party abuses a position of influence over the other for the purpose of obtaining an unfair advantage over the other party;
    (c) fraud: A false representation of a matter of fact, whether by words or by conduct, by false or misleading allegations, or by concealment of that which should have been disclosed, which deceives and is intended to deceive the other party about the consequences of signing the contract;
    (d) unconscionability: Where the terms of the agreement are so one-sided as to oppress one party or unreasonably favour the other;
    (e) fundamental breach: A breach by one party of a basic term on which the whole agreement was based to an extent that makes the whole agreement meaningless; and
    (f) other equitable grounds: The validity of a domestic contract may also be called into question on the grounds of inequality of bargaining power, unfair surprise, mistake, material misrepresentation or non-disclosure.

The Supreme Court of Canada has stated that a domestic contract, which includes a marriage contract or cohabitation agreement, can be set aside if there were problems in the circumstances surrounding the negotiation of the agreement, such as where one or both parties did not have adequate legal (or accounting) advice, or there was oppression, duress or the calculations were made in haste[445]. An agreement can be set aside if it is not in substantial

---

[444] *Demchuk v. Demchuk* (1986), 1 R.F.L. (3d) 176 (Ont. H.C.J.).
[445] *Miglin v. Miglin* (2003), 1. S.C.R. 303 at paragraph 81.

John P. Schuman, C.S., Family Lawyer, Mediator and Arbitrator

compliance with the objectives of the Family Law legislation[446]. The agreement can also be set aside if it results in consequences that the parties did not intend or contemplate[447].

> *Desmond thinks that Eleanor would never agree to sign a marriage contract if she knew how much his store was really worth. He tells his lawyer that he wants to either not tell Eleanor the value of that business, or make up a value that will make Eleanor happy to sign the contract. Desmond's lawyer tells Desmond that is a very bad idea as making complete and accurate financial disclosure protects Desmond. If Eleanor knows what she is giving away, because she saw the financial disclosure, it would be very difficult for her to say the agreement is unfair. If she thinks that, she should not sign the agreement. However, if Eleanor did not get complete and accurate disclosure, she can easily say that she would not have signed the contract if she knew the truth – even if what she believed when she signed the contract was not far from the truth. Worse still, if Eleanor makes complete and accurate disclosure, she may be able to rely on the contract to protect her, even if Desmond cannot rely on the contract to protect him.*
>
> *Understanding that full disclosure is important, Desmond asks his lawyer if there is anything he can do to pressure Eleanor to sign the agreement if she does not want to sign after seeing his disclosure. His lawyer tells him the only option is not to marry Eleanor. Doing anything to pressure Eleanor would allow her to say that she did not sign the contract voluntarily. The courts will never enforce an agreement that was not signed voluntarily.*

---

[446] *Miglin v. Miglin* (2003), 1. S.C.R. 303 at paragraph 84-85, also in *LeVan v. LeVan* 2008 ONCA 388, the Ontario Court of Appeal set aside a Marriage Contract in these types of circumstances.

[447] *Carrier c. Carrier*, 2007 CarswellNB 155 at para 13(N.B. C.A.)

Imposing Punishment for Cheating and Other Lifestyle Clauses

Many celebrities have marriage contracts that impose penalties for infidelity, putting on weight or other types of frowned-upon behaviour. These agreements contract out of the "no fault divorce" system that exists in Ontario[448] (and the rest of Canada[449]) as well as most of the United States. These so-called "Lifestyle Clauses" impose financial penalties for types of behaviour that are specified in the contract. For example, an agreement could contain a clause that if a spouse commits adultery, they must give the other spouse a large sum of money, or they become disentitled to a property division or spousal support payment.

There are no reported Canadian court decisions upholding or setting aside a lifestyle clause in a marriage contract or cohabitation agreement. In her decision in *D'Andrade v. Schrage*, Justice Sachs said, in passing, that marriage contracts are not meant to deal with enforcing personal obligations, such as the obligation to remain faithful.[450] Ontario's family legislation does not specifically ban such clauses. However, there is a strong argument that they should be set aside as against public policy in that they run contrary to Canada's "no fault divorce" system. Anyone considering a lifestyle clause in a marriage contract or cohabitation agreement should keep in mind that a court may not enforce that clause. Parties who choose to include such clauses should also include the necessary terms in the agreement to ensure that the rest of it is enforceable even if the lifestyle clause is not.

Why You Should Never Negotiate A Marriage Contract Right Before the Wedding

The circumstances surrounding the negotiation of any domestic contract are important. With regard to marriage contracts, the circumstances in the last two months before the wedding are very poor circumstances in which to negotiate a marriage contract. The parties are focused on the wedding, not on the contract. One party may feel that he or she cannot get married without the contract in place, which can lead to a situation of duress or undue influence, if it seems like the wedding will have to be called off after the invitations have

---

[448] *Family Law Act*, R.S.O. 1990, c. F-3, s. 5(7), 33(10) as amended.
[449] *Divorce Act*, , R.S.C. 1985, c. 3 (2nd Supp), s. 15.2(5), as amended.
[450] *D'Andrade v. Schrage*, 2011 ONSC 1174 (CanLII) at paragraph 81.

John P. Schuman, C.S., Family Lawyer, Mediator and Arbitrator

gone out and all the payments for the arrangements have been made. A party might sign a bad deal to avoid the embarrassment of cancelling the ceremony.

The parties should start negotiating their marriage contract as far in advance of the wedding as possible. Otherwise, one party might raise the pressure of the looming wedding as a basis for setting the marriage contract aside.

Marriage contracts do not have to be signed before the wedding. They can be signed afterward. They can even be signed long afterward, which can be the case where one spouse is worried about the other's financial habits and needs some protection to stay in the marriage.

If the parties cannot finalize their marriage contract at least two months before the wedding, they should consider a Stand-Still Agreement. A Stand-Still Agreement is a temporary type of marriage contract that states that the parties intend to continue their negotiations after the wedding and, as much as possible, they want to treat each other as if they were unmarried. That means that there will be no spousal support payable or an equalization of the parties' Net Family Properties if they separate in the time allowed to negotiate an agreement.

A Stand Still Agreement is still a marriage contract. All of the restrictions and requirements for a marriage contract apply to a Stand Still Agreement. However, since the Stand Still Agreement usually expires in a matter of months after the marriage ceremony, it is difficult for unanticipated situations to arise that would result in either spouse having a significant claim against the other.

Be Fair, and Careful, About Support Terms

The *Family Law Act* provides that a court may set aside the parts of a marriage contract or a cohabitation agreement that address support or even constitute a waiver of the right to support. If a judge sets aside the terms relating to support, he or she may make an order for support - even though the contract specifically says that the parties do not want a court to do that. A judge can set aside the support provisions of a marriage contract or cohabitation agreement and order support:

1. if the provision for support or the waiver of the right to support results in unconscionable circumstances at the time the matter is before the court (not just at the time the parties signed the agreement);
2. if the provision for support is in favour of, or the waiver of support is by or on behalf of, a dependent who qualifies for an allowance for support out of public money (social assistance, employment insurance, etc.); or
3. if there is default in the payment of support under the contract or agreement at the time the party starts the court proceeding for support[451].

Whether a court will give respect to a provision in a marriage contract or cohabitation agreement either limiting or precluding a claim for future support is very much subject to the discretion of the court at the time an application for support is made. The court can override an agreement that was fair and reasonable when it was executed if it would be unconscionable at the time of a court action to maintain the support agreement. "Unconscionable" means "shocking to the conscience." Generally, judges believe that people who freely entered into their contract should be kept to their bargain, so it should be difficult to convince a judge that an agreement is unconscionable.

In its decision in Miglin, the Supreme Court of Canada gave some guidance about whether agreements should be set aside, and if so, what terms in a contract might be considered unconscionable[452]. The court must first look at the substance of the agreement. This step involves looking at the extent to which the agreement takes into account the factors and objectives of spousal support (as described in Part 2 of this guide). Those factors and objectives are seen to result in a fair sharing of the economic consequences of marriage and its breakdown. If the agreement shows a significant departure from the general objectives of spousal support, the court can change the agreement, even ordering support where there is a release[453].

Pursuant to Miglin, when evaluating a marriage contract or cohabitation agreement, the court must consider the circumstances of the parties at the time one of the spouses starts a court application for support (contrary to the terms of the agreement). It is not just the circumstances at the time of signing the agreement that matter. The judge hearing the case must

---

[451] *Family Law Act*, R.S.O. 1990, c. F-3, s. 33(4) as amended.
[452] Rather than the way the contract was negotiated.
[453] Mig*lin v. Miglin* (2003), 1. S.C.R. 303 at paragraph 85.

John P. Schuman, C.S., Family Lawyer, Mediator and Arbitrator

consider whether, at the time they signed the agreement, the parties contemplated the circumstances that existed at the time of the court application. If the parties did not contemplate their change in circumstances, then the judge must decide whether the agreement should be discounted. The judge must considered whether, in light of these new circumstances, the agreement still reflects the parties' intentions and also still reflects the factors and objectives of spousal support[454].

An Ontario Marriage Contract or Cohabitation Agreement May Not Work Some Place Else

Many couples move to another jurisdiction during their relationship. Ontario's *Family Law Act* recognizes marriage contracts and cohabitation agreements. However, not every jurisdiction does. If the parties separate and pursue their divorce or other Family Law matters in a foreign jurisdiction, the foreign court may not recognize marriage contracts or cohabitation agreements. Further, Ontario's *Family Law Act* states that the division of property on separation will be determined according to the law of the jurisdiction where the parties last lived together[455]. When these agreements are drafted in Ontario, they usually say that the law of Ontario will govern the interpretation of the contract. However, the foreign jurisdiction may still not recognize Ontario Law or a contract made pursuant to Ontario Law. If spouses are moving out of Ontario with a marriage contract or cohabitation agreement, they should speak to a lawyer in the new jurisdiction to make sure the courts there will respect their wishes.

"We Didn't Mean It": Abandoning the Contract

Every marriage contract or cohabitation agreement should contain a clause that says that the contract or agreement can only be changed, or rendered invalid, by a written agreement between the parties. That means that parties cannot get rid of their marriage contract or cohabitation agreement just by telling each other that they are revoking it. Also, if the parties ignore the terms of the agreement, even do things contrary to it, during the course of their relationship, those actions should not invalidate an agreement – especially if the agreement says it can only be changed in writing.

---

[454] *Carrier v. Carrier,* 2007 CarswellNB 155 at para 13 (N.B. C.A.).
[455] *Family Law Act*, R.S.O. 1990, c. F-3, s. 15.

John P. Schuman, C.S., Family Lawyer, Mediator and Arbitrator

However, where the parties' conduct throughout their relationship, or for many years of it, demonstrates that neither of them intended to be bound by the marriage contract or cohabitation agreement, a judge gives little or no weight on the terms of the contract. For example, this might occur in a situation where a marriage contract says that the parties will keep their property separate, but they decide to put all their property in joint names, or one spouse puts virtually all assets in the other spouse's name. If the parties want to do thing differently than as set out in their marriage contract or cohabitation agreement, then they should do a written amending agreement. Otherwise, a court may try to figure out whether the parties abandoned the agreement, or part of it, and the court may get it wrong if the circumstances are confusing.

A Deal is Still A Deal

Much of this part of this guide has been devoted to the circumstances in which courts will not follow a marriage contract or cohabitation agreement. That is because the circumstances under which these agreements can be set aside takes a long time to explain. However, judges like to hold people to their bargain and uphold contracts. This is especially true when the deal is a fair one. Marriage contracts and cohabitation agreements are agreements of utmost good faith[456]. Marrying spouses should want to be fair to each other. As long as one spouse is not using the agreement to try to take advantage of the other spouse and create an unfair situation, the courts will likely respect the terms of the marriage contract or cohabitation agreement.

---

[456] *Dubin v. Dubin* (2003), 34 R.F.L. (5th) at para 35 (Ont. S.C.J.).

John P. Schuman, C.S., Family Lawyer, Mediator and Arbitrator

Part 5: Accusations of Child Abuse or Neglect – What to Do, What Not to Do and When: A Brief Discussion of Child Protection (Cases Brought by Children's Aid Societies)

"Child protection cases" are cases in which a children's aid society is seeking a court order, or a voluntary agreement, in relation to a child and his or her parents. Children's Aid Societies pursue such orders or agreements when the agency believes they are necessary to protect the child's welfare. These cases are considered to be under the umbrella of Family Law. However, child protection cases are very different from divorce, custody/access or support proceedings. Some of the significant differences include, but are not limited to, the following:

1. The children's aid society is the "state" or the government. As these cases involve an interaction between individual people and the state, the *Canadian Charter of Rights and Freedoms* applies to protect the individuals involved in these cases[457].
2. While custody/access cases start with the premise that both parents are capable parents to the children, child protection cases start with a premise that there is something wrong with one or both parent's parenting that requires a children's aid society to step in to protect the children[458].

---

[457] B.(R.). v. *Children's Aid Society of Metropolitan Toronto*, [1995] 1.S.C.R. 315.
[458] *Children's Aid Society of Brant v. L.(J.)*, 2008 CarswellOnt 6306 at paragraphs 15 and 16 (O.C.J.).

3. Child protection proceedings before the courts have very strict timelines, particularly when a child is in the care of the children's aid society rather than his or her parents. Where a child is in the care of a children's aid society, the court proceedings must be set down for trial within three months of the start of the proceedings[459].
4. Except under some very specific, and unusual, circumstances, only the children's aid society can commence child protection proceedings[460].
5. Throughout the initial child protection proceedings, the children's aid society must satisfy the court that it is asking for the least intrusive order possible that still protects the children[461]. This is a different consideration than what is in "the child's best interest."
6. Child protection matters are governed by the *Child and Family Services Act* and not the *Divorce Act* or the *Children's Law Reform Act*, which are the laws that govern custody and access proceedings. Child protection is a very specialized area of law that has unique challenges. By way of example, parents involved in child protection matters are expected to cooperate with the children's aid society to make things better for the children. The parents are expected to cooperate with the children's aid society, even though that agency is suing them. This means that parents cannot take the same adversarial approach in child protection proceedings that they would as opposing parties in any other type of litigation.

You Need Help To Avoid Serious Trouble

Even minor instances of lack of cooperation with the children's aid society can be very detrimental to the parent's case. However, there can be instances where cooperation can also cause problems. For example, if there is a criminal proceeding or criminal investigation that runs parallel to the child protection case, the parents ought to be very careful what they say to the children's aid society, because everything they say will be turned over to the police and may be used to incriminate them. Parents (or other Respondents) may have to walk a very fine line in child protection cases. There is a statutory mechanism available for parents to complain about the behaviour of a children's aid society that is outside the court process[462]. However, all aspects of that process are not

---

[459] *Child and Family Services Act*, R.S.O. 1990, c. C.11, s. 52.
[460] *Child and Family Services Act*, R.S.O. 1990, c. C.11, s. 40(1), 65.1(1).
[461] *Child and Family Services Act*, R.S.O. 1990, c. C.11, s. 1(2)2., 51(3),(3.1).
[462] *Child and Family Services Act*, R.S.O. 1990, c. C.11, s. 68, 68.1.

available while the court proceedings are ongoing[463]. That provision protects parents (and other people involved in the court proceeding), as the children's aid society will likely tell the judge that the complaints are evidence that the parents are not willing to follow the children's aid society's recommendations to improve the life of the child. To avoid getting in trouble in these cases, parents, and others, need advice from a knowledgeable child protection lawyer.

The consequences of child protection proceedings can be more severe than any other type of court proceeding in Canada. Parents can have their children taken out of their care and never see them again if the children are made Crown Wards and placed for adoption. The process of permanently removing a child from that child's parents starts very early on. It is critical that parents retain a child protection lawyer as soon as they know that they will be involved with the children's aid society, so that the parents can avoid making any missteps that could make it very difficult, or impossible, for them to be reunited with their children.

Hiring a child protection lawyer immediately sends several important messages to both the children's aid society and to the court. Those messages are:

1. The parents have sufficient wherewithal, and are sufficiently organized, to be able to retain a lawyer quickly. Parents who hire lawyers immediately do not appear to be parents whose lives are so out of control that they are not able to function as parents;
2. The parents care enough about their children that they are immediately taking steps to get them back;
3. The children's aid society has to play by the rules, which can be very technical and quite onerous; and
4. The parents have legal advisors whose advice they are likely to take, which means the parent is likely to act reasonably.

Having a lawyer right away allows parents to keep the proceedings on track, avoid any pitfalls, and gives them the best chance of convincing the children's aid society and the court that the children should be returned unconditionally to their care.

---

[463] *Child and Family Services Act*, R.S.O. 1990, c. C.11, s. 68(12) and 68.1(8).

John P. Schuman, C.S., Family Lawyer, Mediator and Arbitrator

What To Do When A Children's Aid Society Calls To Investigate

Parents are justified in being worried and scared if a social worker from a children's aid society shows up at their home to investigate concerns of child abuse or whether the parents are a satisfactory parents. Children's aid societies do not do spot checks on parents. If the parents did not invite them, someone has told the agency that they have witnessed something that suggests there is a problem with parenting, or that there is child abuse. When they are investigating child abuse or child neglect, child protection workers have a lot of police-like powers, such as collecting information about the children from various sources without their parents' permission, searching homes and even taking children away immediately. The social worker may be visiting and speaking to the family to collect information to use as the basis for taking children away. However, unlike with police, parents do not necessarily have the right to remain silent. In fact, if the parents refuse to speak to the social worker, or prevent the social worker from speaking to the children alone, that fact can be used as a basis to take the kids away on the assumption the parents are hiding something.

First impressions matter a lot in child protection investigations. If parents make a bad first impression, the children's aid society may stay involved with the family for a long time, even if there aren't legitimate child protection concerns, simply because the worker, or their supervisor, is suspicious. If parents make a really good first impression, the agency may not feel the need to do a full investigation and will close their file quickly. Here is what parents should do if they are contacted by a children's aid society in relation to an investigation of suspected abuse or neglect:

1. Call a child protection lawyer – A parent can only do this if the worker calls before showing up at the house. In this situation, parents should look for a lawyer that practices child protection law and has handled many children's aid society cases. This area of law is very different from other types of family law or criminal law. If a parent treats a child protection worker in the same way they might treat a police officer, the parent will get in trouble. However, if they aren't informed, parents can make mistakes early on that have lasting impact on their case. Each child protection case is unique; parents need specific advice from a lawyer on their specific circumstances. Getting a lawyer involved early can make a huge difference. Just how big a difference is set out later in this Part of the book.

John P. Schuman, C.S., Family Lawyer, Mediator and Arbitrator

2. Do not refuse to speak to or meet with the child protection worker. If parents refuse to meet with the child protection worker, they appear as if they have something to hide. Workers are very suspicious of parents who don't want to talk to them. Parents do not have the right to remain silent - unless they may also face criminal charges in relation to what the worker is investigating. When someone has alleged serious abuse or neglect, the children's aid society will be working closely with the police in their investigation. The worker will report everything the parent says to the police. The police and the Crown Attorney may use those statements to prosecute the parent in criminal court. Parents who may be facing criminal charges must not discuss anything in relation to those allegations with a society worker until they have spoken with a lawyer – even if the social worker considers it "being uncooperative". What parents can and cannot, should and should not, say is a fine balance that requires careful planning to keep the children out of foster care and the parents out of jail.

3. Make sure the house is clean, tidy and kid-friendly. This is part of making a good first impression. Some specific pointers are:

1. If a house is a mess or disorganized, the parents look like they are having difficulty managing or coping, which can lead to concern about whether the parents can manage caring for children. If the house is reasonably tidy, then the parents show that they are "on top of things," which indicates to the worker that the parents have their lives together enough to be appropriate parents.
2. Children's aid society workers also want to see that the house is "baby-proofed" or "child-proofed", meaning that electrical outlets are covered, poisons are locked away, stairs are blocked off where there are young chidden, the house has working smoke and carbon monoxide detectors, there are no safety hazards in the house and nothing else poses a physical danger to the children.
3. The investigating worker will also want to see that there is adequate and appropriate food in the house.
4. It is important for parents to have age-appropriate toys and learning activities in the home.
5. Child protection workers also look to see if there is evidence of a happy and functional family life such as photographs, souvenirs and mementoes that show the family members have close and loving relationships with one another.
6. Finally, child protection workers are required to see the children's rooms to make sure they are furnished appropriately for the children's ages.

John P. Schuman, C.S., Family Lawyer, Mediator and Arbitrator

It can make some workers much more comfortable and at ease if parents offer a tour of the house rather than having to ask. Offering before being asked shows both that the parents are proud and take care of their home, and that they have nothing to hide.

4. Be very nice to the child protection worker. In fact, parents should go out of their way to be nice to the worker and thank the worker for being concerned about the children. This not like dealing with the police, where the person under investigation has no obligation to help the investigation. Children's aid societies, judges and other professionals who may become involved expect parents to cooperate with the children's aid society because everyone's goal should be to work together to do what is best for the children. If parents are not willing to "work together" with the society, child protection workers may think that the children's best interests are not important to the parents, or worse, that the children may be in danger because of this. If the children's aid society does not think it "can work with" the parents, it may take more intrusive actions. The agency may take the children away because it cannot protect them while they remain in the parents' care, or the agency may take the parents to court to get court orders to force the parents to do or not do things. If parents seriously offend the child protection worker, they may proceed with the highest level of intervention that they can justify. It is very important to be nice. If someone has to be mean to the children's aid society or force the agency to play by the rules, it should be a lawyer, so the parents can stay on good terms with the worker.

5. Let the child protection worker speak with your children alone. As part of their investigation, children's aid society workers have the right to speak to the children without parents being present if they are investigating abuse or neglect by the parents.[464] The child can have a lawyer present, but that request

---

[464] Section 15(3) of the *Child and Family Services,* R.S.O. 1990, c. C-11, as amended, sets out the functions of a children's aid society, one of which is to investigate child abuse and neglect. Section 20.1 allows the ministry to set out standards and directives for how those investigations will be carried out. The Ministry publishes standards for children's aid societies. Pages 26 and 27 of those standards require that the child protection worker individually interview each of the children in the family being investigated. The courts have then held that section 15(3) empowers a children's aid society to act pursuant to the standards made under the CFSA, and the court should not interfere with a children's aid society doing what it is required to do pursuant to the established standards. See e.g. Children's Aid Society of Hamilton-Wentworth v. C.(I.), 1993 CanLII 5608 (ON SCDC)

has to come from the child. Workers will be very suspicious if it appears that the child is requesting a lawyer because their parents told them to ask for one. That request must clearly come from the child because the child wants a lawyer and not be the child asking for a lawyer to help the parents. If parents do not allow children to speak to the worker, the worker will be suspicious that parents are trying to "cover up" something. If the worker is having difficulty getting to the child while with the parents, the worker will just go to the child's school, day care, or other activities and speak to the child there. It can cause serious problems if the worker thinks any adult has "put words in the kid's mouth." It is best not to tell the children what to say to the worker and only tell them to "relax and be honest."

6. Speak to a lawyer before signing anything. Ideally, parents should speak to a lawyer before they meet with the worker to go over what they should and should not sign. When parents refuse to sign certain things, it looks like they have something to hide. In most cases, it is alright to sign authorizations to allow the worker to speak to doctors, teachers, activity leaders and similar professionals involved with the children, as the worker already has the power to speak to them as part of a child protection investigation - the authorizations just make it easier. Unless there is a good reason to delay the children's aid society getting that information for a short time, there is rarely harm in signing. However, parents should not to sign any sort of "agreement" with the children's aid society. Those agreements can take away a lot of parents' rights. Parents should never sign any sort of contract or agreement without speaking to a lawyer to make sure they understand what they are signing. If parents are not absolutely certain they know what they are signing, what it fully means, and what it lets the society do, they must speak to a child protection lawyer before signing anything.

7. Ask for file disclosure unless the worker leaves after the meeting saying that the agency intends to close its file. If the investigation is ongoing, parents are entitled to see the children's aid society's file on them. Seeing the file can be important for several reasons. First, it lets the parents know what specific allegations the society is investigating, so the parents will know what the children's aid society is looking for. Second, it lets the parents see on what evidence the agency is basing its concerns, so the parents can address that evidence. Reviewing disclosure can also reveal weaknesses in the society's investigation. Finally, if the society is taking the parents to court, or taking the kids into care, then the parents need the information in the file to challenge the children's aid society's case in court. Because of these reasons, children's aid societies are slow in releasing their file. Often it helps to have a lawyer involved who can assert the parents' rights in this regard as an experienced child protection lawyers will be harder for a children's aid society to push around.

8. Do not assume that the children's aid society is happy until the parents get a letter saying they have closed their file. The investigation is on-going until the parents get a letter telling them it has ended. Workers may be less visible for a time after an initial visit or visits, so they can investigate the family from a distance. It is important to note that once a children's aid society has investigated a parent (even if the agency finds nothing wrong), the children's aid society puts the parent's name into a database that other Ontario children's aid societies can access if they interact with the same parent in the future over concerns of child abuse or neglect. This allows the agencies to see if similar concerns are repeatedly reported about the same parent. Parents must to stay on their best behaviour after a visit from a child protection worker.

Even when parents cooperate fully with a children's aid society, sometimes the allegations or concerns are just too serious for the agency to rely on the parents continuing to cooperate. In other cases, the workers may just be too suspicious of the parents or their motives. When this happens, the children's aid society may feel that the only way to adequately protect the children is to go to court. A children's aid society has to go to court, within 5 days, if the agency brings the children into care.[465] The mandate of a court hearing child protection matters is to provide oversight to make sure the agency is acting fairly and reasonably based on the evidence that it has.

The Basis for the CAS Going to Court: A Child Being In Need Of Protection

Children's Aid Societies are not allowed to forcibly intervene in a family's life just because the agency, represented by one of its social workers, feels that it could do a better job of parenting the children. Before a court can make a final order either placing a child into the care of a children's aid society or allowing that children's aid society to intrude in the family on an ongoing basis, the court must find, as a matter of fact, that the child was in need of protection by the children's aid society to ensure that child's welfare. The onus is a little easier on the children's aid society while its investigation is ongoing. However, before a court can make a temporary order placing a child in the care of a children's aid society or allowing the children's aid society to continue to intrude in the family, the agency must still convince a judge both that there are reasonable grounds on which to believe that the child is in need of protection by the

---

[465] *Child and Family Services Act*, R.S.O. 1990, c. C.11, s. 46(1).

John P. Schuman, C.S., Family Lawyer, Mediator and Arbitrator

children's aid society, and that no less intrusive order will protect the child from harm.

For a judge to find that a child is "in need of protection" the judge must believe that the child was actually harmed, or was at risk of being harmed in a limited number of ways. The list in Section 37 (2) of the *Child and Family Services Act* is exhaustive, meaning that if a child's circumstances do not fall into one of the categories in that section, then the child is not "in need of protection" and the court cannot make a final order in favour of the children's aid society.

There are 12 types of circumstances that would lead a court to find that a child is in need of protection:[466]

1. the child has been physically harmed by a caregiver, either intentionally or by the caregiver failing to adequately care for the child;
2. the child is at risk of physical harm by a caregiver, either intentionally or by the caregiver failing to adequately care for the child;
3. the child has been sexually abused or exploited either by a caregiver, or with the caregiver's knowledge;
4. the child is at risk of being sexually abused or exploited either by a caregiver or with the caregiver's knowledge;
5. the child requires medical or some other form of treatment and the child's caregivers are unable or unwilling to provide that treatment (or allow healthcare professionals to provide it);
6. the child has suffered emotional or psychological harm and the child's caregivers either caused that harm, or were unable to take steps to prevent that harm;
7. the child is at risk of suffering emotional or psychological harm either because of actions of the child's caregivers, or the failure of the child's caregivers to take the steps necessary to protect the child from that harm;
8. the child is likely to suffer emotional or psychological harm that could be prevented by appropriate treatment and the child's caregivers are unable or unwilling to provide that treatment (or allow trained professionals to provide it);

---

[466] This paragraph contains a simplified wording of the statutory grounds for finding a child in need of protection. For the actual wording see: *Child and Family Services Act*, R.S.O. 1990, c. C.11, s. 37(2).

John P. Schuman, C.S., Family Lawyer, Mediator and Arbitrator

9. the child requires treatment for an emotional or psychological condition and the child's caregivers are unable or unwilling to provide that treatment (or allow trained professionals to provide it);
10. the child's caregivers have abandoned the child;
11. the child, who is under 12 years of age, has committed an act that would be considered a serous criminal offence if the child was older, as a result of the child's caregivers failing to provide appropriate supervision for the child; and
12. the parents are unable to care for their child and so are voluntarily placing the child in the care of the children's aid society.

Children Can Be Taken From Their Parents Very Quickly

Children's aid societies have the authority to act rapidly to remove children from their parents care.

A children's aid society must take certain steps if it believes that a child is in one of the circumstances described above such that it is necessary to bring the child into the agency's care. In many cases, a representative of the children's aid society must appear before a Justice of the Peace with a sworn affidavit. The children's aid society must convince the Justice of the Peace that there are reasonable and probable grounds to believe that:

1. the child is in one of the twelve circumstances described above that make a child "in need of protection," and
2. there is no less restrictive course of action, other than placing the child in the care of the children's aid society, that will adequately protect the child.[467]

If the Justice of the Peace is satisfied that those conditions have been met, he or she will issue a warrant to apprehend the child, which allows the children's aid society to take the child away from the child's parents or immediate caregivers.

---

[467] *Child and Family Services Act*, R.S.O. 1990, c. C.11, s. 40(2).

John P. Schuman, C.S., Family Lawyer, Mediator and Arbitrator

However, if the children's aid society believes that there is a real risk that the child will be harmed in the time that it takes to appear before a Justice of the Peace, a child protection worker employed by the children's aid society can apprehend the child without obtaining a warrant.[468]

When a child protection worker is attempting to apprehend a child with a warrant, the worker has authority to enter onto private property and search that private property to locate and remove the child.[469]

After the children's aid society apprehends a child, it can then place the child in a foster home, a hospital, with one of the child's extended relatives, with another member of the child's community, or in the home of another person whose home has been assessed as being a safe environment for the child (usually a group home).[470] These options are called "places of safety" for the child.

Who Can Ask to Care for Kids: People Entitled to Participate at Child Protection Court

Whenever a children's aid society starts a Court Application in relation to the protection of a child, the following people are automatically parties to the court proceeding[471]:

1. the children's aid society;
2. the child's biological or adoptive mother and any people who are believed to be, or have accepted the role of, the child's biological or adoptive father;
3. any person having legal custody of the child, or who has a legal right of access to the child;
4. any person who has, for the previous 12 months, demonstrated a settled intention to treat the child as a child of his or her family; and
5. if the child is Native Canadian, a representative from the child's First Nation or native community.

---

[468] *Child and Family Services Act*, R.S.O. 1990, c. C.11, s. 40(7).
[469] *Child and Family Services Act*, R.S.O. 1990, c. C.11, s. 40(6).
[470] *Child and Family Services Act*, R.S.O. 1990, c. C.11, s. 37(1) (5).
[471] *Child and Family Services Act*, R.S.O. 1990, c. C.11, s. 37(1), 39(1).

John P. Schuman, C.S., Family Lawyer, Mediator and Arbitrator

Foster parents are not automatically parties in a child protection proceeding. This law is in place to avoid a custody fight between the foster parents and the biological or adoptive parents.

In addition to the people listed above, any person who has cared for the child continuously during the six months before court (including a foster parent), is entitled to notice of the court proceedings, to be present at the court (with a lawyer) and to make submissions to the court. However, no order can be made in favour or against these people unless the court decides it should add them as parties to the proceeding[472].

Allowing Children to Have a Voice in Their Future in Child Protection Proceedings

As much as child protection proceedings are court proceedings between the state and parents, they are also court proceedings between the state and the affected children. The outcome of the proceedings will determine whether the children are permitted to have an ongoing relationship with their parents, and where the child will reside. Obviously, these are very important matters for a child.

If the child who is the subject of the proceeding is over 12 years old, he or she has the right to receive notice of the proceedings, and to be present at court[473]. However, if a judge believes that a child over 12 years old would be emotionally harmed by coming to court, the judge can order that the child not receive notice or attend at court. A child who is the subject of the proceeding and who is under 12 years old is not allowed to have notice of the proceedings or come to court unless a judge grants the child permission. Before giving permission, the judge must consider whether the child is capable of understanding the court proceedings and will not suffer emotional harm by being present[474]. Regardless of whether a child is allowed to attend court, he or she is allowed to have a lawyer[475]. The Government of Ontario provides free

---

[472] *Child and Family Services Act*, R.S.O. 1990, c. C.11, s. 39(3). For a discussion of when a person should be made a party to a child protection proceeding see *Catholic Children's Aid Society of Toronto v. S. (R.D.)* (2008), 55 R.F.L. (6th) 132, available at www.devrylaw.ca/ccas-v-rds/ .
[473] *Child and Family Services Act*, R.S.O. 1990, c. C.11, s. 39(4).
[474] *Child and Family Services Act*, R.S.O. 1990, c. C.11, s. 39(5).
[475] *Child and Family Services Act*, R.S.O. 1990, c. C.11, s. 38(1).

John P. Schuman, C.S., Family Lawyer, Mediator and Arbitrator

lawyers for children who are the subject of child protection proceedings. The Office of the Children's Lawyer provides that representation[476].

Meeting With a Judge Right After the Kids Are Taken Away

If the children's aid society apprehends a child and keeps that child in its care, then the children's aid society must bring the matter before the court within five days[477].

Sometimes the children's aid society does not feel that it is necessary to apprehend a child. Instead, the agency feels that the child can remain in the care of their parents, another family member, or another person who is caring for the child, if there is a court order requiring the parents, or other people caring for the child, to abide by certain court-ordered terms. When the children's aid society seeks such an order, the parent, or other people who are caring for the child have up to 30 days to respond to the children's aid society's Court Application[478]. However, if within those 30 days the children's aid society decides that it is necessary to bring the child in the court case into its care, the agency may still apprehend the child. The children's aid society must apprehend the children pursuant to the procedure described above and there must be a court appearance within five days from the date when the child was apprehended.

Every time the matter is before the court, including the first court appearance in less than five days after apprehension, the judge must make the least intrusive order that protects the safety of the child[479]. Until the trial, or an agreement that the child is in "need of protection", the judge should not hear evidence, or consider, what order would be in the child's best interest[480]. The judge is not allowed to determine what order in the child's best interest until after the judge has determined the child is in need of protection[481]. This is to prevent the judge from being influenced by a good plan for the child's care that is only available if the court finds that the child is in need of protection.

---

[476] For information on the Office of the Children's Lawyer see:
http://www.attorneygeneral.jus.gov.on.ca/english/family/ocl/
[477] *Child and Family Services Act*, R.S.O. 1990, c. C.11, s. 46(1).
[478] *Family Law Rules*, Rule 33(1).
[479] *Child and Family Services Act*, R.S.O. 1990, c. C.11, s. 1(2)2., 51(3),(3.1).
[480] *Child and Family Services Act*, R.S.O. 1990, c. C.11, s. 50(2).
[481] *Child and Family Services Act*, R.S.O. 1990, c. C.11, s. 57(1).

John P. Schuman, C.S., Family Lawyer, Mediator and Arbitrator

Parents can get a big advantage if they can get themselves prepared to present a good argument that the child can be protected by a less intrusive order than the child being in the care of the children's aid society. The longer a child has been in the custody of the children's aid society, the harder it can be to get the child back into the care of the parents. There is much to be gained by doing a lot of very intensive work very quickly to argue that the child should be returned to the parents, or somebody else, at the first appearance.

After the first appearance, the child protection proceedings proceed in a manner that is very similar to the process described in Part 1 of this guide. The only exception is that there is generally no Case Conference in child protection proceedings. There are usually few, or no, procedural motions. However, there are Temporary Care and Custody Hearings, which are motions to temporarily change the child's placement (usually out of the care of the children's aid society) before trial. The legal test at such hearings is always: what is the least intrusive order that protects the child[482]? The onus is always on the children's aid society to show that the order it is seeking is the least intrusive order possible.

It is Nobody Else's Business: Child Protection Matters Are Private

Child Protection Proceedings are private proceedings. Members of the public, who are not one of the people listed above, are not allowed in the courtroom[483]. Members of the media are allowed in the courtroom, but their access is restricted[484]. Under no circumstances is anyone allowed to permit any information that identifies the child, who is the subject of the proceedings, to become public information[485].

You Are Entitled to Know: Important Rules for Disclosure

The rules with regard to disclosure are different in child protection proceedings than in custody/access proceedings. This is because, since child protection proceedings are court proceedings between "the state" and ordinary people, the Canadian Charter of Rights and Freedoms applies. The stakes are high in these proceedings, as they may result in parents and children never being able to see each other again. They are very much like the children's aid society prosecuting

---

[482] *Child and Family Services Act*, R.S.O. 1990, c. C.11, s. 1(2)2., 51(3),(3.1).
[483] *Child and Family Services Act*, R.S.O. 1990, c. C.11, s. 45(4), as amended.
[484] *Child and Family Services Act*, R.S.O. 1990, c. C.11, s. 45(5)-(7).
[485] *Child and Family Services Act*, R.S.O. 1990, c. C.11, s. 45(8).

parents for child abuse or neglect. For these reasons, the rules of disclosure in child protection proceedings are similar to those that apply in criminal proceedings.

In child protection proceedings, the parties are allowed to question[486] each other at any time, on any issue, and they do not require the courts permission[487].

Further, the Charter requires that the children's aid society provide prompt, complete, accurate, and ongoing disclosure of all parts of its file that are not covered by solicitor-client privilege[488]. The children's aid society is required to disclose everything, including notes, communications and professional reports that do not support the children's aid society's case, and that upon which the children's aid society would not rely on at trial.

Parents are not restricted to receiving disclosure on only one occasion. They are entitled to receive ongoing disclosure for as long as they are involved with the children's aid society so that they can know and understand the basis for the children's aid society's position, and the weaknesses of that position at all times. The Respondents to the child protection proceeding are also entitled to know if there have been any changes in circumstances (to start their proceedings) that affect what the final outcome should be.

It is crucially important for the Respondents in a child protection proceeding to obtain and review disclosure from the children's aid society throughout the course of the proceedings. That disclosure not only allows the parties to better understand the children's aid society's position, but also to understand the problems with that position. Receiving disclosure is a crucial part of the parents putting together their best defence to the children's aid society's allegations, and coming up with the best possible plan to have a child return to their care. Parents, preferably through their lawyer, should obtain disclosure from the children's aid society early and review it often to obtain the best possible results in their case.

---

[486] Formal Questioning takes place at a court reporter's office to allow a transcript to be prepared for the judge to read. The right to question includes the right to cross-examine. Rule 20(2) of the *Family Law Rules*.
[487] Rule 20(3) of the *Family Law Rules*.
[488] *Children's Aid Society of London & Middlesex v. D.(S.)* (2008), 300 DLR (4th) 123 at para 8 (S.C.J.).

John P. Schuman, C.S., Family Lawyer, Mediator and Arbitrator

The parties in a child protection proceeding should take advantage of their right to question the other party and use it as part of the disclosure process. Questioning allows a party to fully understand the other side's disclosure and the other side's position before the court.

What the Judge Can See and When: The Rules of Evidence are Different in Child Protection Proceedings

Court proceedings, and individual court appearances, generally have strict rules of evidence. The court is only allowed to rely on evidence that meets the criteria for being admissible. For example, "hearsay", which means words said by someone outside of the courtroom as described by a witness in the courtroom, is generally not admissible in court proceedings. There are also other rules such as that witnesses must take an oath or make a solemn affirmation to tell the truth if their words are to be admitted as evidence[489]. These rules are meant to ensure that the court makes the decisions on accurate information as the parties have the opportunity to challenge each other's evidence.

The usual rules of evidence do not apply in the early stages of child protection proceedings. Whenever a court makes a decision about where a child should be placed until trial, a decision that the judge must make in every appearance, the *Child and Family Services Act* allows the judge to rely on information that is "credible and trustworthy", but would not otherwise be admissible as evidence[490]. This allows the children's aid society, or any other party, to rely on hearsay or statements that were not made under oath or affirmation. This is to prevent children being returned to a place where they might be in danger just because the society was not able to put together evidence that meets all the usual rules in the short time period before the children's placement must be reviewed by a court.

At the trial of a child protection matter, the ordinary rules of evidence apply with only a few modifications. The trial judge is not able to rely on information that is just "credible and trustworthy." In addition to evidence that would be admitted in any other case, a judge at a child protection trial can consider evidence regarding a person's past conduct toward children. That evidence might include written reports or a decision in criminal court[491]. While

---

[489] *Evidence Act*, R.S.O. 1990, c. E-23, s. 16-18, as amended.
[490] *Child and Family Services Act*, R.S.O. 1990, c. C.11, s. 1(2)2., 51(7).
[491] *Child and Family Services Act*, R.S.O. 1990, c. C.11, s. 1(2)2., 50(1).

the usual rules of evidence apply in a child protection trial, they may apply in unique ways because of the issues at the trial.

Deciding the Child's Future at Trial

In child protection proceedings, trials come up very fast. When a child is in the children's aid society care, the trial to determine that child's placement is supposed to occur within four months of the apprehension[492]. The parties must start preparing for trial very early in the process. The parties must also decide whether a trial is necessary or they can agree on what court order the court should make.

In the first trial that occurs after a child has been apprehended, the court must determine two things:

1. Whether the child is in need of protection such that it is necessary for the court to make an order to protect the child;[493] and
2. If the child is in need of protection, what court order is in the child's best interest[494]. If the court does not find that the child is in need of protection, the court cannot make a court order placing the child in the care of the children's aid society or somebody else, and it cannot make an order permitting a children's aid society to supervise the placement or impose any other terms on the child's parents. If the court does not find that a child is in need of protection, all of the court orders end, which means that if the child was in the care of someone other than the people who had custody of the child at the time of the apprehension, the child must be immediately returned to whoever had custody of the child immediately before the apprehension.

The finding that a child is in need of protection is an important turning point in the child protection proceedings. As discussed above, before the court makes that finding, the court is required to make the least intrusive order possible that still protects the child. The children's aid society must show that the child cannot be protected if the child is returned to his or her parents or another family member. After the protection finding, the court looks at what

---

[492] *Child and Family Services Act*, R.S.O. 1990, c. C.11, s. 1(2)2., 52. Rule 33(1) of the *Family Law Rules*.
[493] *Child and Family Services Act*, R.S.O. 1990, c. C.11, s. 57(1).
[494] *Child and Family Services Act*, R.S.O. 1990, c. C.11, s. 57(1).

John P. Schuman, C.S., Family Lawyer, Mediator and Arbitrator

order is in the child's best interests. There is no longer a presumption that the child should be returned to his or her parents, if at all possible.

There Are Only a Few Orders a Court Can Make When a Child is in Need of Protection

Once a child has been found to in need of protection, a court can make one of the following eight types of orders:

1. return the child to the parents care without any further order for supervision[495];
2. place the child back in the parents care, but under the supervision of the children's aid society, and with terms that the parents must follow. Such an order must last between three and twelve months;
3. place the child in the care and custody of another person other than the parents (or other person who had custody immediately before the apprehension). Again, this order lasts between three and twelve months;
4. place the child temporarily in the care of the children's aid society (which is called a Society Wardship order). This type of order also lasts between three and twelve months, but is subject to additional limitations, as described below;
5. an order that represents a combination of options 2, 3 and 4, above[496];
6. a permanent order granting custody of the child to a person. This order would have the same effect as making a final custody order in Family Law proceedings between two people (the types of proceedings described in Parts 1 through 3 of this guide);[497]
7. place the child permanently in the care of the children's aid society (by making a cru Order) with visits (or access) permitted between the child and the parent;[498] and

---

[495] *Child and Family Services Act*, R.S.O. 1990, c. C.11, s. 57(9).
[496] *Child and Family Services Act*, R.S.O. 1990, c. C.11, s. 57(1).
[497] *Child and Family Services Act*, R.S.O. 1990, c. C.11, s. 57.1(1). This order cannot be made if it would conflict with an order for custody of the child made pursuant to the *Divorce Act* or if there would be conflict between orders of different levels of court: *Child and Family Services Act*, R.S.O. 1990, c. C.11, s. 57.1(6).
[498] *Child and Family Services Act*, R.S.O. 1990, c. C.11, s. 57(1) and 59(1).

8. place the child permanently in the care of the children's aid society (by making a Crown Wardship Order), but without allowing any further access between the child and his or her parents[499].

If the court makes either of the last two orders, the child is available to be adopted.[500] However, if the society does place a child for adoption, any order that allows on-going visits between the child and the parents ends.[501] That means there will be no further contact between the child and his or her original parents unless the adoptive parents agree to continue the visits[502] or the original parents get an "Openness Order". To get an Openness Order the original parents must start a new court application within 30 days of receiving notice the child will be placed for adoption.[503] A children's aid society cannot place a child with a family to be adopted until it can advise whether the original family is seeking an Openness Order.[504] The proposed adoptive parents do not have to decide whether to accept a specific child into their home for adoption until they know whether they are required to maintain contact between the child and the child's original family.

The court will only allow ongoing contact between the child and the original parents if the following three conditions are met:

1. the Openness Order is in the best interests of the child;
2. the Openness Order will permit the continuation of a relationship with a person that is beneficial and meaningful to the child; and
3. the child has consented to the order, if he or she is 12 years of age or older.[505]

---

[499] *Child and Family Services Act*, R.S.O. 1990, c. C.11, s. 57(1).
[500] *Child and Family Services Act*, R.S.O. 1990, c. C.11, s. 141.1(1) as amended.
[501] *Child and Family Services Act*, R.S.O. 1990, c. C.11, s. 143(1) as amended.
[502] *Child and Family Services Act*, R.S.O. 1990, c. C.11, s. 153.6(1) as amended.
[503] *Child and Family Services Act*, R.S.O. 1990, c. C.11, s. 145.1.2 (1) as amended.
[504] *Child and Family Services Act*, R.S.O. 1990, c. C.11, s. 145.1.2 (3) as amended.
[505] *Child and Family Services Act*, R.S.O. 1990, c. C.11, s. 145.1.2 (6) as amended.

John P. Schuman, C.S., Family Lawyer, Mediator and Arbitrator

How the Judge Decides What Final Order is Right to Protect a Child

In deciding what type of order the court should make, the judge must make the order that is in the child's best interest. However, in reaching that decision, the judge is required to consider:

1. that it may not place the child with someone other than the person who had care of the child at the time of apprehension, unless returning the child would not adequately protect the child;[506]
2. before making an order for Society Wardship or Crown Wardship, whether it is possible to place the child with a relative, neighbour or other member of the child's community[507]. The court must make such a placement, if at all possible, where the child has Native Canadian Heritage[508];
3. whether the child's best interests require that the court stop access between the child and any members of the child's family or community. The presumption is that access will continue unless it is not in the child's best interest[509]; and
4. what efforts the children's aid society made to assist the family to overcome the concerns raised by the agency[510].

There are strict time limits that may result in the court being unable to make some of the orders described above. A child who under six years old can only be in a Society Ward (temporarily in the care of the children's aid society) for less than twelve months in total (regardless of how many individual times the child has been in the care of the children's aid society). Children age six years old and older, cannot be society wards for periods of time that total more than twenty-four months. Once the child has been in the children's aid society's care for that period of time, whether consecutively or non-consecutively, the court must either return the child to his or her parents, or make the child a Crown Ward, which permanently ends the legal parent-child relationship that existed before the apprehension[511].

---

[506] *Child and Family Services Act*, R.S.O. 1990, c. C.11, s. 57(3).
[507] *Child and Family Services Act*, R.S.O. 1990, c. C.11, s. 57(4).
[508] *Child and Family Services Act*, R.S.O. 1990, c. C.11, s. 57(5).
[509] *Child and Family Services Act*, R.S.O. 1990, c. C.11, s. 59(1).
[510] *Child and Family Services Act*, R.S.O. 1990, c. C.11, s. 57(2).
[511] *Child and Family Services Act*, R.S.O. 1990, c. C.11, s. 70.

John P. Schuman, C.S., Family Lawyer, Mediator and Arbitrator

Checking if the Child is Okay: Reviewing the Child's Status

Where the court makes an order placing the child in the care of a person subject to the supervision of the children's aid society or in the care of the children's aid society for a period of time (but not indefinitely), then the court must review the child's situation[512]. When the court has made the child a Crown Ward, but the children's aid society has not managed to place the child for adoption, the child or any of the parties to the original court proceeding can ask the court to review the child's situation[513]. The process for reviewing the child's situation is called a Status Review Application.

At the Status Review Application, the court does not determine whether the child is still in need of protection. It only has to decide what further order is in the child's best interest. While the types of orders that a court can make on a status review are not identical to those that the court can make after the first trial, they are very similar[514]. If the parties cannot agree to an order, then another trial is necessary.

The Status Review process is not available after the child, who has been made a Crown Ward, is placed for adoption[515].

The Last Chance: Appeals

As with other Family Law matters, appeals are permitted in child protection matters. The procedure for the appeal is the same as for other Family Law matters, with the following changes:

1. The Superior Court of Justice hears appeals from orders made in the Ontario Court of Justice. Appeals from the Family Court of the Superior Court of Justice go to the Divisional Court[516].
2. The timeline for filing a Notice of Appeal and perfecting the appeal are shortened in Child Protection Appeals[517].
3. Child Protection Appeals are to be heard quickly – within 60 days of the parties filing their materials for the appeal[518].

---

[512] *Child and Family Services Act*, R.S.O. 1990, c. C.11, s. 64.
[513] *Child and Family Services Act*, R.S.O. 1990, c. C.11, s. 65.1
[514] *Child and Family Services Act*, R.S.O. 1990, c. C.11, s. 65(1) and 65.2(1).
[515] *Child and Family Services Act*, R.S.O. 1990, c. C.11, s. 65.1(9)
[516] *Courts of Justice Act*, R.S.O. c-43, s. 21.9.1.
[517] Rules 38(2) and 38(22) of the *Family Law Rules*.
[518] Rule 38(24) of the *Family Law Rules*.

John P. Schuman, C.S., Family Lawyer, Mediator and Arbitrator

4. The *Child and Family Services Act* specifically allows the appeal court to receive fresh evidence in child protection appeals[519]. As a result, the appeal courts expect to receive an update on the child's situation after the trial, but before making a decision on the appeal.
5. Once a child has been placed for adoption, there is no right to appeal the Crown Wardship Order (or any of the temporary orders in the proceeding) that made the adoption possible.[520]
6. There is no public access to the court in child protection appeals[521].
7. The Trial Judge's order regarding the placement of the child is only stayed for 10 days after a party files a Notice of Appeal. However, there can be another Temporary Care and Custody Hearing in that proceeding before the appeal is heard[522].

Avoiding Court: Alternative Dispute Resolution in Child Protection

If a children's aid society is concerned about whether parents are abusing or neglecting children, then the traditional course of action is to start court proceedings as described above. Although everyone in a child protection proceeding is supposed to be working toward the best interest of the children involved, court is an adversarial process that, by its nature, can inhibit cooperation between the children's aid society and the parents. Court can also be very expensive for all the parties.

The *Child and Family Services Act* promotes two alternatives for addressing child welfare concerns outside of court. The first is voluntary agreements between the parents and the children's aid society. The second is alternative dispute resolution, usually in the form of child protection mediation. In addition, disputes between foster parents or adoptive parents and a children's aid society, or complaints about the society's conduct, are directed to the Child and Family Services Review Board, rather than court[523]. That board tries to keep its hearings less formal and less adversarial then court.

---

[519] *Child and Family Services Act*, R.S.O., c. C-11, s. 69(6).
[520] *Child and Family Services Act*, R.S.O., c. C-11, s. 69(5).
[521] *Child and Family Services Act*, R.S.O., c. C-11, s. 69(8).
[522] *Child and Family Services Act*, R.S.O., c. C-11, s. 69(3)(4)
[523] *Child and Family Services Act*, R.S.O. 1990. c. C-11, s. 68, 144, as amended.

John P. Schuman, C.S., Family Lawyer, Mediator and Arbitrator

If a children's aid society does not believe that immediate intervention is necessary to protect a child from serious harm, it will usually tell the parents the concerns before going to court. If the parents are willing to cooperate with the children's aid society, then the society may decide it is not necessary to go to court. However, to give the children's aid society some reassurance that the parents will continue to cooperate, the agency usually asks the parents to sign an agreement. There are two types of agreements: Voluntary Service Agreements and Temporary Care Agreements.

Voluntary Service Agreements are an agreement to provide services to the family and the children with the children remaining in the home. They set out what services the Society will provide and what measures the parents will take to address the Society's concerns. These agreements have terms similar to what a court might order, but are negotiated between the parents and society allowing both to have more control over the terms than an order imposed by a judge.

If the children's aid society and the parents agree that the children can only be protected if the children are in the care of the children's aid society, then they sign a Temporary Care Agreement[524]. Temporary Care Agreements place a child in the care of the children's aid society for a period of up to six months in the same way that a court order can. The agreement can be extended after six months, but only to a maximum of twelve months[525]. A child over the age of twelve must be a party to a Temporary Care Agreement and no such agreement can be made with respect to a child who is more than sixteen years old[526].

The children's aid society, a parent, or a child over the age of twelve can terminate a Temporary Care Agreement on five days notice to the other parties. A party can terminate the agreement for any reason, although children's aid societies usually terminate agreements either because the parents have fully satisfied all the concerns or the parents are not abiding by the agreement. The five-day notice period allows the children's aid society to apprehend the child upon receiving notice of the termination and have the matter back in court before the child leaves the society's care. A judge can then order that the child stay where she was under the temporary care agreement.

---

[524] *Child and Family Services Act*, R.S.O. 1990. c. C-11, s. 29, as amended.
[525] *Child and Family Services Act*, R.S.O. 1990. c. C-11, s. 29(5).
[526] *Child and Family Services Act*, R.S.O. 1990. c. C-11, s. 29(2).

John P. Schuman, C.S., Family Lawyer, Mediator and Arbitrator

In 2006, the Ontario Government recognized that the adversarial court process might not facilitate cooperation between parents, children's aid societies and other interested parties to protect the best interests of children. It changed the *Child and Family Services Act* to require children's aid societies to consider whether alternative dispute resolution processes, such as mediation or a traditional native dispute resolution process used by a child's band, could assist in resolving any issues related to a child who is, or may be, in need of protection[527]. ADR can be used in child protection even if the matter is before the court. The *Child and Family Services Act* specifically allows judges to adjourn cases to allow the parties to attempt ADR[528]. However, the court cannot order the parties, or a child, to use alternative dispute resolution[529]. The process is entirely voluntary.

Despite the specific legislated direction to children's aid societies to use mediation and other forms of alternative dispute resolution, the establishment of funding for such programs, and the apparent benefits to moving to a non-adversarial process to address child protection concerns, the use of child protection ADR has not caught on[530]. In some areas, children's aid societies have only been willing to agree to mediation if the mediator is sympathetic to the agency. Parents, or other parties, who want to go to try to resolve child protection concerns in a less adversarial way have to insist on mediation by a skilled, objective mediator. Use of such processes may prevent the risk of additional harm to the child associated with court fights.

---

[527] *Child and Family Services Act*, R.S.O. 1990. c. C-11, s. 20/2, as amended.
[528] *Child and Family Services Act*, R.S.O. 1990. c. C-11, s. 51.1, 153.1(10), as amended.
[529] *Child and Family Services Act*, R.S.O. 1990. c. C-11, s. 51.1, 153.1(10), as amended.
[530] Melissa Phillips, *Child Protection Mediation in Ontario: Conquering the Barriers to a Viable and Critical Method of Dispute Resolution* at page 8, available at: http://www.riverdalemediation.com/pdfs/articles/Child_Protection_Mediation_in_Ontario.pdf

John P. Schuman, C.S., Family Lawyer, Mediator and Arbitrator

Sharing the Love and Growing a Family: Adoption

Adoption gives a child a new family. The effect of an Adoption Order is to make the child, for all purposes of law, the child of the adoptive parents. The Adoption Order ends the legal parent-child relationship between the biological parent and the child[531]. An Adoption Order also ends any right of access between the child and any other person[532]. This includes the right to inherit, as a child's original parents will cease to be the child's parents after the Adoption Order. There are processes to allow a continued relationship between the child and his or her original family after the adoption. Everyone affected, including the child, has an opportunity to respond to the request[533]. The order permitting that continued relationship must be in place before the Adoption Order is made[534]. Adoptive parents cannot be forced to allow visits that they did not know would occur at the time they accepted the child into their home.

A child can be adopted by either a family member or a stranger. The process is different, although all adoptions require a court proceeding. Every child over the age of seven years old must give his or her consent to be adopted[535]. Where a child is not a Crown Ward, the adoption requires the consent of every parent to the child, unless it is in the child's best interests that the adoption proceed without a parent's consent, or that parent has received notice of the adoption and chosen not to respond[536].

Stranger Adoptions

There is a different procedure for the adoption of a child by a person who is not a relative of the child or the current spouse of one of the child's parents. That type of adoption requires the involvement of a children's aid society or an

---

[531] *Child and Family Services Act*, R.S.O. 1990, c. C-11, s. 158(2).
[532] *Child and Family Services Act*, R.S.O. 1990, c. C-11, s. 160.
[533] *Child and Family Services Act*, R.S.O. 1990, c. C-11, s. 145.1, 153.6.
[534] *Child and Family Services Act*, R.S.O. 1990, c. C.11, s. 145.1(1), 145.1.1(1), s. 145.1.2(1) as amended.
[535] *Child and Family Services Act*, R.S.O. 1990, c. C-11, s. 137(6). The participation of the Office of the Children's Lawyer is required to ensure that a child (under the age of 18) was fully informed before giving the consent and the consent represents the child's wishes: *Child and Family Services Act*, R.S.O. 1990, c. C-11, s. 137(11).
[536] *Child and Family Services Act*, R.S.O. 1990, c. C-11, s. 137(2) and 138.

John P. Schuman, C.S., Family Lawyer, Mediator and Arbitrator

adoption licensee[537]. In addition, the Ontario Government must approve non-relative adoptions[538].

There is a process by which parents are approved to adopt children. Both children's aid societies and adoption licensees must complete a home study of the proposed adoptive parents[539]. The home study assesses both the ability of the proposed parents to be parents, and the home in which they propose to raise the adopted child or children. The Government of Ontario has set out requirements for home studies. It is not a simple or quick process. The proposed parents must meet with the children's aid society or the adoption licensee several times, provide references, medical reports, police record checks, medical clearance letters, and other materials and information.

When people adopt from a children's aid society, they must also take a course on how to be good adoptive parents. This course serves two purposes: First, it educates the parents. Second, the instructors evaluate the people in the course. That evaluation is part of the assessment of the suitability of the people who want to adopt. Many of the children who are available for adoption through children's aid societies have challenges due to their background. Those challenges mean that adoptive parents must both be special people and have special training to ensure they will grow a close and loving family. Even though children's aid societies run these courses several times each year, there is often a waiting list to get into them. However, they do form an important part of the process of preparing and evaluating people who want to adopt children from children's aid societies.

Once the home study is completed, the children's aid society or adoption licensee places the child with the proposed adoptive parents for at least six months to make sure the placement works for both the adoptive parents and the child. After that period, the children's aid society or the licensee must report to the Government of Ontario regarding the apparent success of the placement. Only when the Government of Ontario approves the adoption

---

[537] An adoption licensee is a person approved by the Government of Ontario to oversee "private adoptions", which are adoptions that are not the adoption of Crown Wards from a children's aid society.
[538] *Child and Family Services Act*, R.S.O. 1990, c. C-11, s. 141(1)(4).
[539] *Child and Family Services Act*, R.S.O. 1990, c. C-11, s. 142(1) and 149(1).

placement can the proposed adoptive parents apply to the court for an Adoption Order[540].

Relative Adoptions

The spouse of a child's parent or a relative can also apply to adopt a child. The idea is to create a stronger, and more permanent, legal relationship between the child and the family member. In making such an Adoption Order, the judge must still agree that it is in the child's best interests[541]. These adoptions do not require the involvement of a children's aid society, or an adoption licensee. They also do not require the approval of the Government of Ontario[542]. Further, relative adoptions do not require a home study report or a report on the child's adjustment to the new home. However, a judge can require those reports to be completed before making an Adoption Order[543].

Relative adoptions still require the consent of every parent to the child and the consent of the child (if that child is over six years old), unless a judge decides that the consent is not required.

Adoptions are a very technical area of law. Private adoptions (those not involving a children's aid society) and relative adoptions require the assistance of a lawyer. It is not common for people adopting from children's aid societies to have their own lawyers unless problems arise with the adoption. If a potential adoptive parent has been approved to adopt a particular child, and the children's aid society or the adoption licensee decides not to proceed with the adoption, that potential parent may have remedies available[544]. That person should discuss their situation with a lawyer familiar with adoption law.

---

[540] *Child and Family Services Act*, R.S.O. 1990, c. C-11, s. 149.
[541] *Child and Family Services Act*, R.S.O. 1990, c. C-11, s. 146(2).
[542] *Child and Family Services Act*, R.S.O. 1990, c. C-11, s. 141(1)(4).
[543] *Child and Family Services Act*, R.S.O. 1990, c. C-11, s. 149(6).
[544] *Child and Family Services Act*, R.S.O. 1990, c. C-11, s. 144.

John P. Schuman, C.S., Family Lawyer, Mediator and Arbitrator

Conclusion: Avoid Saying "I Should Have Done That" – Know Your Options from the Beginning

This guide discusses some of life's most stressful events. These events are stressful, because they involve making big decisions. Not having all of the necessary information to make a big decision makes that process even more stressful. Very few people, essentially all of them Family Lawyers, know how the law affects decisions to live together, get married, create a marriage contract, separate or divorce, or respond to allegations of child abuse/neglect. This guide has covered the basic law that people should know when making any of those important decisions. Many clients have shown up at their lawyers' offices and said, "I wish I had known that before I made the decision." This guide has discussed most of the common major mistakes that people make and how to avoid them.

Separation Does Not Necessarily Mean War

Perhaps the most important lesson to be learned from Part 1, which covered the steps to take after separating, is that there are options. Separating does not automatically mean that former partners have to go to court, or that they have to spend a lot of money. However, it does mean that each partner should go and see a lawyer, independently, to get advice. Going to court to resolve matters should only be reserved for the most difficult and bitter fights. It is expensive both emotionally and financially. The court process can also leave long lasting emotional and financial scars.

Separating spouses or parents can make their lives easier if they commit themselves to avoiding a bitter fight. They may not agree on some issues, but that does not mean they need to go to war. Most issues can be resolved between people who want to a friendly resolution through negotiation; although sometimes a mediator or the Collaborative Practice process is necessary to help those negotiations. Separated spouses who want to work

John P. Schuman, C.S., Family Lawyer, Mediator and Arbitrator

things out without a battle should be able to resolve all the issues between them, or at least be able to determine very discrete issues that they need to submit to an arbitrator to decide in a peaceful, non-destructive manner.

Separation Does Not Have to Hurt the Kids

Research shows that children are not necessarily negatively impacted by a divorce. Children are negatively impacted by conflict between their parents during a divorce. The more intense that conflict, the more the children are harmed and the longer that harm lasts. Protecting the children is another good reason to carefully consider the process options after separation.

The impact of separation and divorce on children can also be lessened when the parents listen to advice of professionals. Parents may want to speak to a psychologist, psychiatrist, social worker or parenting coordinator about the situation facing their children. There is also written advice available to separated parents, the best of which can be found in the Where to Find Out More appendix of this guide.

Knowing the Law Helps a Lot

The discussion of Family Law in this guide should make it clear why courts give little or no weight to a separation agreement if the parties did not have Independent Legal Advice. There are a lot of misconceptions about Family Law. Those misconceptions can result in spouses or parents making bad decisions that they resent later. This guide has covered the most common mistakes that separated partners make and the traps into which they fall.

Knowing the law can also help to resolve issues between separated partners. Some matters that are not controversial in law and so should not result in a fight. For example, when parents of minor children separate, one of those parents will have to pay child support to the other. The exceptions to that rule are very, very rare. It is not a matter worth fighting over. The parties should simply exchange income information and calculate what support is owed between them. The equalization of party's net family properties should also be a straightforward, simple calculation. If the parties exchange the documents showing the value of their assets and liabilities on the date of marriage and the date of separation the calculation can be done quickly. If there is a dispute about the value of an asset or liability it should not be difficult to ask someone make that determination.

When a separated spouse comes to see in a lawyer for an initial consult knowing the financial position of both parties and able to explain, accurately, what the family arrangements were during the marriage, the Family Lawyer can tell that spouse what the final settlement should look like. In almost all cases that advice will be very similar to what a judge orders after a long, bitter court fight. Knowing the law and consulting a lawyer right from the beginning can make life much easier. Parties who want to fight can still to do so, but if they want to fight, they probably also want to win. Hopefully this guide tells separated spouses what position and actions will win a battle in Family Court. Appendix A of this guide details what steps a party can take to lose a Family Court case.

Marriage Contracts Say Good Things about a Marriage

Negotiating a marriage contract is not romantic. However, most couples who negotiate a marriage contract should feel good about their marriage. If the marriage contract was negotiated fairly, then the couple has given some serious thoughts about what it means to be married. They are not entering the marriage blindly without fully understanding what they are getting into. By negotiating a marriage contract before getting married, the couple has already had to work through some difficult issues. Successfully negotiating a marriage contract is an indication that the couple will be able to successfully resolve other difficult issues that come up during the marriage. In addition, as an important goal of marriage contract is to avoid disputes over financial matters after separation. The couple has already committed themselves to trying to resolve difficult issues between them on a friendly basis. That commitment says good things about the likely success of the marriage.

Parents With a Little Bit of Knowledge Keep Their Kid in Child Protection Cases

Doing the right thing from the very beginning can have a big impact in child protection cases. Fortunately, those cases are very rare. Not many people have to know what to do in a child protection proceeding. However the start of a child protection proceeding represents a true emergency. Even in, perhaps especially in, emergencies it is critically important to do the right thing. In those cases, the parties must cooperate and gather as much information from each other as possible, on an ongoing basis, to get the best result. It is easy to lose a child protection case but this guide has provided the essential information necessary to prevent that from happening.

John P. Schuman, C.S., Family Lawyer, Mediator and Arbitrator

Last Thoughts

Family Court Judges often remark about how little the people before them know about Family Law and the Family Court process. Separated spouses often comment they would have done things differently had they known more right when their marriage ended. Very often, Family Lawyers tell clients that they could have done much more to help the client if the client had come in sooner. This guide has discussed very stressful life events. People in stressful situations can only make good decisions if they have the information they need. This book, and advice from a Family Law lawyer, provide the critical information that can make things much better for separated couples and their children.

John P. Schuman, C.S., Family Lawyer, Mediator and Arbitrator

Appendix A: 10 Guaranteed, Sure-Fire Ways to Anger a Judge or Otherwise Blow Your Case in Family Court

1. Involve the Kids in the Fight

Doctors, social workers, psychologists, mediators, counsellors, teachers, principals, swimming lesson instructors, camp counsellors, judges, lawyers and every other professional who works with kids, will tell you that involving the kids in the divorce hurts them. It can actually negatively affect a child's brain development. Nothing angers a judge more than one parent involving the children in the fight. The children should not even know there is a dispute between their parents. All they need to know is what the new situation is when the dispute is over.

2. Don't Pay Child Support

"Child Support is the Right of the Child." Judges expect parents to financially support their children. It is not the children's fault that their parents are not living together. If the children are living most of the time with the other parent, you should continue to make sure they have the financial support they need. Judges are very impressed when a parent voluntarily pays child support.

3. Don't Encourage the Kids to Spend Time With A Parent

Unless a children's aid society has been court sanctioned to cut off access to a parent because of abuse, you must find a way for the kids to know both parents. It is a child's legal right to know both parents. Even murderers and rapists get supervised access, because children benefit from knowing their

---

John P. Schuman, C.S., Family Lawyer, Mediator and Arbitrator

parents. Judges actually take custody away from parents who try to destroy the children's relationship with the other parent.

4. Breach or Ignore Court Orders

Judges work very hard to become judges. They are generally well respected for their wisdom and insight. So, judges expect you to give them respect and do what they say. If you do not want a judge to tell you what to do, you should not be in court. When a judge tells you to do something, it is not like another person telling you. When a judge orders you to do something, you are legally required to do it, or you could go to jail.

5. Secretly Hide Money or Transfer Assets

The law will say how the family's money should be divided. Unless you have a marriage contract, a cohabitation agreement or some other form of agreement, you cannot change that. Moving assets to keep the court from giving them to another party is illegal. It shows the court that you are willing to break the rules and you need to be taught a lesson.

6. Lie

Do not think you can get away with lying - especially when the other party has a Family Lawyer. Family Lawyers get very good at finding out when people are lying. Get caught once, and the court will assume everything you say from then on is a lie. That makes it hard to get your way.

7. Choose Not to Use a Lawyer

Not using a lawyer when you are able to sends the court the message that you do not want to listen to professional advice. That is a bad place to start. Then you try to rely on your judgment when you are involved in a very emotional and stressful event. Add to that you do not know the court rules or the law. Plus, if the other party has a lawyer, there is a person helping him or her make you look bad.

8. Refuse to Give Financial Disclosure

By law, in cases involving support or property division, the other side is allowed to know virtually everything about your financial situation and it is your obligation to tell them. If you fail to provide disclosure quickly, judges will assume that either you are hiding your money (see point 5), trying to lie (see

John P. Schuman, C.S., Family Lawyer, Mediator and Arbitrator

point 6), trying to complicate matters or make them more expensive for everyone, or trying to delay. The law gives judges lots of powers to punish people who refuse to provide financial disclosure quickly.

9. Take Every Opportunity to Slam the Other Party

At one point, you had some sort of relationship with the other party and you at least liked them. So you saw some good qualities (unless the other party is a children's aid society, whose role in protecting children is considered pretty respectable). Attacking the other party at every turn makes you seem angry, vindictive and irrational. Who feels sorry for people like that? Not Family Court Judges.

10. Don't Show Up For Court

If you have been served, the court can make an order against you, even if you do not show up. Sticking your head in the sand will not help you. It will only result in the other party getting what they want, because you did not show up to say why that is wrong. Then, even if you were not there, the court can enforce the order against you if you fail to comply with it. It is like the lottery: you cannot possibly win if you do not play. However, if you show up and behave yourself, you have a good chance of doing well in Family court. At the very least, the judge will explain to you why he or she is making the court orders.

John P. Schuman, C.S., Family Lawyer, Mediator and Arbitrator

Appendix B: Top 10 Reasons to Get a Family Law Lawyer

1.   **People with lawyers know whether their position is reasonable** - Both in court and out of court in settlement discussions, if one side's position is not within the range of what is reasonable, it may get him nowhere. That person will lose credibility before a judge. In settlement discussions, the other side ignores unreasonable suggestions. Family Law matters are often emotional and a person's emotions may cloud her judgment. A related point is that every spouse or parent in a family law dispute needs to know what facts and issues are important and which are not. For example, spousal infidelity probably has no bearing on child custody. Child abuse probably has no effect on property issues. Mixing up what is important and what is not can make everything take a lot longer.

2.   **Lawyers tell their clients what to expect, what they are getting and what they are giving up.** In negotiating or deciding on litigation strategy, every person in the dispute needs to know what the possible outcomes are and whether he could do better using a different course of action. One spouse may want to be generous, or she may want to keep as much her spouse as possible. Without speaking to a lawyer, a party will not know whether he is getting a good deal that will last, or whether he could do better or do worse.

3.   **A marriage contract, cohabitation agreement or separation agreement may not be binding without a lawyer.** People who sign a contract usually want it to hold up. They also want to be able to rely on it and be able to have the court enforce the contract. Judges usually ignore domestic contracts if both parties did not have lawyers. Judges are usually suspicious if one party only saw a lawyer for a few hours to get an ILA Certificate. People who want an enforceable contract ensure that lawyers are involved throughout the negotiations.

John P. Schuman, C.S., Family Lawyer, Mediator and Arbitrator

4.   **Lawyers know the court rules.** The court process is complicated. Judges have expectations about how things will be done in court and those expectations may be based on more than just the *Family Law Rules*. However, judges hold self-represented litigants to the same standard as lawyers. This can place self-represented litigants at a disadvantage.

5.   **There may be options that you have not considered.** Family Lawyers see a lot of cases with a lot of resolutions, and they see the application of the laws in a lot of different situations. A lawyer may have ideas about ways to resolve both the case and her client's problems in ways that the parties have not thought about. A lawyer may also be able to ensure that an unusual resolution is respected and enforced by the courts.

6.   **Family Lawyers can help settle a case - and that saves money.** Lawyers are professional negotiators. Family Lawyers represent individual people, not big businesses or corporations, so Family Lawyers know that the cost of the process is important. Family Lawyers have strategies to get their clients the best possible resolution at the lowest cost possible.

7.   **Family Lawyers let their clients get on with their lives.** Relationship breakdowns are disruptive to people's lives. Doing everything that is required for court, or even negotiating a settlement, can take up an astounding amount of time. Even worse, while a person is doing that work, he has to think about his old relationship. A Family Lawyer can take over that work, and the emotional baggage that goes along with it, so the client can look forward and plan for the future rather than focussing on the past.

8.   **Parents involved with a children's aid society need a professional on their side.** A children's aid society has lots of professionals to help it - lawyers, social workers, psychologists, psychiatrists, doctors and others. The children's aid society uses those professionals to get what it wants. Parents may not have any professionals helping them at first. They need a child protection professional on their side. A child protection lawyer can not only advocate for parents in court, but can help find other professionals to help those parents get what they want.

John P. Schuman, C.S., Family Lawyer, Mediator and Arbitrator

9.   **The paperwork is important and it needs to be filled out correctly**. Unlike on television, Family Court Judges rely (heavily) on the paper that the parties file to make their decision. Except at trial, parties do not get to tell their story by speaking to the judge. Each party tells her story by writing it out on the correct court forms, serving it on the other party, and filing it with the court ahead of time. Lawyers take courses, not just on how to fill out the forms correctly, but how to write persuasively. They do this so judges will be sympathetic to their clients, even before those clients walk into the courtroom. Judges often say that they have a good idea of what their decisions will be after reading the documents and before even meeting the parties or their lawyers.

10.   **An unrepresented party may end up paying for the other party's lawyer!** In Canada, the loser in a lawsuit pays some or all of the winner's lawyer's bill. If one person sues another and looses because she did not know what you was doing, the court will order her to pay for the other party's lawyer. If that happens, the person without a lawyer has not saved any money but the other party (with a lawyer) has saved a lot of money.

John P. Schuman, C.S., Family Lawyer, Mediator and Arbitrator

Appendix C: Why Lawyers Charge by the Hour (and Why Cost is Often Impossible to Predict)

Family Lawyers bill by the hour (or part thereof). That means that when they are working on your case or talking to you, they bill based on the amount of time it takes. Lawyers are selling their time as professionals (in much the same way that psychologists and many other professionals do). Except for very few instances, they cannot predict how much something will cost.

At Devry Smith Frank LLP, we charge $1500.00 for a simple uncontested divorce. That covers the costs of serving the divorce documents on the other side, paying all of the court filing fees, paying for the clearance certificate from the federal government, paying the costs we are charged for the court forms, and a bit of the salary for the person who does the work getting it all together. We can do that because there is nothing to fight about, and no variables. Everything is straightforward and predictable.

Some lawyers will also charge a flat rate to do one particular piece of work – such as draft a document or appear in court for one particular appearance. In these cases, the client is retaining the lawyer to do that one piece of work and nothing else. This approach is called a "limited retainer" or "unbundled services." A lawyer can charge a flat fee because the amount of work is known and predictable. The retainer specifically limits the lawyer from doing any other work. So, the lawyer cannot be "forced" or "dragged into" longer involvement or "continuing the fight" without the client agreeing to a separate retainer to cover those separate steps. This approach is attractive to clients who have limited funds and want to chose how best to use them, or clients who want greater control over how much they spend. However, when a lawyer is on a limited retainer, that lawyer must tell the opposing lawyer, the judge, or the arbitrator that the lawyer is working on a limited retainer and will not be participating further. That can decrease the lawyers' impact because there is no "threat" that the lawyer will take a further step for the client.

John P. Schuman, C.S., Family Lawyer, Mediator and Arbitrator

Aside from uncontested divorces and limited retainers, there are very few circumstances when a Family Lawyer (or any lawyer) knows exactly what the cost will be. It is not like replacing a part in your car where the cost of the part and the mechanics time are known. How long your case will take, and thus how expensive it will be, depends on a number of factors. These factors include:

a. how much the parties want to fight. The bigger the battle, the more costly the war;

b. the complexity of the issues. If a party's financial situation is complex, it will take longer to figure out what the appropriate result should be. A lot of legal issues can arise just in determining the income of someone who is self-employed;

c. whether court is required and what court. The courts have a lot of rules to protect people's rights when they are in court proceedings. While those rules ensure fairness, they also result in time-consuming and expensive procedures to follow. Add to this that some courts are very busy, so lawyers and parties have to sit and wait to be heard. When a lawyer cannot be working on other files, because he or she is in court, then it is only fair that the lawyer bill for his or her time in court;

d. if there is a lot of disclosure to be collected from you or the other-side, that can take a lot of time. The more your lawyer has to chase you to get required documents, the more time he or she will spend and the more it will cost;

e. some clients want to speak to their lawyers frequently and for long periods of time. That can be important to allow the client to understand what is going on, and what the options are. However, if you are speaking to your lawyer for long periods of time, that lawyer cannot get work done for other clients. If what you need is someone to talk to about issues that are not legal ones, then it is less expensive to get a counsellor than speak to your lawyer. Your lawyer should always listen to you, but remember that if you are taking up time, you will have to pay for it; and

f. custody and access disputes are very long, very complex, involve lots of witnesses, lots of professionals and lots of legal issues. For those reasons, they are very expensive. Sometimes you have to fight to look after your kids. However, keep in mind that those fights, which are very important, are by their nature, very complicated and expensive.

John P. Schuman, C.S., Family Lawyer, Mediator and Arbitrator

Family Lawyers know that they are not working for corporations with lots of resources. They are working for people at a time when finances are often stretched already. Family Lawyers know that their fees can cause additional problems. Good Family Lawyers are busy. They have lots of people who need them, so they do not need to make cases complicated. Good Family Lawyers know that it is better for the family to resolve the issues as quickly and inexpensively as possible - while still ensuring that their client is not sacrificing too much. That is what is best for the family - and is what is best for the lawyer, because happy clients refer their friends.

Lawyer's hourly fees range widely. Some lawyers are less than $100 per hour. Some are more than $1000.00 per hour. Usually, you get what you pay for. Lawyers who are more than $300.00 per hour tend to be lawyers with experience and know how to deal with complex issues. They also know how to get to a resolution. Lawyers also know good strategies, which in Canada can result in their opponent paying the legal bills for both sides. If you are self-employed, have a trust, have a complex custody issue, or have some wealth, it is worth your while to find a lawyer who knows how to address those issues. Having a good lawyer from the start, even at a higher hourly rate, will save you money in the end.

John P. Schuman, C.S., Family Lawyer, Mediator and Arbitrator

Appendix D: Questions and Answers about Alternative Dispute Resolution (Mediation, Arbitration and Collaborative Law/Practice)

What is Family Mediation?

Family mediation is a voluntary way of resolving disputes where a trained mediator helps parties to resolve disputes about family issues. The mediator does not decide the case. Instead, the mediator helps the parties reach an agreement that is acceptable to both of them.

Who are Family Mediators?

Mediators are usually social workers, lawyers, psychologists, or other professionals. When these professionals work as family mediators, their job is to help parties reach an agreement on support payments, the division of property, custody of and access to the children, or any other family-related issues. Usually social workers and psychologists are more focussed on resolving parenting issues. Lawyers are often more comfortable with the law as it relates to all of the financial issues, although frequently they address parenting issues too so the parties only have to use one mediator. Mediators do not take sides or make decisions for the parties. They also cannot give legal advice.

Do I Still Need My Own Lawyer if I Want to Mediate?

A party considering mediation should speak to a lawyer before seeing a mediator. It is helpful to know the law and your rights and obligations before mediation starts. Sometimes parties take their lawyers with them to mediation, because they do not feel confident advocating for themselves, or they want legal advice during the course of the mediation to make sure the discussions are on the right track. It is also important for each party to review any agreement

John P. Schuman, C.S., Family Lawyer, Mediator and Arbitrator

reached during mediation with his or her respective lawyer before signing it. Parties who use mediation still need to get Independent Legal Advice, to have a separation agreement that a court is likely to enforce.

Is a Mediation Agreement Binding?

Mediation agreements are not binding until they have been incorporated into a written agreement or a court order.

Both parties should obtain Independent Legal Advice before the agreement is finalized to ensure they understand their rights and obligations, as well as the effect of the proposed agreement.

Can What I Say at Mediation be Used Against Me?

Generally, discussions about settlement are not admissible in court. However, Ontario has two types of mediation in family matters: open and closed.

In closed mediation, all discussions between the parties are confidential and cannot be used as evidence against either party, with very few exceptions (for example, where concerns arise over the welfare of a child). In addition, the mediator will not report to the lawyers or the court on the progress of the mediation or provide an opinion on the issues that have been discussed in mediation to anyone other than the parties themselves.

Open mediation means that the process is not confidential. With open mediation, the agreement to mediate, or mediation contract, may also authorize the mediator to prepare a report once the mediation finishes.

How Long Does Mediation Take?

The mediation process is flexible and can take one session or many. The better prepared the parties are for a mediation meeting, the more productive that meeting will be. It is helpful if the parties have exchanged financial disclosure and figured out the specific areas of disagreement. However, if the issues are complex, a number of meetings may be needed to come to a resolution.

John P. Schuman, C.S., Family Lawyer, Mediator and Arbitrator

How Much Does Mediation Cost?

Mediators charge by the hour. The hourly rate usually depends on the type of professional and his experience. The longer mediation takes, the more it costs. Some mediators also charge administrative fees in relation to the costs of conducting the mediation (obtaining a room, refreshments, access to some computerized Family Law tools, etc.)

Mediation is always less expensive than taking a dispute to trial through the courts.

What is Arbitration?

Where mediators do not impose a decision on the parties, arbitrators do. The arbitrator is usually an experienced Family Lawyer, psychologist or social worker, who knows Family Law well, and also knows the law with regard to the procedure for conducting a formal hearing to decide issues between the parties. With arbitration, the arbitrator makes the decisions after reviewing the evidence of the parties.

The idea behind arbitration is that the parties pick their judge, who is known as the arbitrator. In picking an arbitrator, the parties can choose someone who has the same outlook or values as they do. The parties pay that arbitrator an hourly rate for his or her work. However, arbitration is still usually faster and less expensive than court, as the parties and the arbitrator can agree to streamline the process. Also, because the parties are paying the arbitrator, he or she often spends more time getting to know the parties and their situation. Judges are not always permitted the luxury of having a lot of time to spend on a particular case.

What are Collaborative Family Law and Collaborative Family Practice?

Collaborative Family Law and Collaborative Family Practice are a process options that help people resolve disputes without going to court. A central part of both collaborative options is the parties agreeing that they will not go to court, no matter how difficult things get. In Collaborative Family Law, the parties and their lawyers generally hold a series of meetings to reach a settlement. In Collaborative Practice, the parties jointly hire experts on children or financial matters, or both to help resolve issues in dispute by sharing their expert knowledge on particular issues.

John P. Schuman, C.S., Family Lawyer, Mediator and Arbitrator

In Collaborative Law or Collaborative Practice, the meetings with the parties, the lawyers, and any other professionals are more like brain storming sessions to resolve the issues between the parties, than a traditional negotiation. There are usually a lot more possibilities for solutions.

Are Collaborative Lawyers the Same as Family Lawyers?

Collaborative Lawyers are Family Lawyers who have received additional training in Collaborative Law and Collaborative Practice. The way a lawyer behaves in a Collaborative Meeting is very different from the way lawyers behave in court, or in a traditional negotiation. In a Collaborative Meeting, the main role of lawyers is to facilitate discussion and come up with ideas. They also make sure that the parties are respectful to each other and mindful of each other's feelings. Collaborative Lawyers make sure that the parties do not arrive at an agreement that is contrary to Ontario Law. Additionally, they provide the Independent Legal Advice that is necessary before the parties sign their separation agreements. Collaborative Law leaves the decision-making in the hands of the parties - the lawyers do not make the decisions.

If the Collaborative Process breaks down, then a rule in Collaborative Law and Collaborative Practice is that the parties must get new lawyers to go to court. This allows the parties to speak freely at the meetings without worrying that the other party's lawyer will use what they say against them. It also gives the parties a disincentive from walking away and going to court.

John P. Schuman, C.S., Family Lawyer, Mediator and Arbitrator

Where to Find Out More: References and Bibliography

This guide is a starting point for learning about Ontario Family Law. The footnotes in this guide give the legal authority for the principles discussed. This list of references provides information about where to get more detailed information.

Statutes (Family Law Legislation)

All of the Family Law Legislation that applies in Ontario is available on the Internet. They can be found at the following web addresses:

Arbitration Act:

http://www.e-laws.gov.on.ca/html/statutes/english/elaws_statutes_91a17_e.htm

Child and Family Services Act:

http://www.e-laws.gov.on.ca/html/statutes/english/elaws_statutes_90c11_e.htm

Children's Law Reform Act:

http://www.e-laws.gov.on.ca/html/statutes/english/elaws_statutes_90c12_e.htm

Child Support Guidelines (Ontario):

http://www.e-laws.gov.on.ca/html/regs/english/elaws_regs_970391_e.htm

Divorce Act (Canada):

http://laws.justice.gc.ca/en/D-3.4/index.html

Family Law Act:

http://www.e-laws.gov.on.ca/html/statutes/english/elaws_statutes_90f03_e.htm

Family Law Rules:

http://www.e-laws.gov.on.ca/html/regs/english/elaws_regs_990114_e.htm

Court Decisions

Many court decisions are now publically available on the Internet for free. All of the Supreme Court of Canada decisions are available at http://scc-csc.lexum.com/scc-csc/scc-csc/en/nav_date.do. Ontario Court of Appeal decisions from 1998 to the present are available on that court's website at: http://www.ontariocourts.on.ca/decisions_index/en/. Other Ontario court Decisions are available through CanLii: http://www.canlii.org/en/on/. Decisions that are not available through those sources will be available through law libraries.

Some of the important decisions mentioned in this guide are available at the following web addresses:

Contino v. Leonelli Contino:

http://scc-csc.lexum.com/scc-csc/scc-csc/en/item/2244/index.do?r=AAAAAQAHY29udGlubwAAAAB

D.B.S. v. S.R.G.; L.J.W. v. T.A.R.; Henry v. Henry; Hiemstra v. Hiemstra:

http://scc-csc.lexum.com/scc-csc/scc-csc/en/item/2311/index.do?r=AAAAAQAISGllbXN0cmEAAAAAAQ

John P. Schuman, C.S., Family Lawyer, Mediator and Arbitrator

Miglin v. Miglin:

http://scc-csc.lexum.com/scc-csc/scc-csc/en/item/2055/index.do?r=AAAAAQAGbWlnbGluAAAAAAE

Other Useful Reference Available On the Internet:

Ontario Family Court Forms (Official Website in English):

http://www.ontariocourtforms.on.ca/english/family

Ontario Family Court Forms (Official Website in French):

http://www.ontariocourtforms.on.ca/french/family

Child Support Guidelines Calculator:

http://www.justice.gc.ca/eng/pi/fcy-fea/lib-bib/tool-util/apps/look-rech/index.asp

Family Responsibility Office:

http://www.theFRO.ca

Revenue Canada:

http://www.cra.gc.ca

Ontario Collaborative Law Federation:

http://www.oclf.ca/

Collaborative Practice Toronto:

http://www.collaborativepracticetoronto.com/

York Collaborative Practice:

http://www.yorkcollaborativepractice.com/

Families Change (Information for parents and children)

John P. Schuman, C.S., Family Lawyer, Mediator and Arbitrator

http://www.familieschange.ca/

What Happens Next? Information for Kids About Separation and Divorce:

http://www.justice.gc.ca/eng/rp-pr/fl-lf/famil/book-livre/pdf/book-livre.pdf

Cooperative Parenting Institute:

http://www.cooperativeparenting.com/

Association of Family and Conciliation Courts Resource Centre for Families:

http://www.afccnet.org/resource-center/resources-for-families/categoryid/1

Devry Smith Frank LLP Family Law Group:

http://www.devrylaw.ca/personal-expertise/family-law/

Helpful Books about Separation, Divorce, Children and Family Court

Justice Harvey Brownstone, Tug of War (Toronto: ECW Press, 2009).

Marc Brown, Dinosaurs Divorce, (Little, Brown Books for Young Readers, 1988).

Joanne Pedro-Carroll, Putting Children First: Proven Parenting Strategies for Helping Children Thrive Through Divorce (Avery, 2010).

Kids First Organization, Kids First What Kids Want Grown-ups to Know About Separation and Divorce (Tower Publishing, 2008).

Parenting Resources

Triple P Positive Parenting Program (Quick Tips for Parenting):
http://www.triplepontario.ca/en/practitioner_regions/north.aspx

The New Dad Manual (in the style of a car manual):
http://www.newdadmanual.ca/

Index

1

18 years old, 26, 90, 135, 148

A

Abandoning the Contract, 182
access, 12, 17, 25, 26, 34, 36, 58, 60, 66, 68, 70, 71, 73, 75, 76, 79, 80, 82, 83, 84, 85, 112, 148, 149, 150, 173, 174, 185, 186, 192, 195, 198, 202, 203, 204, 206, 209, 217, 226, 229, 231
Access Parent, 79
access to information, 79
accountant, 31, 95, 96, 104, 147
accurate, 16, 25, 26, 35, 37, 51, 146, 154, 155, 177, 178, 199, 200
acting reasonably, 19
adequate provisions, 18
adoption, 31, 75, 86, 187, 203, 205, 206, 209, 210, 211
adoption licensee, 210, 211
Adoption Order, 209, 211
adoptive parents, 11, 12, 80, 86, 87, 98, 132, 196, 203, 206, 209, 210
ADR, 6, 52, 59, 60, 208, 249
adultery, 18, 179
adversarial, 33, 35, 50, 186, 206, 208
affection, 75
affidavit, 19, 26, 27, 31, 32, 34, 35, 37, 40, 164, 194
affidavits, 26, 35, 36, 38, 51, 162
agreement, 4, 5, 15, 16, 17, 24, 27, 29, 32, 36, 42, 52, 53, 54, 55, 56, 57, 60, 61, 62, 63, 64, 65, 66, 74, 75, 78, 79, 81, 90, 98, 100, 104, 112, 115, 116, 120, 121, 133, 137, 141, 142, 143, 144, 147, 149, 150, 151, 152, 153, 154, 155, 156, 157, 158, 159, 160, 163, 164, 165, 166, 167, 171, 172, 173, 174, 175, 176, 177, 178, 179, 180, 181, 182, 183, 185, 191, 197, 207, 214, 218, 221, 229, 230, 232
alternative dispute resolution, 4, 6, 52, 206, 208, 229
amending agreement, 163, 164, 183
Answer, 24, 25, 27, 28, 31, 32, 34, 162
anxiety, 69
appeals, 48, 59, 205
Applicant, 31, 32, 44
Application, 24, 25, 27, 28, 31, 32, 107, 134, 162, 195, 197, 205
apprehension of bias, 62
apprehension of child, 201, 202, 204
apprehensionn of child, 197
arbitration, 9, 24, 52, 57, 59, 60, 61, 62, 63, 165, 167, 229, 231, 233
arbitration hearing, 58, 59
arbitrator, 52, 53, 57, 58, 59, 61, 62, 63, 65, 68, 69, 84, 103, 150, 157, 214, 231, 249
assessor, 69, 84, 85
assets, 13, 15, 16, 26, 27, 28, 36, 37, 105, 107, 108, 109, 110, 114, 116, 118, 124, 126, 129, 143, 159, 167, 168, 172, 177, 183, 214, 218
attack, 50
award, 5, 44, 53, 57, 59, 60, 61, 62, 63, 103, 115, 129, 130, 142, 152, 155, 156, 165, 169

B

bad faith, 43, 65
bail, 133
bank, 29, 105, 110, 119, 121, 125, 126, 134, 168
bank accounts, 105, 125, 126
bankrupt, 127, 128, 129, 130, 131
bargain, 181, 183
beneficial owner, 123
benefits, 11, 19, 28, 60, 64, 67, 94, 95, 117, 123, 162, 164, 208
best interests of the child, 17, 76, 166, 173, 174, 203
best interests of the children, 75, 149
beyond a reasonable doubt, 168
bill, 6, 223, 225, 226
binding, 24, 33, 39, 42, 57, 59, 66, 136, 221, 230
biological parents, 12, 75
bitterness, 15
brainwashing, 76
breakdown, 15, 80, 98, 152, 154, 175, 181
briefs, 48, 56
business, 28, 38, 41, 51, 58, 124, 147, 173, 178

C

calculation, 66, 67, 86, 95, 96, 103, 109, 113, 115, 143, 144, 145, 147, 214
calculation service, 52, 66
Canada Pension Plan, 105, 112, 134
Canada Revenue Agency, 27, 28, 66, 95, 111, 113, 144
Canadian Charter of Rights and Freedoms, 185, 198
capacity, 10, 14
capital gains, 117
case conference, 30, 33, 34, 35, 39, 161, 162, 198
change in circumstances, 136, 142, 150, 151, 154, 157, 158, 160, 166, 168, 182
changing a child's name, 78
chattels, 125
child abuse, 185
Child and Family Services Act, 186, 187, 192, 193, 194, 195, 196, 197, 198, 200, 201, 202, 203, 204, 205, 206, 207, 208, 209, 210, 211, 233

Child and Family Services Review Board, 206
child professionals, 80
child protection, 3, 5, 25, 51, 185, 186, 187, 188, 189, 190, 191, 192, 195, 196, 197, 198, 199, 200, 201, 205, 206, 208, 215, 222, 249
child protection proceedings, 186
child protection worker, 188, 189, 190, 192, 195
child support, 4, 12, 15, 17, 19, 27, 52, 66, 67, 68, 73, 77, 82, 86, 87, 88, 89, 90, 91, 92, 93, 94, 95, 96, 97, 98, 109, 117, 127, 131, 135, 136, 142, 143, 144, 145, 146, 147, 148, 161, 162, 164, 166, 167, 173, 174, 214, 217
Child Support Guidelines, 17, 19, 28, 37, 66, 67, 82, 86, 88, 90, 92, 93, 94, 95, 96, 97, 98, 102, 137, 143, 145, 148, 162, 164, 166, 173, 174, 234, 235
child welfare, 84, 206
child's parents, 80, 88, 187, 194, 201, 209
child's relationship with other people, 71, 75, 81, 87, 169
child's views, 69, 71, 76, 85, 120
child-centred mental health XE "mental health" professional, 84
childless, 103
children, 1, 2, 3, 4, 5, 9, 13, 14, 15, 17, 18, 19, 25, 26, 33, 34, 36, 37, 46, 49, 50, 58, 60, 64, 66, 67, 68, 69, 70, 71, 75, 76, 77, 78, 79, 80, 81, 82, 83, 84, 85, 86, 89, 91, 92, 93, 94, 95, 97, 98, 100, 120, 128, 129, 132, 135, 136, 137, 138, 145, 147, 149, 150, 162, 164, 165, 166, 169, 172, 173, 174, 175, 185, 186, 187, 188, 189, 190, 191, 192, 193, 194, 195, 196, 197, 198, 199, 200, 201, 202, 203, 204, 205, 206, 207, 208, 209, 210, 211, 214, 216, 217, 219, 222, 229, 231, 235, 249
children's aid society, 3, 5, 25, 26, 185, 186, 187, 188, 189, 190, 191, 192, 193, 194, 195, 197, 198, 199, 200, 201, 202, 203, 204, 205, 206, 207, 209, 210, 211, 217, 219, 222, 249
Children's Law Reform Act, 12, 26, 50, 53, 68, 69, 75, 76, 79, 80, 82, 83, 84, 86, 87, 131, 132, 135, 138, 141, 149, 150, 174, 186, 233
clinical Investigation, 85
clinical issues, 84

closed mediation, 53, 230
closing statements, 41
coercion, 76
cohabitation agreement, 3, 5, 150, 153, 171, 172, 173, 175, 176, 177, 180, 181, 182, 183, 218, 221
cohabitation agreements, 5, 100, 171, 172, 174, 176, 179, 182, 183
Collaborative Family Law, 4, 63, 231
Collaborative Family Practice, 231
common law relationships, 9, 11, 14, 16, 20, 107, 111, 118, 132
communication, 54, 60, 80
community, 81, 195, 204
compensatory spousal support, 99, 100
compensatory support spousal support, 99, 100
complaining about a children's aid society, 186, 206
complexity, 15, 43, 71, 90, 225
concealing, 36, 65
conduct, 136, 177, 183, 200, 206
confidential, 39, 230
conflict, 1, 9, 60, 66, 68, 70, 71, 78, 80, 81, 83, 84, 202, 214
consequences, 16, 18, 98, 130, 154, 177, 178, 181, 187
Consumer Price Index, 151
contempt, 168
contested divorce, 19
continued cohabitation, 18
contract issues, 74
contract law, 154
contribution to the relationship, 98
cooperate, 15, 80, 186, 190, 192, 207, 215
costs, 28, 31, 42, 43, 49, 51, 52, 66, 89, 90, 91, 92, 94, 126, 130, 144, 225, 231
court appearance, 19, 32, 33, 34, 161, 197
court case, 24, 27, 33, 34, 59, 70, 132, 197
court decision, 7
court documents, 21, 51
court order, 30, 31, 36, 38, 47, 59, 60, 61, 77, 78, 79, 81, 82, 83, 105, 115, 121, 126, 130, 133, 142, 143, 149, 150, 151, 152, 153, 155, 156, 157, 160, 161, 162, 163, 164, 165, 166, 167, 168, 169, 175, 185, 197, 201, 207, 230
court proceeding, 5, 21, 24, 25, 26, 32, 33, 42, 61, 74, 126, 133, 137, 153, 181, 187, 195, 205, 209
court reporter, 37, 58, 59, 199

CRA, 66, 95, 144
creative solutions, 36, 50, 65
credibility, 35, 50, 162, 221
credit rating, 167
creditor, 111, 129
Criminal Code of Canada, 70, 132, 133
Criminal Harassment, 133
criminal investigation, 186
criminal proceedings, 25, 168, 199
cross examinations, 41
Crown Ward, 204, 205, 209
Crown Wardship, 202, 203, 204, 206
cruelly, 18
cruelty, 18
custody, 4, 12, 17, 25, 26, 34, 36, 51, 67, 68, 70, 73, 75, 76, 77, 78, 79, 80, 82, 83, 84, 85, 92, 94, 95, 132, 138, 145, 148, 149, 150, 173, 174, 185, 186, 195, 196, 198, 201, 202, 217, 221, 226, 227, 229
custody/access assessment, 84, 85

D

date of separation, 13, 16, 29, 108, 109, 110, 112, 114, 117, 134, 135, 137, 214
de facto custody, 79
deadline, 31, 32
deal, 21, 33, 50, 54, 55, 56, 74, 112, 120, 141, 158, 167, 179, 180, 183, 221, 226
death, 109, 121, 134, 136, 137, 138, 155
debt, 105, 108, 111, 128, 129
default, 90, 119, 153, 167, 181
defence, 199
dependent, 19, 87, 95, 128, 137, 153, 181
detriment, 46, 69, 122, 125
disclosure, 16, 24, 28, 29, 30, 31, 34, 36, 37, 38, 39, 56, 65, 66, 126, 134, 144, 147, 152, 154, 155, 156, 159, 161, 163, 165, 166, 169, 177, 178, 191, 198, 199, 200, 218, 226, 230
dishonest, 30, 65
dismissal, 150, 152
disproportionately large, 110
Dispute Resolution Officer, 161
divide, 20, 92, 107, 110, 115, 116
divorce, 3, 5, 14, 17, 18, 19, 20, 21, 32, 38, 45, 63, 68, 83, 112, 117, 121, 127, 134, 138, 158, 164, 166, 171, 175, 179, 182, 185, 213, 214, 217, 225
Divorce Act, 13, 17, 18, 21, 50, 75, 78, 79, 81, 86, 90, 98, 99, 107, 135, 141, 147,

148, 149, 150, 151, 153, 156, 174, 179, 186, 202, 234
Divorce Order, 17, 19, 138
DNA testing, 12, 87
domestic contract, 16, 98, 119, 151, 153, 163, 173, 177, 179
driver's licence, 105, 167
duress, 16, 154, 156, 159, 177, 179

E

economic advantages, 98
economic disadvantage, 124
economic reasons, 13
economic self sufficiency, 99
education, 67, 76, 77, 79, 88, 89, 90, 91, 139, 145, 173, 174
educational decisions, 77
elative adoption, 211
emergency, 32, 77, 215, 249
emotional harm, 71, 196
emotional or psychological harm, 193
emotional ties, 75
emotionally draining, 41
employment, 11, 67, 89, 90, 103, 139, 143, 145, 149, 153, 173, 181
encumber, 119, 174
endorsement, 40, 47
enforcement, 52, 106, 126, 127, 144, 163, 164, 168
entitled to information, 78
entitlement, 79, 99, 100, 101, 103, 123
entitlement to spousal support, 100
equal parents, 80
equalization, 4, 28, 99, 100, 107, 108, 109, 110, 111, 113, 114, 115, 117, 118, 120, 123, 124, 125, 126, 130, 131, 137, 143, 158, 159, 172, 180, 214
equally and fairly, 58, 62, 63
equitable, 123, 124, 154, 177
equity, 122, 123, 124, 125
estate, 29, 54, 119, 121, 136, 137, 138
estate taxes, 121
evidence, 31, 35, 39, 40, 41, 44, 45, 46, 58, 70, 121, 133, 155, 161, 166, 187, 189, 191, 192, 197, 200, 206, 230, 231, 249
exceptional circumstances, 20, 35, 47, 48, 50, 51, 62, 70, 102, 151, 162
excluded, 109
exhibits, 48

expensive, 6, 18, 30, 36, 44, 48, 51, 145, 150, 206, 213, 218, 225, 226, 231
expert, 6, 41, 45, 231
exploited, 193
extended family, 12, 75
extracurricular activities, 66, 77, 144
Extraordinary expenses, 88, 91

F

factum, 35
failed to disclose, 110
fair, 27, 54, 55, 63, 93, 110, 118, 141, 158, 181, 183, 226
fair and reasonable, 181
fairly, 41, 58, 62, 63, 125, 157, 192, 215
family income, 89, 92
Family Law Act, 10, 11, 12, 13, 15, 16, 17, 20, 50, 53, 55, 57, 60, 61, 66, 67, 79, 90, 98, 99, 104, 107, 108, 109, 110, 111, 112, 116, 118, 119, 120, 121, 122, 124, 126, 131, 132, 134, 136, 137, 141, 144, 147, 148, 149, 151, 152, 153, 154, 156, 158, 159, 162, 163, 164, 166, 167, 169, 171, 172, 173, 174, 175, 176, 179, 180, 181, 182, 234
family law issues, 57
Family Law proceeding, 4, 36, 37
Family Lawyer, 3, 6, 7, 53, 103, 213, 215, 216, 218, 222, 225, 226, 231, 232
family life, 3, 189
family member, 5, 81, 141, 142, 189, 197, 201, 209, 211
family property, 4, 99, 108, 109, 110, 111, 113, 114, 116, 117, 119, 123
Family Responsibility Office, 66, 67, 90, 104, 106, 129, 131, 144, 167, 169, 235
father, 87, 195
final order, 34, 47, 142, 159, 192, 193
final resolution, 5, 71, 158
finality, 63, 141, 155
finances, 13, 30, 38, 147, 172, 226
financial contribution, 77
financial disclosure, 28, 36, 56, 178, 218
financial hardship, 99, 127
financial issues, 15, 26, 54, 103, 127, 229
financial situation, 27, 28, 29, 30, 99, 127, 218, 225
financial statement, 26, 27, 31, 34, 126, 168
financial support, 18, 217

financially independent, 90
findings of fact, 48
fine, 120, 186, 189
First Nation, 195
follow-up question, 6
foreign, 57, 182
form, 2, 10, 14, 25, 26, 27, 38, 47, 58, 63, 70, 88, 106, 109, 115, 118, 123, 125, 126, 130, 150, 163, 193, 206, 210, 218
formal court order, 47
foster home, 195
fraud, 19, 45, 143, 152, 159, 177
fully employed, 97
fundamental breach, 177
future, 222

G

gaming, 105
garnishment, 126
gift, 109, 123, 133
government, 20, 67, 78, 102, 104, 185, 225
Government of Ontario, 86, 143, 196, 210, 211
gross salary, 96
gross taxable income, 96
grosses up, 96
guidance, 5, 54, 76, 142, 181
guilt, 69, 71

H

harass, 132
harassing, 131, 132
health, 19, 53, 66, 69, 79, 84, 88, 91, 135, 139, 144
health insurance, 19
healthcare, 77, 193
hearsay, 200
higher income, 92
home study, 210, 211
hospital, 195, 249
hourly rate, 227, 231

I

imprisonment, 106, 120, 167, 168
improvidently depleted, 110
in need of protection, 192, 193, 194, 197, 201, 202, 205, 208

inaccurate, 26
income, 11, 13, 16, 26, 27, 29, 36, 37, 38, 66, 67, 86, 87, 88, 89, 91, 92, 93, 94, 95, 96, 97, 99, 100, 102, 103, 109, 114, 116, 117, 118, 123, 124, 127, 128, 129, 134, 136, 143, 144, 145, 146, 147, 148, 155, 156, 157, 161, 168, 177, 214, 225
income information, 146
income tax, 66
Income Tax Act, 95, 113, 174, 175
Income tax returns, 28
Independent Legal Advice, 16, 154, 163, 176, 214, 230, 232
infirmity, 90
inheritance, 109, 110
injury, 74, 109, 135, 139
injustice, 122
insurance, 88, 89, 109, 153, 173, 181
insurance policy, 109
intention, 12, 14, 195
intentionally, 32, 97, 127, 134, 193
interview, 68, 69, 70, 190
intrusive, 70, 186, 190, 193, 197, 198, 201
investigate, 67, 69, 188, 190, 192
investigated, 190, 192
investigation, 3, 188, 189, 190, 191, 192
investment, 29, 112, 113
irrational, 14, 219
irreparably harmed, 35
issue, 14, 27, 28, 34, 36, 43, 47, 48, 49, 51, 52, 58, 59, 66, 70, 71, 74, 77, 86, 87, 94, 97, 103, 108, 114, 130, 135, 166, 175, 194, 199, 227
issues, 4, 6, 12, 14, 15, 16, 17, 20, 24, 26, 30, 32, 33, 34, 36, 37, 38, 39, 40, 41, 43, 44, 51, 52, 53, 54, 56, 57, 58, 59, 60, 62, 63, 64, 65, 66, 67, 68, 73, 74, 75, 76, 78, 83, 84, 85, 90, 91, 97, 103, 115, 117, 118, 129, 130, 139, 144, 149, 158, 159, 161, 162, 163, 165, 166, 169, 171, 172, 173, 201, 208, 213, 214, 215, 221, 225, 226, 229, 230, 231, 232, 249
issuing and entering, 47

J

joint asset, 109
joint custody, 80
Joint Family Venture, 124, 125
joint tenants, 121, 138

judge, 4, 10, 13, 14, 16, 17, 19, 25, 32, 33, 34, 35, 39, 40, 41, 42, 43, 44, 45, 46, 47, 48, 49, 50, 51, 53, 57, 59, 60, 61, 62, 63, 65, 66, 68, 69, 70, 75, 78, 81, 83, 84, 85, 87, 90, 94, 97, 103, 104, 106, 115, 127, 131, 135, 137, 145, 146, 150, 151, 152, 153, 157, 158, 159, 161, 162, 164, 167, 169, 170, 173, 180, 181, 183, 187, 192, 193, 196, 197, 199, 200, 204, 207, 211, 215, 217, 218, 219, 221, 223, 231
Judge's comments, 40
judge's decision, 43, 47, 48
judgment, 2, 47, 126, 218, 221
judgment-debtor examinations, 126
Justice, 17, 33, 45, 48, 59, 69, 85, 96, 112, 122, 126, 141, 165, 179, 194, 195, 205, 236
Justice of the Peace, 194

L

land, 105, 125, 128, 134
last place the spouses lived together, 107
last will and testament, 138
law of contract, 16, 154, 163
lawyer, 2, 4, 5, 6, 16, 21, 27, 30, 31, 37, 38, 43, 44, 45, 46, 47, 49, 51, 54, 55, 58, 59, 71, 83, 85, 87, 93, 94, 95, 96, 97, 104, 117, 122, 123, 131, 132, 133, 136, 138, 139, 141, 169, 175, 176, 178, 182, 187, 188, 189, 190, 191, 196, 199, 211, 213, 215, 216, 218, 221, 222, 223, 225, 226, 227, 229, 232
leading questions, 44
leave to appeal, 48
legal authorities, 6
legal fees, 42, 43, 44, 148
legal name change, 78
legal significance, 16, 176
legally binding, 15
legally separated, 4, 13, 14
legitimate, 19, 30, 38, 82, 149, 188
legitimate reasons, 19, 82
less adversarial, 35, 208
less than five years, 110
Less than six months, 67, 145
liabilities, 15, 16, 26, 27, 28, 36, 107, 110, 116, 159, 172, 177, 214
lie, 218
life insurance, 109, 112, 128
lifestyle, 99, 156, 179

lifestyle clause, 179
line 150, 86, 95, 97
loan, 29, 111
loan documents, 111
long term relationships, 124
lottery, 105, 158, 219
love, 14, 75, 94
love, affection and emotional ties, 75
lower income, 91
lower taxed jurisdiction, 96
lump sum, 97, 103, 115, 116, 137, 150, 152
lump sum payment, 150

M

major change, 3
manipulation, 76
marriage, 3, 5, 9, 10, 16, 18, 20, 27, 29, 32, 79, 80, 98, 99, 100, 103, 107, 108, 109, 110, 111, 112, 113, 114, 116, 125, 130, 137, 147, 148, 150, 152, 153, 154, 157, 171, 172, 173, 174, 175, 176, 177, 178, 179, 180, 181, 182, 183, 213, 214, 215, 216, 218, 221
marriage contract, 3, 5, 109, 150, 153, 171, 172, 173, 174, 175, 176, 177, 178, 179, 180, 181, 182, 183, 213, 215, 218, 221
married, 4, 9, 10, 11, 13, 14, 17, 19, 20, 45, 79, 90, 98, 99, 100, 107, 108, 110, 111, 118, 119, 120, 121, 122, 124, 125, 132, 135, 136, 137, 138, 156, 171, 174, 175, 179, 213, 215
married spouses, 108, 122, 174
material change, 142, 150, 151, 156, 157, 158, 166, 168
matrimonial home, 79, 108, 109, 110, 118, 119, 120, 121, 122, 172, 173, 174, 175
meaningful relationship, 78
media, 2, 198, 249
mediate, 40, 42, 52, 54, 59, 60, 230
mediation, 4, 5, 6, 15, 33, 52, 53, 54, 55, 56, 59, 60, 150, 160, 163, 165, 206, 208, 229, 230, 231, 249
mediation/arbitration, 52, 60
mediator, 3, 52, 53, 55, 56, 59, 165, 208, 214, 229, 230, 249
mediator/arbitrator, 59
medical, 66, 77, 87, 88, 144, 193, 210, 249
medical clearance, 210
medical decisions, 77
meeting room, 33

mental health, 84
mental illness, 14
Miglin, 16, 152, 153, 154, 155, 156, 159, 163, 165, 177, 178, 181, 235
misled, 152
mistake, 82, 103, 120, 143, 152, 159, 177
mortgage, 119, 120, 121, 129, 174
mother, 87, 195
motion, 30, 34, 35, 36, 42, 43, 44, 47, 50, 90, 147, 159, 160, 161, 165, 168, 169
Motion to Change, 106, 129, 136, 161, 162, 164, 166

N

name changes, 73
native, 195, 208
Native Canadian, 195, 204
necessaries of life, 76
need and ability to pay, 99
negotiation, 4, 16, 33, 60, 63, 156, 159, 163, 177, 179, 213, 232
net family property, 109, 111, 113, 123
new partner, 120, 121
no longer living together as spouses, 13
no reasonable prospect, 13, 18
non-compensatory spousal support, 99
notice, 31, 45, 106, 145, 159, 160, 196, 203, 207, 209
Notice of Motion, 61

O

objection (to evidnece), 45
objective observer, 13, 62
objectives, 16, 94, 96, 153, 154, 155, 156, 178, 181, 182
offence, 120, 194
Offer to Settle, 42, 43
Offers to Settle, 39, 41, 42, 43, 49
Office of the Children's Lawyer, 69, 85, 197, 209
officiant, 10
one year, 18
ongoing relationship, 196
Ontario Court of Justice, 126, 166, 205
Ontario Family Law, 2, 4, 9, 10, 11, 13, 15, 133, 233
Ontario Law, 10, 12, 13, 14, 74, 80, 182, 232
Ontario Superior Court of Justice, 126

open court, 33
opening statement, 44
Openness Order, 203
opinion, 38, 39, 45, 68, 76, 84, 85, 169, 230
opposing lawyer, 38, 44
oppressed, 16
oppression, 74, 154, 159, 177
oppression remedies, 74
original agreement, 154, 163
outstanding taxes, 111

P

parent, 10, 12, 19, 26, 32, 34, 66, 67, 69, 70, 71, 75, 76, 77, 78, 79, 80, 81, 82, 83, 84, 85, 86, 87, 88, 90, 91, 92, 93, 94, 95, 96, 97, 132, 133, 135, 136, 137, 138, 143, 144, 145, 146, 147, 148, 149, 168, 175, 185, 186, 187, 188, 189, 192, 196, 197, 202, 204, 207, 209, 211, 217, 221
parent's consent, 78, 209
parent's contribution, 88
parent's income, 95, 96, 146, 147
parent's time, 77
parental conflict, 68
parenting, 4, 14, 26, 31, 36, 53, 60, 65, 70, 71, 73, 75, 76, 78, 79, 80, 81, 82, 83, 84, 86, 94, 130, 143, 149, 150, 161, 165, 166, 168, 169, 174, 185, 188, 192, 214, 229
Parenting Affidavit, 25
parenting agreement, 75
parenting coordination, 84, 150
parenting coordinator, 60, 84, 150
parenting order, 60, 169
parenting plan, 60, 83, 84
parents' care, 190
parents' consent, 78
parents' income tax, 66
parents' rights, 67, 191
parents' tax returns, 67
parole, 133
participant, 18
participate, 12, 31, 62, 77, 79, 144, 149, 165
Participation Agreement, 64
parties' intentions, 11, 155, 182
Partition and Sale Act, 122
Partition and Sale of Property, 121
paternity, 73
payment of money, 125, 126, 168
payment of support, 86, 103, 153, 181

pension, 28, 112, 113, 114, 115, 116, 117, 128
period of cohabitation, 99
periodic, 97, 103, 130, 137, 151, 156
periodic payments, 151
perjury, 35
permanence and stability, 76
plans for the child's care and upbringing, 76
pleadings, 24, 38, 40
police, 26, 82, 83, 132, 133, 186, 188, 189, 190, 210
police records check, 26
position, 4, 33, 35, 39, 56, 63, 71, 85, 120, 177, 199, 200, 215, 221
possession, 36, 119, 120, 121, 174
post-secondary, 67, 88, 90, 91, 145
power imbalance, 52, 54
precedent, 35
preferential share, 138
prejudice, 19
pre-nups, 5
prescription medication, 19
present circumstances, 155
Preservation Order, 126
pressure, 154, 178, 180
pre-trial, *41*
primarily reside, 21, 67, 76, 89, 92, 124, 148
primary parent, 80
private, 28, 29, 51, 57, 64, 69, 195, 198, 210
probation, 133
procedural options, 165, 168
procedural order, 34
procedural steps, 40, 57, 59
process, 4, 9, 13, 15, 24, 32, 33, 34, 35, 37, 39, 41, 47, 50, 51, 52, 53, 54, 57, 58, 59, 60, 61, 62, 63, 64, 65, 66, 69, 70, 84, 85, 90, 102, 104, 108, 109, 111, 117, 122, 141, 143, 147, 150, 161, 163, 164, 165, 172, 173, 186, 187, 198, 200, 201, 205, 206, 208, 209, 210, 213, 214, 216, 222, 230, 231
process server, 51
professional report, 199
profit sharing, 28, 112, 117, 118
property, 4, 11, 16, 20, 26, 27, 34, 37, 67, 73, 103, 105, 107, 108, 109, 111, 115, 117, 118, 119, 121, 122, 123, 124, 125, 126, 128, 129, 130, 137, 138, 141, 143, 145, 158, 159, 171, 172, 173, 179, 182, 183, 195, 218, 221, 229

property division, 11, 27, 171, 179, 218
property issues, 4
prosecute, 189
psychiatrist, 214
psychologist, 54, 214, 231

Q

quasi-criminal, 168
Questioning, 36, 37, 38, 39, 199, 200, 249
questions, 3, 4, 6, 26, 37, 38, 44, 56, 59, 71, 161

R

rapport, 41
real estate, 119
real property, 121, 125
reasonable and probable grounds, 194
reasonable grounds, 132, 192
recalculation, 68, 145, 146, 147
registered a designation, 118
registering the child for activities, 78
relationship, 11, 12, 13, 14, 15, 54, 71, 75, 80, 81, 82, 87, 98, 99, 100, 107, 111, 122, 124, 132, 135, 138, 169, 171, 172, 175, 176, 182, 183, 203, 204, 209, 211, 217, 219, 222
relationship issues, 54
relationship of some permanence, 98, 107
relationship with the other parent, 75, 81, 217
relative adoption, 210, 211
releases, 152, 160
relevant, 35, 36, 43, 46, 139, 165
religion, 19
religious barriers to remarriage, 18, 73
religious upbringing, 77, 78
relocate, 15
remarriage, 156
remarry, 17, 19, 20, 32
rent, 14, 125
rental property, 67, 145
Reply, 24, 25, 162
reports, 53, 66, 68, 114, 117, 144, 199, 200, 210, 211, 249
reputation, 3, 36
Research, 68, 214
residential schedule, 148, 149
resolution, 5, 24, 34, 37, 52, 57, 59, 60, 64, 65, 66, 158, 208, 213, 222, 227, 230

Respondent, 31, 32, 44, 186, 199
restraining orders, 11, 73, 130
Restraining/Non-Harassment Orders, 131, 159
Resulting Trust, 123
resume cohabitation, 13, 18
review of spousal support, 156
reviewed, 61, 142, 151, 156, 157, 158, 200
rights, 2, 11, 20, 50, 57, 62, 63, 64, 76, 78, 79, 107, 119, 120, 121, 133, 136, 145, 168, 169, 172, 226, 229, 230, 249
risk, 117, 160, 176, 193, 195, 208

S

safeguards, 168
safety, 132, 133, 189, 195, 197
salary, 38, 67, 95, 96, 117, 225
sanctions, 36, 38
scars, 50, 213
scholarships, bursaries, or grants, 91
school, 71, 77, 84, 88, 90, 91, 148, 149, 191
search, 82, 195
secondary parent, 80
Section 37, 193
Section 7, 66, 67, 88, 90, 144, 148
security, 126, 128, 130, 167
self-employed, 28, 29, 30, 38, 95, 96, 147, 225, 227
self-represented, 222
sell, 117, 119, 174
separate, 4, 5, 9, 11, 12, 13, 14, 16, 18, 19, 33, 68, 71, 74, 76, 80, 86, 97, 107, 108, 109, 110, 121, 135, 171, 172, 175, 180, 182, 183, 213, 214
separate and apart, 9, 13, 14, 18
separate residences, 13
separated, 4, 5, 6, 9, 11, 13, 14, 15, 17, 18, 20, 27, 33, 45, 50, 66, 67, 74, 78, 79, 84, 86, 88, 114, 115, 120, 121, 127, 130, 133, 135, 137, 138, 142, 175, 214, 215, 216, 249
separated couples, 15, 57
separating, 6, 14, 57, 68, 85, 86, 115, 118, 138, 139, 171, 213, 249
separation, 3, 4, 5, 14, 15, 16, 17, 20, 24, 33, 42, 53, 54, 55, 56, 57, 63, 65, 68, 71, 73, 74, 75, 76, 78, 79, 80, 83, 100, 104, 108, 112, 114, 115, 116, 117, 118, 119, 120, 125, 127, 131, 135, 137, 138, 142, 144, 150, 153, 155, 156, 158, 163, 164, 165, 166, 171, 172, 173, 174, 175, 182, 214, 215, 221, 230, 232
Separation Agreement, 15, 17, 42, 54, 73, 74, 142, 153, 163, 164, 165, 166
served, 21, 31, 43, 51, 62, 219
service, 21, 66, 207
settle, 4, 38, 39, 40, 41, 42, 43, 44, 50, 55, 56, 59, 64, 166, 222
settlement, 17, 24, 29, 34, 39, 40, 41, 42, 53, 54, 55, 56, 64, 100, 103, 115, 163, 164, 169, 173, 215, 221, 222, 230, 231
settlement conference, 34, 39, 40
sever the joint tenancy, 138
shared custody, 67, 92, 94, 95, 145
Sheriff, 168
shocking, 153, 181
short, 71, 110, 125, 132, 155, 191, 200
short duration, 110
shorten, 20
shorter, 31, 103
shortly, 39, 41
sign, 57, 64, 66, 106, 116, 119, 144, 163, 171, 174, 178, 180, 191, 207, 221, 232
signature, 15, 42, 43, 176
signed, 15, 42, 52, 61, 111, 118, 121, 150, 153, 155, 159, 171, 176, 178, 180, 181
similar circumstances, 32, 96
simplified procedure, 60, 146, 161, 162
simplified wording, 193
social worker, 54, 69, 85, 188, 189, 214, 231
Society Wardship, 202, 204
sole custody, 80
solicitor-client privilege, 199
special and extraordinary expenses, 89, 90, 92, 131, 143
Special Expenses, 88
special needs, 25, 27, 76, 88
special or extraordinary expenses, 88, 90, 143
split custody, 67, 95, 145
sports, 88
spousal support, 4, 11, 27, 73, 94, 97, 98, 102, 103, 104, 116, 121, 128, 129, 130, 131, 143, 146, 150, 151, 152, 153, 154, 155, 156, 157, 158, 164, 167, 171, 172, 175, 179, 180, 181, 182
Spousal Support Advisory Guidelines, 102, 103, 157
spouses, 1, 4, 5, 9, 10, 11, 13, 16, 17, 18, 19, 20, 27, 30, 32, 33, 49, 50, 51, 52, 54, 64, 71, 79, 85, 86, 98, 99, 100, 107, 108,

109, 110, 111, 112, 113, 114, 115, 118, 119, 120, 121, 122, 124, 125, 126, 127, 130, 131, 132, 133, 135, 137, 138, 141, 142, 152, 153, 157, 172, 174, 181, 182, 183, 213, 214, 215, 216
stable home environment, 76
stalkers, 132
Stand-Still Agreement, 180
Status Review, 205
statutory, 6, 186, 193
step parent, 86, 87
stock, 117, 118
stock options, 117, 118
stranger, 49, 209
Stranger Adoptions, 209
suitable and affordable accommodation, 120
Superior Court, 17, 21, 33, 48, 59, 122, 126, 141, 165, 169, 205
supervision, 194, 202, 205
support, 13, 19, 20, 24, 26, 27, 29, 34, 35, 37, 38, 52, 58, 59, 66, 67, 68, 82, 86, 87, 88, 89, 90, 91, 92, 93, 94, 95, 96, 97, 98, 99, 100, 101, 102, 103, 104, 105, 106, 110, 116, 117, 118, 120, 124, 125, 126, 128, 129, 130, 134, 135, 136, 137, 141, 143, 144, 145, 146, 147, 148, 150, 151, 152, 153, 154, 155, 156, 157, 158, 160, 161, 162, 164, 166, 167, 168, 169, 172, 173, 174, 175, 180, 181, 185, 199, 214, 217, 218, 229
Support Calculation, 52, 66
support obligation, 93, 126, 148
support order, 20, 106, 125, 129, 151, 153, 157, 167
support payor, 91, 102, 104, 105, 106, 126, 146, 147, 148, 161, 167, 173
Supreme Court of Canada, 3, 16, 92, 94, 116, 124, 130, 135, 153, 177, 181, 234, 249
sworn documents, 26, 35

T

Table Amount, 86, 87
tax, 11, 13, 27, 28, 37, 38, 51, 54, 66, 67, 86, 90, 94, 95, 96, 97, 104, 105, 113, 114, 115, 116, 117, 118, 123, 144, 145, 175
taxed at a lower rate, 96, 117
Temporary Care Agreement, 207
temporary custody, 79

terms of the agreement, 16, 142, 155, 156, 157, 164, 176, 182
testify, 35, 40, 45, 48, 59, 162
third parties, 36, 119
third party, 109, 111
timelines, 20, 31, 36, 186
title, 105, 118, 119, 121, 123, 124, 134
tort, 74, 109
total income, 86
traced, 109
trauma, 69
treatment, 77, 96, 135, 193, 194, 249
trial, 4, 18, 24, 32, 34, 37, 38, 39, 40, 41, 42, 44, 45, 46, 47, 48, 50, 51, 58, 85, 99, 161, 162, 169, 186, 197, 198, 199, 200, 201, 205, 206, 223, 231
Trial Judge, 38, 39, 40, 42, 45, 46, 48, 85, 206
Trial Management Conference, 34, 39, 40
Trial Management Conference Briefs, 40
Trial Management Conference Judge, 40
trust remedies, 123
trustworthy, 200
truth, 26, 37, 44, 178, 200
truthful, 26, 37
tuition, 66, 91, 144

U

unconscionable, 16, 153, 181
Uncontested Trial, 31
uncooperative, 35, 189
under the same roof, 13, 79
underemployed, 97
undertaking, 36, 38
undue influence, 177, 179
unemployed, 97
unequal, *111*
unfair, 62, 63, 116, 130, 141, 177, 178, 183
unfairly prejudiced, 18
uniformity, 96
unimpeachable circumstances, 163
unmarried, 107, 122, 124, 138, 180
untruthful, 26
urgency, 20, 35

V

vacation, 13, 82, 118
valuation date, 13
value, 13, 38, 58, 102, 108, 109, 110, 112, 113, 114, 115, 116, 117, 118, 119, 123, 124, 125, 128, 172, 175, 178, 214
values, 27, 49, 53, 57, 102, 177, 231
vexatiously, 167
violence, 52, 59, 120
Voluntary Service Agreement, 207
vulnerabilities, 154

W

waiver, 153, 180, 181
war, 41, 68, 213, 225
warrant, 194, 195
wedding, 10, 179, 180
wherewithal, 187
wills, 5, 138
winnings, 105

witness, 35, 37, 38, 41, 44, 45, 46, 48, 68, 85, 200
witnessed, 15, 42, 159, 163, 176, 188
witnesses, 40, 41, 43, 44, 45, 46, 47, 48, 58, 162, 170, 200, 226, 249
work schedule, 149
writing, 2, 15, 27, 30, 38, 42, 46, 53, 59, 92, 159, 163, 176, 182, 223
writs of seizure and sale, 126, 169
written agreement, 182
written opening, 41
written request, 30
written statements, 45
written summary, 35

Y

year, 18, 20, 21, 32, 37, 46, 67, 89, 90, 92, 95, 113, 143, 145, 146, 210, 249
young children, 68

John P. Schuman, C.S., Family Lawyer, Mediator and Arbitrator

About the Author

John Schuman received his Honours B.A. from Queens University in 1994. He obtained his EMCA (paramedic designation) in 1995. John attended Law School at the University of Windsor, graduating in 1998. He then went on to complete his LL.M. in child and family law in 1999. John's thesis on Questioning child witnesses was published that same year and remains a frequently cited authority on to obtaining the evidence of children.

John has always practised in the areas of family law and children's rights. He articled at a prominent Toronto litigation firm. After John was called to the bar in 2001, he practised at a firm known for its work in children's legal issues and family law. He was also counsel for a children's aid society before joining a prominent Toronto family law litigation boutique. He joined Devry Smith & Frank in 2009, where he practices mostly in the area of family law.

John has litigated before every level of court in Ontario, several tribunals and the Supreme Court of Canada. Several of John's cases have been reported in law reports. John's cases involving children's rights have been reported in the national media.

John also helps separating couples resolve their matters outside of court as a family mediator and arbitrator. As a family mediator, John has received recognition for both his knowledge of family law and his effective mediation style that allows parties to reach amicable settlements that effectively address their concerns

John has published articles in legal journals on the Questioning of child witnesses, allegations of abuse when parents have separated, and the rights of children to direct their own medical treatment. He is also writes the "Child in the Courtroom" chapter of Wilson on Children and the Law. John co-authors the child protection chapter of Evidence in Family Law.

John is a member of the Law Society of Upper Canada, the Ontario Association of Family Mediators, the ADR Institute of Ontario, the Association of Family and Conciliation Courts, Collaborative Practice Toronto. Outside of the practice of law, he is an avid swimmer, paddler and cyclist and retains an interest in pre-hospital emergency care.

John can be reached at Devry Smith Frank LLP in Toronto, Ontario. (416) 446-5080, www.devrylaw.ca, john.schuman@devrylaw.ca

John P. Schuman, C.S., Family Lawyer, Mediator and Arbitrator

Made in the USA
Monee, IL
30 June 2022